W. Som...
P...

For Services Rendered, The Letter, Home and Beauty, Lady Frederick

Lady Frederick was Somerset Maugham's first great theatrical hit and established his reputation as a master of the English social comedy in the tradition of Oscar Wilde. The three other plays in this selection provide equal proof of his powers as a dramatist and include some of his later more acerbic work. *For Services Rendered*, now hailed by many as one of his finest plays, sheds a harrowing light on provincial middle-class England in the Depression after the First World War. *The Letter*, adapted by Maugham from his short story, is a tense drama of sexual passion set in the Malay States, and shows Maugham as the colonial storyteller. In contrast, *Home and Beauty* treats the marital complications facing a returning war hero with Mozartian *joie de vivre*.

William Somerset Maugham was born in 1874 and lived in Paris until he was ten. He studied medicine at St Thomas's Hospital until the success of his first novel, *Liza of Lambeth*, in 1897 launched his career as a writer. His reputation was further established by novels such as *Of Human Bondage* (1915), *The Moon and Sixpence* (1919), *The Painted Veil* (1925), *Cakes and Ale* (1930), *The Razor's Edge* (1944) and his fame as a short story writer by collections such as *The Trembling of a Leaf*, subtitled *Little Stories of the South Sea Islands* (1921). His first major theatrical success was *Lady Frederick* in 1907, followed by a series of other successes before and after the First World War, including *Our Betters* (1917), *Home and Beauty* (1919), *The Circle* (1921), *East of Suez* (1922), *The Constant Wife* (1926), *The Sacred Flame* (1928), *For Services Rendered* (1932) and culminating in *Sheppey* in 1933. His other works include travel books such as *On a Chinese Screen* and *Don Fernando*, essays, criticism, and the autobiographical *The Summing Up* and *A Writer's Notebook*. He settled in the South of France in 1927 and lived there until his death in 1965.

W. SOMERSET MAUGHAM

Plays: Two

For Services Rendered
The Letter
Home and Beauty
Lady Frederick

introduced by Anthony Curtis

METHUEN DRAMA

METHUEN WORLD CLASSICS

1 3 5 7 9 10 8 6 4 2

These plays were first published in Great Britain by
William Heinemann Ltd:
For Services Rendered in 1932, *The Letter* in 1927,
Home and Beauty in 1923, *Lady Frederick* in 1931
This selection first published by Mandarin Paperbacks
in 1996 as *For Services Rendered & Other Plays*
Reissued in this series with a new Introduction in 1999
by Methuen Publishing Ltd
20 Vauxhall Bridge Road, London SW1V 2SA
and Australia, New Zealand and South Africa

ISBN 0 413 71310 5

Methuen Publishing Limited Reg. No. 3543167

A CIP catalogue record for this book
is available from the British Library

Typeset by Intype Typesetting Ltd, London
Printed and bound in Great Britain by
Cox & Wyman Ltd, Reading, Berkshire

Contents

William Somerset Maugham:
A Chronology

1874	25 January: born in British Embassy in Paris where his father Robert Maugham, a solicitor, is partner in British law firm.
1884	Both parents die by the time he is eleven (his mother in 1882, his father two years later). Willie (as he was always known) is sent to be brought up by his uncle, the Reverend Henry Macdonald Maugham and his German-born wife, in his vicarage at Whitstable in Kent.
1885	May: enters the King's School, Canterbury. He is teased and bullied because of his stammer and small stature. An attack of pleurisy in winter 1888 causes him to be absent for a whole term. While recuperating at Hyères on French Riviera he determines to leave school as soon as possible and not attempt to go to Cambridge like his elder brother Frederic Herbert (who became Lord Chancellor of England).
1889	Leaves the King's School.
1890	At the suggestion of his German foster-mother aunt he goes to Heidelberg and, aged sixteen, enrols at the University. Attends philosophy lectures, sees plays by Ibsen and Henri Becque and music dramas by Wagner. Meets Ellingham Brooks, a cultivated twenty-four-year-old homosexual Englishman. He seduces Maugham.
1892	Returns to Whitstable. Literary ambition has already taken hold. Small private income (£150 p.a.) not sufficient to live off comfortably in his view. Considers various alternative professions as safety-net while establishing himself as a writer. Settles for medicine.
1892	27 September: enters St Thomas's Hospital,

Chronology

South London. Starts to keep a notebook (later published in part as *A Writer's Notebook*) in which he jots down ideas for stories and plays. Takes Walter Pater for his model as a prose-stylist.

1894   Spends six weeks of Easter break in Italy. Start of lifelong love of European and Far Eastern travel.

1895   Oscar Wilde trials in London. Verdict sends shock waves through Britain's gay community. Authors like Maugham and E. M. Forster conceal their sexual preferences thereafter. Maugham visits Capri, a refuge at this time for homosexual men and women.

1896   Gains practical experience in midwifery. On call during night hours and delivers babies born to the working-class mothers of Lambeth.

1897   Qualifies as a doctor; at the same time gives up medicine and commits himself to full-time writing. Pater rejected in favour of a plain prose-style using short sentences that becomes his trademark. Leads Bohemian life in Paris. Learns about Gauguin. Studies narrative technique by intensive reading of Maupassant. *Liza of Lambeth*, a short novel full of Cockney dialect, appears to some favourable reviews.

1898–1907   Writes *The Artistic Temperament of Stephen Carey* based on his Whitstable and Canterbury youth; this novel rejected by several publishers and set aside. Short stories printed in *Punch* and other journals, collected in *Orientations* (1899), followed by novels, *The Hero* (1901), *Mrs Craddock* (1902), *The Merry-Go-Round* (1904), *The Bishop's Apron* (1906), and a travel book about Spain, *The Land of the Blessed Virgin* (1905).

1902   One-act play *Schiffbrüchig* (*Shipwrecked*) given a café-production in Berlin.

1903   *A Man of Honour*, drama about a misalliance, put on by the Stage Society.

1907   *Lady Frederick* staged at Court Theatre in Chelsea, intended as a stop-gap but runs for more than a year. Formerly rejected plays, *Jack Straw*, *Mrs Dot*, *The Explorer* (adapted from his novel) join *Lady Frederick* with West End productions in 1908. Portrait painted by Gerald Kelly, a friend from Paris. Financial anxieties lessen.

1911   Meets fashionable interior decorator Syrie Wellcome. She is the daughter of Dr Barnado, wife of American drug-baron Henry Wellcome, and mistress of Gordon Selfridge. She and Maugham become lovers. Their child Liza born September 1915.

1908–1917   Maugham acclaimed as most successful British playwright with stream of society comedies including *Penelope* and *Smith* (1909), *Loaves and Fishes* (1911), *Caroline* (1916), *Our Betters* (1917). Takes a year off play-writing to re-cast and expand earlier autobiographical novel; it is published 1915 as *Of Human Bondage*.

1916 ff   Works behind the Allied front-line in France as member of ambulance unit. Meets handsome American driver, Gerald Haxton, with whom he falls in love. Recruited as intelligence agent and sent to Switzerland; then on mission to St Petersburg. On return to England de-briefed and recovers from lung-trouble in TB sanatorium in Scotland. Sails to Tahiti in search of material about Gauguin with Haxton, first of many voyages together in South Seas and Far East.

1917   Syrie's divorce from Wellcome absolute. Marries Maugham May 26 in Jersey City, US.

1919   *The Moon and Sixpence* (Gauguin novel) heralds period of prolific literary activity. Plays, novels, books of travel appear from his pen each season in a steady flow. Main titles: *Home and Beauty* (1920); *The Circle* (1921); *The Trembling of a Leaf* (1921), short stories of South Sea Islands including 'Rain'; *On a Chinese Screen* (1922), travel sketches; *The Casuarina Tree* (1926), stories with Borneo and Malayan settings; *The Constant Wife* (1927); *The Letter* (1927); *Ashenden* (1930), wartime spy stories; *Cakes and Ale* (1930), in which his literary rival Hugh Walpole was savagely satirised; *The Breadwinner* (1932); *For Services Rendered* (1932); *Sheppey* (1933); *Theatre* (1937); *The Summing Up* (1938), autobiography; *Christmas Holiday* (1939).

1926	Marriage breaks up. Maugham moves to the Villa Mauresque at Cap Ferrat with Haxton. Puts Arabic sign to ward off evil eye on entrance to Villa. It becomes logo stamped on all his books.
1929	Divorces Syrie. Sustains morning work routine every day without let; afternoons and evenings devoted to entertaining many smart friends and neighbours who after Abdication include Duke and Duchess of Windsor. Plays much Bridge. Maugham's hospitality topped by ultra-strong dry martinis mixed by Haxton.
1933	Maugham retires from playwriting to concentrate on short stories, novels and travel books. *Don Fernando* on Spanish temperament and culture appears in 1935.
1938	Has injection of serum from sheep's cell aimed at patient's rejuvenation and longevity from Swiss doctor, Paul Niehans.
1939	On outbreak of war remains in France at request of British Government doing propaganda work; then at Occupation escapes to England via North Africa and Lisbon in colliery vessel.

1940   Briefly in London then sent by British
        Government to America to try to counter anti-
        British sentiment by articles and public
        appearances. Tours entire country. Visits
        Hollywood, sees Aldous Huxley and Isherwood.
        Settles in Parker's Ferry, Yemasee, South
        Carolina, with Haxton in house built for him by
        Doubleday, his American publisher. Hour's
        drive to Charleston, nearest city. Works on
        novel based on pre-war visit to Indian ashram
        using abandoned play *The Road Uphill* for plot.

1944   September: *The Razor's Edge*, a best-seller on
        both sides of Atlantic. November: Haxton dies
        aged fifty-two in a New York hospital.

1946   Returns to Mauresque with Alan Searle, forty-
        one, a Londoner and prison visitor Maugham
        had known before the war. Searle becomes his
        secretary-companion for rest of Maugham's life.

1948   *Greatest Novelists and their Novels*, criticism
        (republished 1954 as *Ten Novels and their
        Authors*). Four of his short stories filmed as
        Quartet followed by *Trio* and *Encore*. Appears
        in movie on terrace of Mauresque to introduce
        them. 'The old party', he describes himself.

1949   *A Writer's Notebook*, heavily excised version of
        his journals.

1952   *The Vagrant Mood*, literary memoirs.

1962   Friendship with Riviera neighbour, Lord
        Beaverbrook, ripens. Persuades Maugham to let
        him serialise volume of autobiography, *Purely
        For My Pleasure*, in *Sunday Express*. Extracts
        over several Sundays, in which the now dead
        Syrie is viciously attacked, deeply shock
        Coward, Beverley Nichols and other old friends.
        Maugham's sanity questioned. Paintings from
        Villa (by Picasso, Lautrec etc.) sold at
        Sotheby's. Liza sues for share of proceeds.
        Maugham's attempt to adopt Searle as his son

vetoed by French court. Maugham quarrels with his British publisher, A. S. Frere of Heinemann, who reports him to be suffering from violent outbursts of paranoia. Searle is not allowed to leave Maugham's sight for more than a few minutes.

Introduction

The first ten years of Somerset Maugham's life from 1874 were spent in Paris where his beautiful mother was the darling of the Faubourg St Honoré and his father served the British Embassy as its official solicitor. French became the boy's language as much as English. During this period Victorien Sardou sustained a play-writing tradition he inherited from Eugène Scribe of meticulously crafted comedies and dramas largely designed to display the histrionic genius of such sacred monsters as Sarah Bernhardt, then at the height of her glory. It was a propitious time and place in which to be growing up for someone who would one day make an outstanding contribution to the mainstream British theatre.

Young Willie Maugham (he never used the name Somerset) had his own puppet theatre in which he performed plays to an audience of other British children. Somehow he had been made aware of a large world of theatre outside the confines of the Embassy and on his seventh birthday, given a twenty-franc piece by his mother's friend Lady Anglesey, the boy said he wanted to spend it in going to see Sarah Bernhardt. He was duly taken by an older brother to observe her in Sardou's *Nana Sahib*, a lurid melodrama he found 'wonderfully thrilling'.

Such treats came suddenly to an end when both his parents died within two years of each other and the lad, six months into double figures, was whisked away from the Paris of the Third Republic to provincial class-conscious Victorian England. There was no theatre on offer near his uncle's vicarage in the oyster town of Whitstable nor, during those grim days of British public school life, at the King's School, Canterbury, where he was sent to be educated. His love of romance was satisfied only through solitary readings of the *Arabian Nights*, one of very few books unconnected with Christian doctrine to be found in his new home.

Introduction

His theatrical ambition remained in abeyance until aged sixteen he broke away to become a student at the University of Heidelberg. Here he found a cultural ferment in progress whose intensity was only exceeded by that of the bohemian world he discovered when he returned to Paris ten years later. At Heidelberg there were productions of Ibsen, among the earliest performances of his work outside Norway. What interested Maugham was not so much the playwright's revolutionary ideas as his technique. He noted how the plays were constructed on the principle of someone coming into a stuffy room and opening a window to let in a disruptive breath of fresh air. The same strategy was to serve him well when in his own comedies a returning planter or country cousin effects a similar glaring exposure of the hypocrisies of English society.

Maugham's mental horizon was widened immeasurably by the culture-shock of Germany and his latent homosexuality awakened by an older English friend named Ellingham Brooks. Maugham knew already that in the long term what he wanted to be was a writer but he felt he had, in spite of the £150 a year left him by his father, to adopt some more financially certain profession. After toying with the law, the traditional Maugham vocation, he chose medicine and went through the five-year training at St Thomas's Hospital in South London. When he was not making anatomical drawings or working in the operating theatre, he filled pages of notebooks with dramatic dialogue as a preparation for writing plays. In his free evenings he went to the other theatre on Shaftesbury Avenue to learn how the operation of a smash-hit was achieved.

By the time he had qualified in 1897 the reception of his short novel about Cockney life, *Liza of Lambeth*, had given him the confidence he had initially lacked. He determined henceforth to take his chance as a professional writer. He was never to use his medical qualification to practise as a doctor. Soon his name became known in literary circles. The fashionable playwright Henry Arthur Jones (whose younger daughter Sue was remembered by Maugham in 1930 as Rosie in *Cakes and Ale*) gave it as his considered opinion that this young novelist could write for the stage.

Jones, author of *The Liars* (1897) and *Mrs Dane's Defence* (1900), was one of a small group of playwrights whose work monopolised the West End theatre at the turn of the century. The young Bernard Shaw, wielding his critical lash in the *Saturday Review* during the 1890s, and a sworn enemy of these writers' 'Sardoodleism', nevertheless praised Jones's craftsmanship. Among the dramatists in what was known as the Ring were R. C. Carton, author of the hugely popular *Lord and Lady Algy* (1898), and one whose work is still revived, A. W. Pinero.

Maugham did not underestimate the difficulty of breaking into this sodality. He had his eyes on a theatrical model temporarily out of service, the work of Oscar Wilde whose brilliant comedies had been summarily withdrawn after his disgrace at the Old Bailey in 1895. Maugham noted the current drama's obsession with Society; so many plays turned on an individual's punitive exclusion from it because of some violation of its moral code. In *A Man of Honour* (1898) he studied the fate of a literary gentleman whose marriage to the barmaid he has made pregnant meant social exile. It was given two performances by the Stage Society with Harley Granville Barker playing the hero. The play was revived a year later by a commercial management when it ran for twenty-eight performances.

At last Maugham was off the mark, even if he was still a long way from his goal of being able to live solely on the income from his plays. Max Beerbohm who attended some of the same social gatherings in London as Maugham at this period, and who took over from Shaw as the *Saturday Review*'s drama critic in 1898, strongly advised Maugham to stick to fiction for his livelihood. But Maugham was not to be deterred. As an apprentice playwright he had found rehearsals most instructive. There was one lighter scene in *A Man of Honour* that raised so many laughs it convinced Maugham that he had it in him to write a full-length comedy and he set about turning out several comedies tailored to what

Introduction

he conceived to be the requirements of London managements. But he had no luck with them; throughout the 1890s these managements were unyielding in their rejection of his scripts. He was also writing much fiction, and with slightly more success. Sometimes he would turn a rejected play into a novel, as with *Loaves and Fishes*, or a published novel into a play, as with *The Explorer*. His facility was only equalled by his unflagging industry. Then, after a long spell of writing, he would go on a working holiday to Italy or Spain both of which he grew to love.

In 1907 Maugham was in Sicily inspecting classical ruins, a trip funded by £20 he had received for a short story, almost all of which he had now got through. He received an urgent message from his agent saying that Otho Stuart had decided to put on his comedy *Lady Frederick*, written five years earlier. Stuart ran the small Court Theatre at Sloane Square (where *Candida* and *Major Barbara* had been performed). The play he had planned to do had fallen through and he thought Maugham's comedy would serve as a stop-gap while he found something else.

Maugham rushed back to England, arriving just in time to see the play when it opened in October. After the first night and the following morning's reviews he knew that the success that had so long eluded him was now in his grasp. In March his play went to a larger theatre in central London, the Garrick, from where it went to the Criterion in April, to the New in June, finally arriving at the Haymarket Theatre in August. By which time it had been joined by three more scripts resuscitated from the bottom drawer of his writing-desk: *Mrs Dot*, *Jack Straw* and *The Explorer*. Maugham had become not merely a success but a phenomenal success. Up to then no other dramatist had had four plays performed in the West End at the same time. *Punch* printed a drawing showing a wall covered in playbills advertising the four productions with a scowling Shakespeare standing in front of it biting his thumb.

Maugham was gratified but he did not let it go to his head. It had taken him ten years to realise his ambition. He knew that he was going to have to work like blazes (as he put it) if he was going to keep it up. His success was largely an imitative success. If his comedies were not mere carbon copies of Wilde and Pinero, they showed how the model could be taken over and subtly modified. He planned now to scrap the unwieldy Victorian vehicle altogether and find a leaner one that would illuminate contemporary marriage (something he himself was to embark on in 1917) in a concentrated, piquant format; he looked across the Channel not to Sardou whose *Divorçons* (*Let's Get Divorced*) had struck an audacious new comic note in the 1880s, but to Henri Becque whose *La Parisienne* (*Woman of Paris*) had a decade later paved the way for a realistic comedy format, using a small cast and one setting, known as *comédie rosse* (abrasive comedy).

Maugham's abrasive comedies turned on the war between the sexes whose battleground was the bedroom, whose weapons were sharp tongues and whose spoils were diamond and emerald brooches. The heroine who always ended as the victor often lent her name as the play's title, *Penelope* (1909), *Caroline* (1915), *Home and Beauty* (1919, which might easily have been called Victoria). These creatures, around whom the plot pivoted in a flurry of one-liners, were articulated by such mistresses of comic timing as Marie Tempest, Irene Vanburgh, Marie Löhr. With such gifted performers in charge, the plays were perfect fodder for middle-class West End audiences before the war, and were invariably successful at the box-office; the flow of them continued into the war when Maugham's profession of playwright became, as readers of *Ashenden* will recall, his cover for spying activities in Switzerland, and they even survived after it was over in *Home and Beauty*, the most delightful of them. In between came *Our Betters*, a swingeing attack on Society. Maugham had been fêted by Society; as its most fashionable playwright he had for several years been the theatrical toast of the town. By now he was thoroughly bored with all that and frequently felt subversive. He wrote *The Constant Wife* with its explosive punch-line likening the modern wife to a prostitute who failed

Introduction

to deliver the goods. In mellower mood he also wrote what many consider his masterpiece, *The Circle*, with its satisfying symmetry, its nostalgia for Edwardian graciousness.

By the mid-1920s Maugham was in demand for a play by every leading lady in the English theatre, but he was becoming weary of the form he had as a young writer felt to be so full of possibility. He now preferred to write long short stories rather than plays. In them he had freer scope to depict the behaviour of his characters under duress, particularly the men and the wives of the men, administering parts of the British and other colonial empires; the people who were shouldering 'the white man's burden'. After Kipling, Maugham was their most assiduous chronicler. He made good use of the copious material he had gathered on his travels East of Suez (title of yet another Maugham play) with his companion Gerald Haxton.

When two journalists approached him for permission to adapt his story 'Rain' for the stage, he agreed somewhat reluctantly and was pleasantly surprised by the enormously successful outcome. When Gladys Cooper asked him for a new play he took another of his exotic tales, 'The Letter', and adapted it for the stage himself. By the time he wrote *The Sacred Flame* in 1928, in which she also starred, Maugham was well into his fifties, producing fiction and travel-books in tandem with his work for the theatre. He began to make noises about giving up playwriting altogether. It was essentially a young man's job, he said, forgetting Sophocles, still writing plays in his nineties, like Shaw. After his great run of theatrical successes Maugham was content to withdraw from the limelight in favour of the young Noël Coward, writer of a smart clipped dialogue in a bright modern manner he had no wish to emulate.

Before the precise moment for retirement dawned Maugham still had a few more plays left in him that he wanted to write. These were plays that eschewed those sugary happy endings that had sent the audience home pleased with life, harsher plays that had grown out of his own mature experience. In spite of his immense success and large fortune,

Introduction

Maugham's life had not been a happy one on the domestic front. His marriage to Syrie Wellcome, the interior decorator who made white drawing-rooms fashionable, was tempestuous, to put it mildly. He wrote a play concerning a middle-aged city stockbroker weighed down by family responsibilities who decides to escape to a life of freedom like Gauguin (*The Breadwinner*). Maugham looked at the England of the Depression that had succeeded the war. He wrote a play about the fate of those who had fought in that war and survived (*For Services Rendered*). Then Maugham returned to the teaching of Christ whose gospels he had been required to study so diligently as a boy. He decided to make a drama out of Christ's command to the rich man '. . . go and sell that thou hast and give to the poor' (*Matthew*, 19), by imagining what might happen if this were taken seriously by one contemporary individual in possession of a small fortune (*Sheppey*). He knew that the plays he wrote on these themes would not have the popular success of his earlier comedies but he decided to write them and have them produced nonetheless.

After *Sheppey* was performed in 1933 with Ralph Richardson as the London barber who sees 'a great white light', Maugham vowed he would never write another play and though he lived for another thirty-two years of productive life he was as good as his word. As he had reckoned, these last plays disappointed audiences when they were originally presented; but out of all of his thirty or more plays, they seem most in harmony with our taste in the theatre today.

For Services Rendered

This play was first performed in London at the Globe Theatre in 1932; the penultimate work of the four last plays Maugham said he wrote for artistic fulfilment rather than commercial gain, the final one being *Sheppey* (see *Plays: One*).

England after the Great War is its theme. By the time he

Introduction

wrote the play Maugham had ceased to have direct experience of the England he was writing about. In 1926 he had gone to live permanently abroad at the Villa Mauresque on Cap Ferrat in the South of France. His life there with Gerald Haxton, his companion and lover, was very different from the Ardsleys' at 'Rambleton' in Kent near the cathedral city of 'Stanbury' (Canterbury) where the play is set. Here and in the novel *Cakes and Ale* (1930), Maugham wrote England, particularly the England of his boyhood in Kent, out of his system and never returned to it as a setting except as the background to a short story.

Leonard Ardsley, Rambleton's resident lawyer, is a ponderous family solicitor straight out of Galsworthy or Granville Barker. Ardsley's comfortable roomy house, with its french windows leading to the garden, terrace and tennis court, and his office where he sees his clients, is an emblem of middle-class English life between the wars. (Settings in different parts of the house are given for each of the three acts; but, as in the 1993 revival at the Salisbury Playhouse, these may all be combined nowadays into one.)

Save for the middle daughter, all the members of Ardsley's family still live at home. As we meet them we seem to be in for a sentimental Dodie Smith-style family drama, cosily and reassuringly English. A play with these characters, to whom we are introduced at a tennis party, as in a conventional drawing-room comedy of the period, could have been written mainly for smiles. But here the traditional plot is turned on its head. Instead of being given a lump in the throat we get a smack – a series of smacks – in the chops, scabrous anti-comedy on the present condition of England.

Fifteen years after the Armistice in 1918, what has happened to 'the land fit for heroes' promised by Lloyd George? Sydney Ardsley was awarded the Military Cross for a gallant foray that made him blind. He spends his time at home these days in pastimes such as tatting (lace-macking) or playing chess with his sister Eva, a sour spinster whose fiancé was killed in the war, now martyring herself to her brother. Sydney answers Maugham's underlying question early in the play:

Everything goes on in the same old way, except that we're all broke to the wide and a few hundred thousand fellows like me have had our chance of making a good job of life snatched away from us.

Another such fellow is Collie Stratton, commander of a destroyer during the war, now axed from the Navy, and proprietor of a local garage. This venture in which he has invested all his savings has been a disaster. He begs a loan from Wilfred Cedar, a prosperous local businessman, to stave off his creditors. Wilfred flatly turns down Collie's request to borrow £200 off him. With savage irony Maugham shows Wilfred, in the next scene, begging the Ardsley's pretty youngest daughter Lois, whom he covets for his mistress, to let him spend several times that sum on her to set her up in her own flat, and giving her an expensive string of pearls. The married Ardsley daughter lives nearby with her husband on their farm; that is not a success either and he has taken heavily to the bottle. To make the family's troubles complete, Mrs Ardsley is dying of cancer.

No one who shelters under the Ardsley's roof, except possibly the housemaid, escapes untraumatised. This really is *Heartbreak House* but instead of a Chekhovian or Shavian talking-shop Maugham provides a series of stunning climaxes – Eva's erupting rage as she overthrows the chessboard, Lois's gradual capitulation to the dirty old man who desires her, the farmer's alcoholic fugues, Mrs Ardsley's stoical acceptances of the inevitable diagnosis, the last-ditch attempt of Eva to get Collie to propose to her. When she fails, Eva's ultimate derangement ensues. She sings the National Anthem with mounting hysteria as the final curtain descends. In this role, Flora Robson gave by all accounts the performance of her career and Joan Miller was equally moving when the play was revived in 1946 at the little New Lindsey Theatre in Notting Hill Gate.

But in 1932, in spite of the presence alongside Robson of C. V. France (one of Maugham's favourite and frequently used actors) as the solicitor, Louise Hampton as his wife, and

Introduction

Ralph Richardson and Marda Vanne to represent the next generation, the London critics damned it with qualified praise. The theatre-going public could not take much of it either and the play closed after 78 performances. 'Mr Maugham has given us an enthralling theatrical entertainment, if nothing more,' wrote Charles Morgan (anonymously) in *The Times*. His was one of the more favourable notices. In the *Spectator* Peter Fleming made the point that has been made many times since. The agony, he claimed, was piled on much too copiously to carry conviction; and moreover not all of it could be attributed to the effect of the war. As he put it:

> *Post bellum* [after the war] is not necessarily *propter bellum* [because of the war]. If the war decreed that Mrs Ardsley should find post-war life a sad and silly business, no longer in the best of taste, it is not the war's fault that she must shortly leave it.

The playwright became the subject of personal attack led by the novelist Cecil Roberts in the *Daily Express*. 'Should Maugham Get Away With It?' was the heading of his article. 'It is worse than a bad play,' he fulminated. 'It is a play of malevolent propaganda against those who live with courage and hope . . .' A few days later 'Bunny' Austin, the young Wimbledon tennis champion, wrote to the paper defending the play as zealously as Roberts had denigrated it.

At this distance of time, the play appears as a microcosmic image of what Auden later described as 'a low dishonest decade'. Historically it came midway between the hilarity of Coward's *Private Lives* (1931) and Priestley's jocular *When We Are Married* (1938), both of which enjoyed long runs. In that context it put the record poignantly straight. When it was performed by the Royal National Theatre in 1979 it was hailed, by Francis King in the *Sunday Telegraph* and others, as Maugham's theatrical masterpiece.

Introduction

The Letter

This and *Sheppey* are the only plays that Maugham adapted from his short stories – and here the adaptation closely follows the original. 'The Letter' appeared first in 1924 in magazines on both sides of the Atlantic and in 1926 it reappeared as the final story of the six that made up *The Casuarina Tree* set in Malaya and Borneo. The dramatised version was written at the request of Gladys Cooper who wanted a vehicle she could star in when she took over the Playhouse as its actor-manager in 1927. Maugham's play opened there in February of that year with Cooper as the heroine and Leslie Faber as her lawyer.

The plot has its origin in the fate of Ethel Proudlock, a member of the British community in the Federated Malay States, who shot her lover on a verandah in 1911 and was found guilty at her subsequent trial. The actress Dulcie Gray, whose childhood was spent in Malaya, remembers the case as a much discussed scandal among her parents' circle. Maugham heard about it when he and Haxton were on their travels in the Far East fifteen years after it had occurred. He discovered Ethel had been sentenced to death but thanks to strenuous efforts on her behalf by her friends a pardon had been granted.

Maugham moulded the facts to a narrative in which the adulterous woman's guilt begins to emerge soon after the shooting. It is confirmed by an incriminating letter she wrote to the man she killed. After the curtain has gone up on her bungalow we see shots being fired and the lover slumping to his death. In the story this event is recalled in a conversation with her lawyer. There are a number of other alterations of viewpoint from story to play for a student of narrative technique to note.

Either way – read or seen – it is a riveting piece of work. The heroine's iron self-control as she gives her fictitious account of the attack on her virtue by the dead man slowly disintegrates, a chilling spectacle on both page and stage. The part offers superb opportunities for a leading lady seized by

Introduction

Cooper, by now Maugham's ace performer. Ivor Brown in the *Saturday Review* compared her to a tigress; she played the part 'with a compression of fury and despair'. Most of those who have followed in her wake have found the role just as rewarding. Kathleen Cornell, who like Cooper made a corner in Maugham roles, played it on Broadway; and it was filmed with Jeanne Eagels interpreting the heroine; then it was re-made as a film directed by William Wyler in 1940, with Bette Davis in the tigress role, articulated as much by mute close-ups of Davis's terrifying face as through Maugham's truncated dialogue. Of this version Pauline Kael wrote in *5001 Nights at the Movies*: 'Davis gives what is very likely the best study of female sexual hypocrisy in film history.'

The role of the husband offers rather less scope, consisting initially of brief interjections, 'the swine', 'the brute', 'the cur . . . the filthy cur'; but he does have his moment in the final act when the truth comes out after another long confession from his wife. In an alternative version of the final scene printed here as an appendix, this second recital from Leslie is interrupted by a flashback to the events surrounding the shooting, thus extending the minimal role of the lover in the play.

Among the male roles is it that of the lawyer who soldiers on even after his initial scepticism has burgeoned into proof positive of his client's guilt, and his Chinese confidential clerk, who are given the acting opportunities. Maugham is supposed to have based Mr Joyce's character on the lawyer he stayed with in Singapore from whom he first heard about the case. The impression given by the play of the widespread prevalence of sleaze in the FMS under the British administration understandably angered those upright officials shouldering the white man's burden who had extended generous hospitality to Maugham and Haxton while they were there.

Home and Beauty

Performed in the US as *Too Many Husbands*, this comedy
finds its setting and inspiration in England just after the Great
War has ended. During the war Maugham had been sent on a
secret service mission to Russia. While he was there the
Revolution had broken out (see the story 'Mr Harrington's
Washing' in *Ashenden*). He returned to England for a de-
briefing by Lloyd George and his intelligence chiefs. While in
Russia Maugham had contracted tuberculosis of the lungs and
they were alarmed when they saw his state of health.
Invalided out of the service, he went to a hospital in the north
of Scotland for treatment (see the story 'Sanatorium' in
Creatures of Circumstance). The clinical régime suited him;
not only did he soon recover, he found it the ideal conditions
for work:

> I was sent to bed every day at six o'clock, and an early
> dinner gave me a long evening to myself. The cold
> windless night entered the room through the wide-open
> windows, and with mittens on my hands so that I could
> comfortably hold a pen, it was an admirable opportunity to
> write a farce. For *Home and Beauty* pretends to be no
> more.

Maugham's farce is still good for continual laughter if
performed with the requisite skill. The patina of period detail
in which it has become coated enhances its charm as we re-
live the Armistice period with its shortages of everything from
fuel to domestic servants. The soldier presumed dead, who
returns to the land of the living, was a motif used with due
solemnity by several English and French playwrights at this
time. It was only Maugham who saw it had a funny side, if
husband number one DSO, should come back home to find
his sweet little wife, in reality a monster of selfishness and
vanity, married to his best friend, husband number two
DSO. In the event both husbands desperately desire their
release from marriage to Victoria.

Maugham may be seen here as part of an English comic

tradition in the theatre that begins with Wilde and ends with Coward, comedies light and silken to the touch but as durable as finely spun steel. *Home and Beauty* echoes *The Importance of Being Ernest* in its symmetry of plot, its hilarious penetrating throwaway dialogue, and it looks forward to Coward's disillusioned dissections of modern marriage. In *Blithe Spirit* the central figure also discovers by the end of Act One that marriages entered into serially have become simultaneous. Apart from the bigamous trio centre-stage, whose lines are scored with Mozartian precision, Maugham's play is full of fine cameo roles, the war-profiteer limbering up to become husband number three, and the divorce lawyer with his lady of accommodation in tow with whom he arranges the necessary evidence of adultery.

It all seemed just a little too British for the first audience in New York in 1919, with Estelle Winwood as Victoria, and it closed rapidly after only 15 performances despite an appreciative review from Alexander Woolcott in the *New York Times*. But in London later in the year, with Gladys Cooper in the lead, it ran for 235 performances after a crop of laudatory reviews. One of them was by Aldous Huxley, making his name as a literary journalist on the ultra-highbrow journal the *Athenaeum* edited by Middleton Murry. Huxley loved the play and praised the work of Charles Hawtrey as the returning war hero and Jean Cadell as the stooge adultery lady; but he felt that Cooper hardly did justice to the main part of Victoria. She 'was too impassive, too statuesque, playing all the time as though she were Galatea, newly unpetrified and still unused to the ways of the living world.' Since then the part has been interpreted in a more lively and unpetrified fashion, by, among many others, Brenda Bruce soon after the Second World War, and twenty years later Geraldine McEwan at the National Theatre, by which time the play had become part of social history.

Introduction

Lady Frederick

This was Maugham's first great hit, in 1907, though written, as we have seen, five years earlier. It is sub-Wildean, unlike *Home and Beauty* which is a twentieth-century counterpart of Wilde. It takes us back to Wilde's period of the 1890s when a group of leisured, languid, titled English people are enjoying a sojourn in the Hôtel de Paris at Monte Carlo. Some productions, like the successful 1946 revival at the Savoy Theatre with Coral Browne, have pushed it back to the 1880s at the behest of the costume designer; but a decade or so either way does not make much odds so long as the world of the idle rich with their endemic social snobbery, and their heedless extravagance which has delivered them into the clutches of the money-lenders, is fully evoked. Maugham homes in on one of the stock figures of the period, the Adventuress. Maugham adds to her traditional heart of gold an Irish brogue, an indomitable cheerfulness and an innate magnanimity. The usual plot is followed, whereby this allegedly wicked woman is discovered to be in possession of a bundle of incriminating letters she can use to get her own back on those in the higher ranks of society who have slighted her. Disdaining such vulgar tactics, Lady Frederick throws the letters into the fire before their very eyes quite early in the play.

Maugham said that as a budding, largely unperformed, playwright his plan was to write a meaty central role that would tempt a great lady of the theatre into wanting to perform it; and then, as women are more persuasive than men – he continued – the aforesaid great lady would compel a management to put it on. But the idea backfired because of what in retrospect has become the most memorable part of the comedy. This is the scene in the third act in Lady Frederick's dressing-room played while she is giving her face its early morning going-over with paint and rouge. She has asked the young Lord Mereston who is deeply in love with her to attend her *toilette*, as a way of making him see the impossibility of a marriage between them. She aims to disillusion him about her beauty by showing him her real face stripped of its cosmetic mask. The trouble was that no actress of the time wanted to expose herself to such humiliation even in a comedy.

Nor was it a totally new idea. Scribe and Legouvé's *Adrienne Lecouvreur*, which Maugham must surely have seen in Paris, opens with the Princess de Bouillon in her boudoir making up her face and applying beauty-spots to it while she listens to her friend the Abbé de Choiseul retailing all the latest court gossip. She even asks him to position one of the beauty-spots for her. Maugham staged the ritual of the *maquillage* much more fully. When Ethel Irving was persuaded to perform the role of Lady Frederick she had a triumph in it.

The critics who had hailed Maugham a year or two earlier as the promising author of the sombre *A Man of Honour* took a little time to adjust to the fact that he had it in him to write a mainstream comedy of this order and they were patronising. 'This pleasant little play . . .' was the line taken by J. T. Grein in the *Sunday Times*; but neither he nor anyone else was in any doubt as to the strength of the performances in both major and minor roles. One of the most enthusiastic reviews came appropriately enough from Oscar Wilde's (and Maugham's) friend Reginald Turner in the *Academy*. 'It was a delicious evening,' he said, 'full of delight from start to finish.'

Anthony Curtis
1997

Further reading

The prefaces to the six volumes of *The Plays of Somerset Maugham*, published from 1931 to 1934, contain Maugham's recollections of the composition of each work. His account of play-writing as a profession is given at length in *The Summing*

Up (1938). A further summing-up through a fictitious leading lady of the London stage is the theme of the novel *Theatre* (1937). The most comprehensive guide to Maugham's play-writing activities is the invaluable *The Theatrical Companion to the Plays of Maugham* (1955) by Raymond Mander and Joe Mitchenson. It includes extracts from contemporary reviews. More of these are to be found in *W. Somerset Maugham: The Critical Heritage* (1987) edited by Anthony Curtis and John Whitehead.

For Services Rendered

A PLAY IN THREE ACTS

Characters

Leonard Ardsley	
Charlotte Ardsley	his wife
Sydney	his son
Eva	his unmarried
Lois	daughters
Ethel Bartlett	his married daughter
Howard Bartlett	her husband
Collie Stratton	Commander, R.N.
Wilfred Cedar	
Gwen	his wife
Dr Prentice	Mrs Ardsley's brother
Gertrude	the Ardsley's parlour maid

The action of the play takes place in the Ardsley's house at Rambleston, a small country town in Kent near the cathedral city of Stanbury.

Act I

The scene is a terrace at the back of the Ardsley's house. French windows lead out on it from the house, and beyond is the garden.

Leonard Ardsley *is the only solicitor in Rambleston and his house faces the village street. Part of it is used as his office.*

Tea is laid. It is five o'clock on a warm afternoon in September.

Mrs Ardsley *is sitting in a chair, hemming a napkin. She is a thin, grey-haired woman of more than sixty, with a severe face but kind eyes. She is very quietly dressed.*

The Maid *brings in the tea.*

Mrs Ardsley: Is it tea-time?

Gertrude: The church clock's striking now, ma'am.

Mrs Ardsley (*getting up and putting her sewing aside*): Go down to the tennis court and tell them that tea is ready.

Gertrude: Very good, ma'am.

Mrs Ardsley: Have you told Mr Sydney?

Gertrude: Yes, ma'am.

> *She goes out into the garden.* **Mrs Ardsley** *brings two or three light chairs up to the table.* **Sydney** *comes in from the house. He is a heavy man of hard on forty, with a big, fat face. He is blind and walks with a stick, but he knows his way about and moves with little hesitation.*

Mrs Ardsley: Where would you like to sit, dear?

Sydney: Anywhere.

3

He lets himself down into a chair by the table and puts down his stick.

Mrs Ardsley: What have you been doing all the afternoon?

Sydney: Nothing very much. Knitting a bit.

Mrs Ardsley: Ethel's here. Howard's coming to fetch her on his way home from Stanbury. He's gone to the cattle-market.

Sydney: I suppose he'll be as tight as a drum.

Mrs Ardsley: Sydney!

Sydney (*with a little chuckle*): What rot it all is. Does Ethel really think we don't know he drinks?

Mrs Ardsley: She's proud. She doesn't want to admit that she made a mistake.

Sydney: I shall never stop asking myself what on earth she saw in him.

Mrs Ardsley: Everything was so different then. He looked very nice in uniform. He was an officer.

Sydney: You and father ought to have put your foot down.

Mrs Ardsley: They were madly in love with one another. When all that slaughter was going on it seemed so snobbish to object to a man because he was just a small tenant farmer.

Sydney: Did you think the war was going on for ever?

Mrs Ardsley: No, but it looked as though the world would be a changed place when it stopped.

Sydney: It's funny when you think of it. Everything goes on in the same old way, except that we're all broke to the wide and a few hundred thousand fellows like me have had our chance of making a good job of life snatched away from us. (**Mrs Ardsley** *gives a sigh and makes an unhappy gesture.* **Sydney** *utters a little sardonic chuckle.*) Cheer up, mother. You must console yourself by thinking that you've got a hero for a son. M.C. and mentioned in despatches. No one can say I didn't do my bit.

Mrs Ardsley: They're just coming.

> **Gwen Cedar** *and* **Ethel Bartlett** *come in from the garden.* **Ethel Bartlett,** *Mrs Ardsley's second daughter, is a handsome woman of thirty-five with regular features and fine eyes.* **Gwen Cedar** *is fifty, a good deal painted, with dyed hair; she is too smartly dressed in a manner hardly becoming to her age. She has the mechanical brightness of a woman who is desperately hanging on to the remains of her youth.*

Ethel: The others are coming as soon as they've finished the set. Hulloa, Sydney.

Sydney: Hulloa.

Gwen (*shaking hands with him*): How are you to-day, Sydney? You're looking very well.

Sydney: Oh, I'm all right, thanks.

Gwen: Busy as a bee as usual, I suppose. You're simply amazing.

Mrs Ardsley (*trying to head her off*): Let me give you some tea.

Gwen: I do admire you. I mean, you must have great strength of character.

Sydney (*with a grin*): A will of iron.

Gwen: I remember when I was ill last spring and they kept me in a darkened room for nearly a week, it was quite intolerable. But I kept on saying to myself, well, it's nothing compared to what poor Sydney has to put up with.

Sydney: And you were right.

Mrs Ardsley: One lump of sugar?

Gwen: Oh, no, I never take sugar. It's Lent all the year round for me (*brightly attacking Sydney again*). It's a marvel to me how you pass the time.

Sydney: Charming women like you are very sweet to

5

me, and my sisters are good enough to play chess with me. I improve my mind by reading.

Gwen: Oh, yes, Braille. I love reading. I always read at least one novel a day. Of course I've got a head like a sieve. D'you know, it's often happened to me to read a novel right through and never remember till the end that I'd read it before. It always makes me so angry. I mean, it's such a waste of time.

Sydney: How's the farm, Ethel?

Ethel: We're making the most of the fine weather.

Gwen: It must be so interesting, living on a farm. Making butter and all that sort of thing.

Ethel: One's at it from morning till night. It keeps one from thinking.

Gwen: But of course you have people to do all the rough work for you.

Ethel: What makes you think that?

Gwen: You don't mean to say you do it yourself. How on earth d'you keep your hands?

Ethel (*with a glance at them, smiling*): I don't.

There is a sound of voices from the garden.

Mrs Ardsley: Here are the others.

Her two daughters come in with the two men they have been playing with. These are **Wilfred Cedar** *and* **Collie Stratton**. **Wilfred Cedar** *is a stout, elderly man, but well preserved, with a red face and grey, crisply curling hair. He is stout, jovial, breezy, and sensual. He is out to enjoy all the good things of life.* **Collie Stratton** *is between thirty-five and forty. He has been in the Royal Navy and has the rather school-boyish manner of those men who have never quite grown up. He has a pleasant, frank look.* **Eva** *is Mrs Ardsley's eldest daughter. She is thin and of a somewhat haggard appearance. She is very gentle, a trifle subdued, but she does not give you the*

*impression of being at peace with herself.
Behind the placidity is a strange restlessness.
She is thirty-nine.* **Lois Ardsley** *is the
youngest of the family. She is twenty-six, but
the peaceful, monotonous life she has led has
preserved her youth and she looks little more
than twenty. She is gay and natural. She is a
very pretty young woman, but what is even
more attractive in her than her blue eyes and
straight nose is the air she has of immense
healthiness.*

Lois: Tea. Tea. Tea.

Wilfred: By George, they made us run about. Hulloa,
Sydney.

Mrs Ardsley: How were you playing?

Wilfred: Lois and me against Eva and Collie.

Eva: Of course Wilfred's in a different class from us.

Collie: That forehand drive of yours is devilish.

Wilfred: I've had a lot of practice, you know, playing
in tournaments on the Riviera and so on.

Gwen: Of course he was too old for singles, but a few
years ago he was one of the best doubles players
in Cannes.

Wilfred (*not too pleased*): I don't know that I play
any worse than I played a few years ago.

Gwen: Well, you can't expect to get across the court
as you used to when you were young. I mean,
that's silly.

Wilfred: Gwen always talks as if I was a hundred.
What I say is, a woman's as old as she looks and a
man as old as he feels.

Sydney: It has been said before.

Mrs Ardsley (*to* **Wilfred**): How do you like your tea?

Lois: Oh, mother, I'm sure they want a drink.

Wilfred: Clever girl.

Mrs Ardsley: What would you like?

7

Wilfred: Well, a glass of beer sounds good to me. What about you, Collie?

Collie: Suits me.

Eva: I'll tell Gertrude.

Mrs Ardsley (*as Eva is going*): Tell your father that if he wants any tea he'd better come now.

Eva: Very well. (*She goes into the house.*)

Wilfred: Damned convenient for your husband having his office in the house.

Lois: He's got a private door so that he can slip away without the clients seeing him.

Gwen: Evie's looking a little tired, I think.

Mrs Ardsley: She's been rather nervy lately. I've wanted her uncle to have a look at her, but she won't let him.

Gwen: So sad the man she was engaged to being killed in the war.

Mrs Ardsley: They were very much in love with one another.

Ethel: She's never really got over it, poor dear.

Gwen: Pity she never found any one else she liked.

Mrs Ardsley: In a place like this she could hardly hope to. By the end of the war there were very few young men left. And girls were growing up all the time.

Gwen: I heard there *was* someone.

Mrs Ardsley: Not very desirable. I believe he did ask her, but she refused him.

Gwen: I'm told he wasn't quite, quite. It's always a mistake to marry out of one's own class. It's never a success.

> **Gwen** *has dropped a brick.* **Ethel** *has married beneath her.*

Lois: Oh, what nonsense. As if that sort of thing mattered any more. It depends on the people, not on their class.

> **Gwen** *suddenly realises what she has said,*

8

gives **Ethel** *a hurried look and tries to make
everything right.*

Gwen: Oh, of course. I didn't mean that. All sorts of
people keep shops nowadays and go in for poultry
farming and things like that. I don't mind what a
man is as long as he's a gentleman.

Collie: It's a relief to hear you say that as I run a
garage.

Gwen: That's just what I mean. It doesn't matter
your running a garage. After all you were in the
navy and you commanded a destroyer.

Sydney: To say nothing of having the D.S.O. and the
Legion of Honour.

Wilfred: In point of fact what made you go into the
motor business when you were axed, Collie?

Collie: I had to do something. I was a pretty good
mechanic. I got a bonus, you know, and I thought
I might just as well put it into that as anything
else.

Wilfred: I suppose you do pretty well out of the motor
buses.

Collie: Lot of expenses, you know.

> **Gertrude** *comes out of the house with two
> tankards of beer on a tray.*

Wilfred: Look what's here.

> *He takes one of the tankards and takes a great
> pull at it.* **Eva** *comes back.*

Eva: Father's just coming. He wants to see you,
Collie.

Collie: Oh, does he?

Wilfred: That doesn't look too good, old man. When
a solicitor wants to see you it's generally that he
has something disagreeable to say to you.

Lois: Hurry up and finish your beer and we'll give
them their revenge. It'll be getting dark soon.

9

Gwen: Oh, are you going to play again, Wilfred? Don't you think it's time we went home?

Wilfred: What's the hurry? You take the car. I'll have another set and I'll walk back.

Gwen: Oh, if you're not coming, I'll wait.

Wilfred (*trying to hide his irritation behind his joviality*): Oh, come on, you can trust me out of your sight just this once. I promise to be a good boy.

> *A little look passes between them. She stifles a sigh and smiles brightly.*

Gwen: Oh, all right. A brisk walk won't do your figure any harm. (*She turns towards* **Mrs Ardsley** *to say good-bye.*)

Mrs Ardsley: I'll come as far as the door with you.

> *The two of them go out.*

Sydney: Where's my stick, Evie? (*She gives it to him and he gets up.*) I think I'll totter down to the court and see how you all play.

Ethel: I'll come with you, shall I?

Eva: I think I'd better get some fresh tea for father.

Lois: Hurry up, then, or the light'll be going.

Eva: I shan't be a minute. (*She goes into the house.*)

Lois: What should we do in this house without Evie?

Sydney: What would Evie do without us? You can't sacrifice yourself unless there's someone about whom you can sacrifice yourself for.

Wilfred: You're a cynical bloke.

Lois (*with a smile*): And ungrateful.

Sydney: Not at all. It's jam for Evie to have an invalid to look after. If she could make me see by saying a magic word, d'you think she'd say it? Not on your life. Nature destined her to be a saint and it's damned lucky for her that I'm around to give her the opportunity of earning a heavenly crown.

Ethel (*with a chuckle*): Come on, give me your arm.

Sydney (*putting on a cockney accent*): Spare a copper for a poor blind man, sir. (*They go out.*)

Lois: I'll just go and hunt for that ball. I think I know more or less where it is.

Wilfred: I'd come with you if I weren't so lazy.

Lois: No, stay there. You'll only wreck the flower-beds with your big feet.

Wilfred: I like that. I flatter myself not many men of my size have smaller feet than I have.

Lois: Modest fellow, aren't you? Give me a shout when Evie comes. (*She disappears into the garden.*)

Wilfred: Good-looking girl that. Nice too. And she's got a head on her shoulders.

Collie: Plays a good game of tennis.

Wilfred: Funny she shouldn't have been snapped up before now. If I was a young fellow and single I shouldn't hesitate.

Collie: She hasn't got much chance here, poor thing. Who the devil is there she can marry in a place like this?

Wilfred: I wonder you don't have a cut in yourself.

Collie: I'm fifteen years older than she is. And I haven't got a bean.

Wilfred: Girls nowadays who live in the country have to take what they can get.

Collie: Nothing doing as far as I'm concerned.

Wilfred (*with a shrewd look at him*): Oh!

Collie: Why d'you want to know?

Wilfred: Only that she's a nice girl and I'd like to see her settled.

Collie: I say, old man, I suppose you wouldn't do me a favour.

Wilfred: Of course, I will, old boy. What is it?

Collie: Well, to tell you the truth, I'm in a bit of a hole.

Wilfred: Sorry to hear that. What's it all about?

Collie: Business has been rotten lately.

Wilfred: I know it has. And I don't know when things
are going to improve. I can tell you I'm damned
glad I got out when the going was good.

Collie: I expect you are.

Wilfred: Every one told me I was a fool to retire. But
I smelt a rat. I said, no, I've worked a good many
years and I've made a packet. Now I'm going to live
like a gentleman. I sold out at the top of the
market. Just in time.

Collie: Lucky.

Wilfred: Lucky be damned. Clever, I call it.

Collie: Look here, old man, I hate asking you, but
I'm terribly hard up just now. I should be awfully
grateful if you could lend me a bit.

Wilfred (*very heartily*): Why, my dear old boy, of
course I will. I'm always glad to oblige a friend.
How much d'you want?

Collie: That's awfully kind of you. Could you
manage two hundred pounds?

Wilfred: Oh, I say, that's real money. I thought you
were going to say a tenner. Two hundred pounds
is quite another story.

Collie: It's not very much for you.

Wilfred: I'm not made of money, you know. My
investments have gone down like everybody
else's. Believe me, I haven't got more than I can
spend.

Collie: I'm in a most awful jam.

Wilfred: Why don't you go to the bank?

Collie: I'm overdrawn already. They won't lend me
a bob.

Wilfred: But haven't you got any security?

Collie: Not that they'll accept.

Wilfred: Then what d'you expect me to lend you the
money on?

Collie: I'll give you my word of honour to return it
as soon as ever I can.

Wilfred: My dear old boy, you're a damned good chap

and a D.S.O. and all that sort of thing, but this is business.

Collie: You've known me for six months now. You must know I'm honest.

Wilfred: I took a furnished house down here for my wife's health, and when I heard you'd been in the navy of course I came to you for my petrol and tyres and repairs. I know it's hard for you fellows who've been axed. I've paid all my bills on the nail.

Collie: I've given you good service.

Wilfred: I know you have. I'm very sorry your garage hasn't proved a good proposition. If you'd been a business man you'd have known it was crazy to settle down in a little tin-pot place like this. But I really don't see that I'm called upon to make you a present of two hundred pounds.

Collie: I'm not asking it as a present.

Wilfred: It comes to the same thing. I've lent dozens of fellows money and they never pay it back. I think it's a bit thick to ask me to lend you a sum like that.

Collie: You don't think I like it. I tell you I'm absolutely up against it. It means life and death to me.

Wilfred: I'm awfully sorry, old boy, but there's nothing doing . . . I wonder if Lois has found that ball yet.

He gets up and goes into the garden. **Collie** *sits on dejectedly. In a moment* **Eva** *comes in with the teapot.*

Eva: What's the matter? You're looking terribly depressed.

Collie (*trying to collect himself*): I'm sorry.

Eva: Are they waiting for us?

Collie (*with a slight sigh*): I suppose so.

Eva: Tell me what the matter is.

Collie (*forcing a smile*): It wouldn't interest you.

Eva: Why do you say that? Don't you know that anything that concerns you interests me.

Collie: That's very sweet of you.

Eva: I suppose I'm rather reserved. It's difficult for me to show my feelings. I should like you to look upon me as a friend.

Collie: I do.

Eva: Tell me what it is then. Perhaps I can help you.

Collie: I'm afraid not. I think you've got troubles enough of your own without sharing mine.

Eva: You mean looking after Sydney. I don't look upon that as a trouble. I'm glad to do what I can for the poor boy. When I think of what the war did to him, it's only right that I should sacrifice myself.

Collie: It's very good of you, all the same.

Eva: You see, Ethel was married and Lois was so young. Mother isn't very strong. Looking after Sydney helped me to bear the loss of poor Ted.

Collie: That was the man you were engaged to?

Eva: Yes. I was terribly unhappy when he was killed. I'm afraid I was rather morbid about it. One can't afford to give in, can one? I mean, life is given to us, and it's our duty to make the best we can out of it.

Collie (*rather vaguely*): Naturally one gets over everything in course of time.

Eva: I suppose one ought to consider oneself fortunate that one can. And I think a girl ought to marry, don't you? I mean, it's a woman's province to have a home of her own and children to look after.

Collie: Yes, I suppose it is.

There is a moment's pause.

Eva: It's rather strange that you should never have married, Collie.

Collie (*with a grin*): I never had anything to marry on.

Eva: Oh, money isn't everything. A clever woman can manage on very little. (*Brightly*) I must have a look round and see if I can't find someone to suit you.

Collie: I'm afraid I'm too old now.

Eva: Oh, what nonsense. You're just the same age as I am. Every woman loves a sailor. Between you and me and the gate-post I don't believe there's a girl here who wouldn't jump at the chance if you asked her.

Collie (*a trifle embarrased*): I'm not likely to do that.

Eva: Are you waiting for her to ask you? That's wanting almost too much.

Collie: I suppose it is really.

Eva: After all, a nice girl can't do much more than show a man she's not indifferent to him and leave him to draw what conclusions he pleases.

Collie: I've got an awful headache. I wonder if you'd tell the others that I can't play tennis again to-day. Perhaps Ethel will make a four.

Eva: Oh, my dear. I am sorry. Of course you mustn't play. That's quite all right. (**Leonard Ardsley** *comes out from the house. He is a red-faced, hearty man of sixty-five, with blue eyes and white hair. He looks more like the old-fashioned sporting squire than the country solicitor. He is on familiar terms with the local gentry and in the season enjoys a day's shooting.*) Oh, there you are, father. We've all had tea.

Ardsley: I had somebody with me. (*With a nod to him*) How are you, Stratton? Run along, Evie, I'll help myself. I want to have a word with our young friend.

Eva: Oh, all right. (*She goes out into the garden.*)

Ardsley: I've just seen Radley.

Collie: Yes.

Ardsley: I'm afraid I haven't got very good news for you.

Collie: He won't wait?

Ardsley: He can't wait.

Collie: Then what's to be done?

Ardsley: The only sensible thing is to file your petition.

Collie: It's ridiculous. It's only a matter of a hundred and eighty-seven pounds. I'm sure if I can hang on a little longer I can manage. When does Radley want to be paid?

Ardsley: The first of the month.

Collie: I've just got to get the money before then, that's all.

Ardsley: You've had a hard struggle and you've deserved to succeed. Believe me, no one will be sorrier than I if you're beaten. You know, you needn't worry about my fees. We'll forget about them.

Collie: That's very kind of you.

Ardsley: Not a bit of it. I think it's very tough on you fellows who've been kicked out of the navy. A man with your record. You put all your eggs in the one basket, didn't you?

Collie: Everything. If I go bust I haven't a shilling. I'll be thankful if I can get a job driving a motor bus.

Ardsley (*cheerily*): Oh, I hope it won't come to that. It would be rather a come-down for a man who's commanded a destroyer and has all the ribands you have. (**Mrs Ardsley** *comes out of the house with* **Dr Prentice.** *He is a thin, elderly man with iron-grey hair, a stern face and searching eyes*) Hulloa, Charlie.

Prentice: How are you? Oh, Stratton.

Ardsley: Just in time for a cup of tea. (*to* **Collie**) Don't you bother about us if you want to go and play tennis.

16

Collie: No, I'm not playing any more. I'll hop it. Goodbye, Mrs Ardsley.

Mrs Ardsley: Are you going already?

Collie: I'm afraid I must.

Mrs Ardsley: Well, good-bye. Come again soon.

Collie: Good-bye.

> *He nods to the two men and goes out through the house.*

Mrs Ardsley (*to Prentice*): Will you have some tea?

Prentice: No, thank you.

Mrs Ardsley: Collie looks rather worried. Is anything the matter?

Prentice: I'm told his garage isn't doing any too well.

Ardsley: It's the same old story. All these ex-officers. They go into business without knowing anything about it. And by the time they've learnt how many beans make five they've lost every bob they'd got.

Mrs Ardsley: It's very hard on them.

Ardsley: Of course it is. But what's to be done about it? The nation can't afford itself the luxury of supporting an army of officers it has no use for.

Prentice: The unfortunate thing is that the lives they've led in the service has unfitted them for the rough and tumble of ordinary life.

Ardsley: Well, I must get back to my office. Is this just a friendly call, Charlie, or are you hunting a patient? Personally, I am in robust health, thank you very much.

Prentice (*with grim humour*): That's what you say. I expect your blood pressure's awful.

Ardsley: Get along with you. I've never had a day's illness in my life.

Prentice: Well, don't blame me if you have a stroke. I always have my suspicions about a man who looks as well as you do.

Mrs Ardsley: As a matter of fact, I wanted to have a

little talk with Charlie about Eva. She's been very
jumpy lately.

Ardsley: Oh, that's only your fancy, my dear. She's
getting a little old maidish. The great thing is to give
her occupation. Fortunately Sydney gives her
plenty to do.

Prentice: Sydney keeping pretty fit?

Mrs Ardsley: As fit as can be expected.

Ardsley: Poor old Sydney. The only thing we can do
is to make things as easy for him as we can. It's
been a great blow to me. I was hoping he'd go into
the business. He'd have been able to take a lot of
the work off my hands now. I've paid for the war
all right.

Prentice (*with a twinkle in his eye*): He has too, in
a way.

Ardsley: Of course. But he's got used to it. Invalids
do, you know. Well, it's lucky I've got my health
and strength. Anyhow, I must go back and do a job
of work. (*He nods to the doctor and goes into the
house.*)

Prentice: Leonard's a wonderful fellow. He always
looks at the bright side of things.

Mrs Ardsley: It's a strength.

Prentice: You've spoilt him.

Mrs Ardsley: I've loved him.

Prentice: I wonder why.

Mrs Ardsley (*with a smile*): I can't imagine. I suppose
because he can never see further than the end of
his nose and I've always had to take care that he
didn't trip over the obvious and hurt himself.

Prentice: You've been a good wife and mother,
Charlotte. There aren't many left like you now.

Mrs Ardsley: Times are difficult. I think one should
make allowances for all these young things who
are faced with problems that we never dreamed of.

Prentice: What did you want to say to me about Evie?

Mrs Ardsley: I want her to come and see you. She's been losing weight. I'm rather uneasy about her.

Prentice: I dare say she wants a holiday. I'll have to talk to her. But you know I'm more concerned about you. I don't like this pain you've been complaining of.

Mrs Ardsley: I don't think it's very important. It's just pain, you know. I suppose most women of my age have it now and then.

Prentice: I've been thinking about it. I want you to let me make a proper examination.

Mrs Ardsley: I'd hate it.

Prentice: I'm not a bad doctor, you know, even though I am your brother.

Mrs Ardsley: You can't do anything for me. When the pain gets bad I take some aspirin. It's no good making a fuss.

Prentice: If you won't let me examine you I shall go to Leonard.

Mrs Ardsley: No, don't do that. He'll have a fit.

Prentice: Come along, then.

Mrs Ardsley: Now?

Prentice: Yes, now.

Mrs Ardsley: I disliked you when you were a little boy and used to make me bowl to you, and every year that has passed since then has made me dislike you more.

Prentice: You're a wrinkled old hag, Charlotte, and women ought to be young and pretty, but upon my word there's something about you that I can't help liking.

Mrs Ardsley (*smiling*): You fool.

> **Lois** and **Wilfred Cedar** *saunter in from the garden.*

Lois: Hulloa, Uncle Charlie. Tennis is off. Evie says Collie's got a bad head.

Mrs Ardsley: He's gone home.

Prentice: I'm just taking your mother off to have a look at her.

Lois: Oh, mother, you're not ill?

Mrs Ardsley: No, darling, of course not. Uncle Charlie's an old fuss-pot.

They go off into the house.

Wilfred: D'you want me to take myself off?

Lois: No, sit down. Would you like a drink?

Wilfred: Not at the moment. Let's have a talk.

Lois: The days are drawing in. Oh, how I hate the winter.

Wilfred: It must be pretty grim down here.

Lois: The wind! When d'you go south?

Wilfred: Oh, not for another month.

Lois: Shall you take a house here again next year?

Wilfred: I don't know. Would you like me to?

Lois: Naturally. It's awful when there's no one at the Manor.

Wilfred: D'you know, you're a very pretty girl.

Lois: It doesn't do me much good.

Wilfred: I wonder you don't go on the stage.

Lois: One can't go on the stage just like that.

Wilfred: With your looks you could always get a job in the chorus.

Lois: Can you see father's face if I suggested it?

Wilfred: You haven't got much chance of marrying in a place like this.

Lois: Oh, I don't know. Someone might turn up.

Wilfred: I believe you'd be a success on the stage.

Lois: One has to have training. At least a year. I'd have to live in London. It costs money.

Wilfred: I'll pay.

Lois: You? What *do* you mean?

Wilfred: Well, I'm not exactly a poor man. I can't bear the thought of your going to seed in a rotten little hole like this.

Lois: Don't be silly. How can I take money from you?

Wilfred: Why not? I mean, it's absurd at this time of day to be conventional.

Lois: What do you think Gwen would say?

Wilfred: She needn't know.

Lois: Anyhow, it's too late. I'm twenty-six. One has to start at eighteen . . . It's extraordinary how the years slip by. I didn't realize I was growing up till I was twenty. I vaguely thought of becoming a typist or a hospital nurse. But I never got beyond thinking of it. I suppose I thought I'd marry.

Wilfred: What'll you do if you don't?

Lois: Become an old maid. Be the solace of my parents' declining years.

Wilfred: I don't think much of that.

Lois: I'm not complaining, you know. Life's so monotonous here. Time slips by without your noticing it.

Wilfred: Has no one ever asked you to marry him?

Lois: Oh, yes. An assistant of Uncle Charlie's did. An odious little man. And there was a widower with three children and no money. I didn't think that much catch.

Wilfred: I don't blame you.

Lois: What made you suggest that just now? Paying for my training?

Wilfred: Oh, I don't know. I was sorry for you.

Lois: You don't give me the impression of a philanthropist.

Wilfred: Well, if you must know, I'm crazy about you.

Lois: And you thought I'd show my gratitude in the usual way.

Wilfred: I never thought about it.

Lois: Oh, come off it.

Wilfred: You're not angry with me? It's not my fault if I'm just dotty about you.

Lois: After all, you are old enough to be my father.

Wilfred: I know. You needn't rub it in.

Lois: I think it's just as well that you're going away in a month.

Wilfred: I'd do anything in the world for you, Lois.

Lois: Thank you very much, but there's nothing you can do.

Wilfred: You don't know what you're talking about. You're just mouldering away here. I can give you a better time than you've ever dreamed of. Paris. You've never been there, have you? By God, you'd go mad over the clothes. You could buy as many as you liked. Cannes and Monte. And what price Venice? Gwen and I spent the summer before last at the Lido. It was a riot, I can tell you.

Lois: You're a monstrous old man. If I were a properly brought up young woman I should ring for a flunkey and have you shown the door.

Wilfred: I'm not a bad sort. I'm sure I could make you happy. You know, you could turn me round your little finger.

Lois (*looking at her fingers*): Blazing with jewels?

Wilfred: Rather.

Lois (*with a laugh*): You fool.

Wilfred: God, how I love you. It's a relief to be able to say it at all events. I can't make out how you never guessed it.

Lois: It never occurred to me. Does Gwen know?

Wilfred: Oh, no, she never sees anything. She hasn't got the brains of a louse.

Lois: You're not going to make a nuisance of yourself, are you?

Wilfred: No, I'm going to leave you to think about it.

Lois: That's not necessary. There's nothing doing. I can tell you that at once. Take care, there's someone coming.

> **Howard Bartlett** *comes in from the house. He is a big, fine man of forty, somewhat on the stout side, but still with the dashing good*

*looks that had attracted **Ethel** during the war.
He wears rather shabby plus-fours and a golf
coat of rather too loud a pattern. He is
altogether a little showy. He does not drop his
aiches often, but his accent is slightly
common. At the moment he is not quite sober.
You would not say he was drunk, but the
liquor he has had during the day has made
him jovial.*

Howard: Well, here I am.

Lois: Hulloa, Howard.

Howard: I've caught you, have I? What are you doing
with my sister-in-law, Cedar? Eh? You be careful of
that man, Lois. He's up to no good.

Lois (*with a laugh*): Oh, shut up, Howard.

Howard: I know him. He's just the kind of fellow to
lead a poor girl astray.

Lois (*coolly*): Howard, you've had a couple.

Howard: I know I have, and I'm feeling all the better
for it. (*Harking back*) Don't you listen to a word
he says. He's a wicked old man.

Wilfred: Go on. I like flattery.

Howard: You know, his intentions aren't
honourable. (*To* **Wilfred**) Now, as one man to
another, are your intentions honourable?

Wilfred: If you put it like that . . .

Howard: One man to another, mind you.

Wilfred: I don't mind telling you they're not.

Howard: There: Lois, what did I tell you?

Lois: At all events, I know where I am now.

Howard: Don't say I didn't warn you. When you're
walking the streets of London, with a baby on your
arm and no home to go to, don't say, Howard never
warned me.

Lois: Ethel's waiting for you Howard. She wants to
go home.

Howard: No place like home and home's a woman's place.

Lois: You'll find her somewhere in the garden.

Howard: A good woman. You always know where to find her. She's not one of your gad-abouts. One of the best. And a lady, mind you. (*To* **Wilfred**) I don't mind telling you I'm not a gentleman by birth.

Wilfred: Aren't you?

Howard: The king made me a gentleman. His Majesty. I may be only a farmer now, but I've been an officer and a gentleman. And don't you forget it.

Lois: You're drivelling, Howard.

Howard: What I mean to say is, leave the girl alone, Cedar. A poor motherless child. An innocent village maiden. I appeal to your better nature.

Wilfred: D'you know what's the matter with you, Bartlett?

Howard: I do not.

Wilfred: You're tight.

Howard: Me? I'm as sober as a judge. How many drinks d'you think I've had to-day?

Wilfred: More than you can count.

Howard: On the fingers of one hand, maybe. (*With triumph*) But not on the fingers of two. It wants more than that to make me tight.

Wilfred: You're getting older. You can't carry your liquor like you used to.

Howard: Do you know, when I was an officer and a gentleman, I could drink a bottle of whisky at a sitting and not turn a hair. (*He sees* **Mrs Ardsley** *and* **Dr Prentice** *coming through the drawing-room*) Here's the doctor. We'll ask him.

They come out.

Mrs Ardsley: Oh, Howard, I didn't know you were here.

Howard: As large as life.

Prentice: Been in to Stanbury?

Howard: Market-day to-day.

Prentice: Do any business?

Howard: Business is rotten. Just wasting my time, I am. Farming's gone all to hell.

Mrs Ardsley: You look tired, Howard. Would you like me to have a cup of tea made for you?

Howard: Tired? I'm never tired. (*Pointing to* **Wilfred**) Do you know what this chap says? He says I'm tight.

Wilfred: I was only joking.

Howard (*solemnly*): I'm going to get a professional opinion. Uncle Charlie and Dr Prentice, as one man to another, tell me, am I tight? Don't mind hurting my feelings. I'll bear it. Whatever you say, like an officer and a gentleman. 'Shun.

Prentice: I've seen men a lot tighter.

Howard: You examine me. I want to get to the bottom of this. Tell me to say British Constitution.

Prentice: Say British Constitution.

Howard: I've already said it. You can't catch me that way. Now what about the chalk line?

Prentice: What about it?

Howard: Look here, do you want me to teach you your business? Draw a chalk line and make me walk along it. That'll prove it. Go on. Draw a chalk line. Draw it straight, mind you.

Prentice: I don't happen to have any chalk.

Howard: You haven't got any chalk?

Prentice: No.

Howard: Then I shall never know if I'm tight or not.

> **Sydney** *comes from the garden, accompanied by* **Ethel**. *A moment later* **Eva** *follows them.*

Ethel: Howard. Had a good day?

Sydney: Hulloa.

Howard: Yes, I met a lot of good chaps, white men, fine upstanding fellows. Straight as a die. Pick of the British nation.

25

Ethel gives a little start as she realizes that he is tipsy, but pretends to notice nothing.

Ethel (*brightly*): How was business?

Howard: Rotten. Everybody's broke. Farming – what a game! What I ask you is, why the Government don't do something.

Ethel: Well, they've promised to.

Howard: Are they going to keep their promises? You know they're not, I know they're not, and they know they're not.

Ethel: Then the only thing is to grin and bear it as we've grinned and borne it all these years.

Howard: Are we the backbone of the country or not?

Sydney: I've never heard a Member of Parliament who didn't say so.

Howard (*about to get angry*): I know what I'm talking about.

Ethel (*soothingly*): Of course you do.

Howard: Then why does he contradict me?

Sydney: I wasn't contradicting you. I was agreeing with you.

Howard (*mollified*): Were you, old boy? Well, that's damned nice of you. You're a sport. I've always liked you, Sydney.

Sydney: Good.

Howard: I was born on a farm. Born and bred. Except when I was an officer and a gentleman, I've been a farmer all me life. Shall I tell you what's wrong with farming?

Sydney: No.

Howard: No?

Sydney: No.

Howard: All right, I won't.

He sinks back, comatose, into his chair. At that moment **Gwen Cedar** *comes in from the drawing-room, she has a fixed bright smile on her face.*

Mrs Ardsley (*a little surprised*): Oh, Gwen!

Gwen: I'm like a bad penny. I was just passing your door and the maid told me Wilfred was still here, so I thought I'd step in for him.

Mrs Ardsley: Of course.

> **Wilfred's** *face is sullen with anger.*

Wilfred: What's the idea, Gwen?

Gwen: I didn't think you'd want to walk all that way.

Wilfred: You said you were going home.

Gwen: I remembered I had some things to do.

Wilfred: I prefer to walk.

Gwen (*with a bright smile*): Why?

Wilfred: Good God, surely I don't have to explain why I want a walk.

Gwen: It seems so silly when the car is there.

Wilfred: I need the exercise.

Gwen: You've had lots of exercise.

Wilfred: You're making a fool of yourself, Gwen.

Gwen: How rude you are, Wilfred.

Wilfred: It's maddening that you can never trust me out of your sight for ten minutes.

Gwen (*still very bright*): You're so fascinating. I'm always afraid some bold bad woman will be running after you.

Wilfred (*surly*): Come on, then. Let's go.

Gwen (*turning to shake hands with* **Mrs Ardsley**): Tiresome creatures men are, aren't they?

Wilfred: Good-bye, Mrs Ardsley. Thank you very much.

Gwen: It's been a lovely afternoon. So kind of you to ask us.

Mrs Ardsley: I hope you'll come again very soon.

> **Wilfred** *gives a sullen nod to the others. He waits at the window for his wife and when she flutters out he follows her.*

Sydney: What's the trouble?

Lois: What a fool of a woman.

Sydney: I bet he gives her hell in the car.

> **Howard** *gives a little snore. He has fallen into a drunken sleep.* **Ethel** *gives a start.*

Ethel: Listen to Howard. He's tired out, poor dear. One of the cows has something the matter with her and he was up at five this morning.

Mrs Ardsley: Let him sleep for a little, Ethel. Sydney, hadn't you better come in. It's beginning to get quite chilly.

Sydney: All right.

> **Mrs Ardsley, Dr Prentice** *and* **Sydney** *go into the house.*

Prentice (*as they go*): How has the neuralgia been lately?

Sydney: Bearable, you know.

> *Mrs Ardsley's three daughters are left with the drunken, sleeping man.*

Ethel: Poor Howard, he works so hard. I'm glad to see him get a few minutes' rest.

Eva: You work hard too and you get no rest.

Ethel: I love it. I'm so interested in it, and Howard's a wonderful person to work with.

Eva: Would you marry him over again if you could put the clock back?

Ethel: Why, of course. He's been a wonderful husband.

> **Mrs Ardsley** *comes to the door of the drawing-room.*

Mrs Ardsley: Evie, Sydney would like a game of chess.

Eva: All right, mother. I'll come.

> **Mrs Ardsley** *withdraws into the room.* **Eva** *gets up.*

Lois: Don't you hate chess?

Eva: I loathe it.

Ethel: Poor Evie.

Eva: It's one of the few games Sydney can play. I'm glad to do anything I can to make life a little easier for him.

Ethel: That horrible war.

Lois: And the chances are that it'll go on like this till we're all weary old women.

> **Howard** *gives another snore.*

Eva: I'll go. (*She makes her way into the house.*)

Lois: At all events you've got your children.

Ethel: I've got nothing to complain of.

> **Lois** *gets up and bending over* **Ethel** *kisses her on the cheek. Then she saunters away into the darkening garden.* **Ethel** *looks at her husband and the tears flow down her cheeks. She takes out her handkerchief and nervously pulls it about as she tries to control herself.*

CURTAIN

Act II

The scene represents the dining-room of the Ardsley's house. It is furnished in an old-fashioned style, with a mahogany sideboard, mahogany chairs with leather seats and backs, and a solid mahogany dining-table. On each side of the fireplace are two easy chairs, one with arms for the master of the house and one without for the mistress. On the walls are large framed engravings of academy pictures. There is a bow window, looking on the High Street, and here **Eva** *and* **Sydney** *are seated, playing chess. Luncheon is just over and* **Gertrude**, *the maid, is* *clearing away.* **Mrs Ardsley** *is sitting in her easy chair reading the paper.*

Eva: Uncle Charlie's car has just driven up.

Sydney: Do attend to the game, Evie.

Eva: It's your move.

Mrs Ardsley: You'd better go and open the door, Gertrude.

Gertrude: Very good, ma'am. (*She goes out.*)

Eva: He's been here rather often lately.

Mrs Ardsley: You know what he is. He will fuss.

Sydney: You're not ill, mother, are you?

Mrs Ardsley: No, only old.

Sydney: I doubt whether even Uncle Charlie can do much about that.

Mrs Ardsley: That's what I tell him.

> **Gertrude** *shows in* **Dr Prentice**.

Gertrude: Dr Prentice.

> *He comes in, kisses* **Mrs Ardsley** *and waves to the others.*

Prentice: How are you? Don't let me disturb your game.

Sydney: D'you want us to leave you?

Prentice: No. This isn't a doctor's visit. I'm only stopping a minute.

Sydney: Queen's knight to queen's bishop's third.

> **Eva** *moves the piece he indicates. The* **Doctor** *sits down and holds out his hands to the fire.*

Prentice: Chilly to-day.

Mrs Ardsley: Have you arranged something?

Prentice: Yes, three o'clock to-morrow afternoon.

Mrs Ardsley: That'll suit very well.

Prentice: Where's Lois?

Mrs Ardsley: She's playing golf. She thought it would be a rush to get back, so she lunched at the club house.

Sydney: She's playing with Wilfred. She said she'd bring him back with her, and Collie's coming in so that we can have a rubber or two of bridge.

Mrs Ardsley: Oh, that'll be nice for you, Sydney.

Sydney: Is there a fire in the drawing-room?

Mrs Ardsley: I'll have one lit. Gertrude.

> **Gertrude** *has been clearing the rest of the things away and now has finished.*

Gertrude: Very good, ma'am. (*She puts the table-cloth away in the sideboard drawer and goes out.*)

Mrs Ardsley (*to* **Dr Prentice**): Can't you stay and have a man's four.

Prentice: I wish I could. I'm too busy.

Eva: King's knight to queen's third.

Sydney: That's an idiotic move, Evie.

Eva: There's no reason why I shouldn't make it if I want to.

Sydney: You must protect your bishop.

Eva: Play your own game and let me play mine.

Mrs Ardsley: Evie.

Sydney: You won't look ahead.

Eva (*violently*): Good God, don't I spend my life looking ahead. And a damned cheerful prospect it is.

Sydney: My dear, what on earth's the matter with you?

Eva (*regaining her self-control*): Oh, nothing. I'm sorry. I'll protect my bishop. Queen's bishop's pawn to bishop's fourth.

Sydney: I'm afraid that's not a very good move.

Eva: It'll do.

Sydney: There's not the least use playing chess unless you're prepared to give it some attention.

Eva: Oh, can't you stop nagging. It's enough to drive one insane.

Sydney: I didn't mean to nag. I won't say another word.

Eva: Oh, I'm sick of it. (*She takes the board and throws all the pieces on the floor.*)

Mrs Ardsley: Evie!

Eva: Damn it. Damn it. Damn it.

Mrs Ardsley: Evie, what's the matter with you? You mustn't lose your temper because you're losing a game. That's childish.

Eva: As if I cared whether I lost or won. I hate the filthy game.

Prentice (*soothingly*): I think it's very boring myself.

Mrs Ardsley: Sydney has so few amusements.

Eva: Why should I be sacrificed all the time?

Sydney (*with an amused smile*): My dear, we thought you liked it.

Eva: I'm sick of being a drudge.

Mrs Ardsley: I'm sorry, I never knew you looked at it like that. I thought you wanted to do everything you could for Sydney.

Eva: I'm very sorry he's blind. But it's not my fault. I'm not responsible for the war. He ought to go into a home.

Mrs Ardsley: Oh, how cruel. How callous.

Eva: He took his chance like the rest of them. He's lucky not to have been killed.

Sydney: That of course is a matter of opinion.

Eva: It's monstrous that he should try to prevent any one else from having a good time.

Mrs Ardsley: I thought it was a privilege to be able to do what we could to make life easier for him when he gave so much for us. And I felt that it wasn't only for him we were doing it, but also for all those others who, for our sakes, and for what at least they thought was honour, have sacrificed so much of what makes life happy and good to live.

Eva: I've given enough. I gave the man I was going to marry. I adored him. I might have had a home of my own and children. I never had another chance. And now . . . now. Oh, I'm so unhappy.

*Bursting into tears, she rushes out of the room.
There is a moment's awkward pause.*

Mrs Ardsley: What's the matter with her?

Sydney: She wants a man, that's all.

Mrs Ardsley: Oh, Sydney, don't. That's horrible.

Sydney: But not unnatural.

Mrs Ardsley: You mustn't take any notice of what
she said to you.

Sydney (*with an indulgent smile*): Oh, my dear, I
knew it already. The day's long past since I was a
wounded hero for whom nothing was good enough.
Fifteen years is a long time.

Mrs Ardsley: If you could bear it there's no reason
why others shouldn't.

Sydney: It was easier for me, you know. Being blind
is an occupation in itself. It's astonishing how
quickly the time passes. But of course it's hard on
the others. At first it gives them a sort of
exaltation to look after you, then it becomes a habit
and they take you as a matter of course, but in the
end, human nature being what it is, you become
just a damned bore.

Mrs Ardsley: You'll never be a bore to me, Sydney.

Sydney (*affectionately*): I know. You've got that
queer, incomprehensible thing that's called the
mother instinct.

Mrs Ardsley: I can't live for ever. It was a comfort to
me to think that you'd always be safe with Evie.

Sydney (*almost gaily*): Oh, don't bother about me,
mother. I shall be all right. They say suffering
enobles. It hasn't enobled me. It's made me sly and
cunning. Evie says I'm selfish. I am. But I'm
damned artful. I know how to get people to do
things for me by working on their sympathy.
Evie'll settle down. I shall be as safe as a house.

Mrs Ardsley: Her not marrying and all that. It seemed
so natural that she should look after you. Ethel's

got her husband and children. Lois is so much younger. She doesn't understand. She's hard.

Sydney (*with a good-natured shrug of the shoulders*): Oh, I don't know. She's got the healthy, normal selfishness of youth. There's no harm in that. She doesn't see why she should be bothered with me, and she damned well isn't going to. I don't blame her. I know exactly where I am with her.

Mrs Ardsley: I suppose I ought to go to Evie.

Prentice: I'd leave her alone for a little longer.

> **Gertrude** *comes in with a note.*

Gertrude: Mrs Cedar asked me to give you this, ma'am.

Mrs Ardsley: Oh. (*She opens the letter and reads it*) Is she in the drawing-room?

Gertrude: No ma'am. She's waiting in her car.

Mrs Ardsley: Ask her to come in.

Gertrude: Very good, ma'am. (*She goes out.*)

Mrs Ardsley: How very strange.

Prentice: What is it?

Mrs Ardsley: It's from Gwen. She asks if she can see me alone for a few minutes.

Sydney: I'll get out then. (*He rises, takes his stick and stamps out of the room.*)

Prentice: I'll go too.

Mrs Ardsley: I wonder what she wants.

Prentice: Probably an address or something.

Mrs Ardsley: She could have telephoned.

Prentice: Am I right in thinking she's a very silly woman?

Mrs Ardsley: Quite right.

> **Dr Prentice** *has been watching* **Sydney** *go and as soon as the door is closed on him he changes his manner.*

Prentice: I've had a long talk with Murray.

34

Mrs Ardsley: I hate this consultation that you've forced me into.

Prentice: My dear, it's essential. I don't want to alarm you, but I must tell you I'm not satisfied with your condition.

Mrs Ardsley: Oh, well. It's at three o'clock to-morrow afternoon?

Prentice: Yes. He's promised to ring me up after he's seen you.

Mrs Ardsley (*giving him her hand*): You're very nice to me.

Prentice (*kissing her cheek*): I'm very fond of you.

> *He goes out. In a minute* **Gertrude** *shows* **Gwen Cedar** *into the room, and after announcing her, goes out.*

Gertrude: Mrs Cedar.

Mrs Ardsley: How d'you do.

Gwen: I hope you don't think it very strange my sending in a note like that. I simply had to see you.

Mrs Ardsley: Do sit down. We shan't be disturbed.

Gwen: I thought I'd better talk it over with you. I mean, I thought it only fair to you.

Mrs Ardsley: Yes?

Gwen: I think I'd better come straight to the point.

Mrs Ardsley (*with a little smile*): It's always a good plan.

Gwen: You know that I'm Wilfred's second wife.

Mrs Ardsley: No, I didn't.

Gwen: He's my second husband. We fell very much in love with one another. And there were divorce proceedings. We've been married for twelve years. It's all so long ago, I didn't see any reason to say anything about it when we came down here.

Mrs Ardsley: It was nobody's business but your own.

Gwen: We've been awfully happy together. It's been a great success.

35

Mrs Ardsley: I imagine he's a very easy man to get on with.

Gwen: Of course he's always been very attractive to women.

Mrs Ardsley: That's a thing I'm no judge about.

Gwen: He's got a way with him that takes them. And he pays them all kinds of little attentions that flatter them. But of course it doesn't mean anything.

Mrs Ardsley: It seldom does.

Gwen: All women don't know that. It's the kind of thing that's quite likely to turn a girl's head. It would be silly to take him seriously. After all he's a married man and *I* would never divorce him whatever he did. Never.

Mrs Ardsley: My dear, you said you were coming straight to the point. Aren't you beating about the bush a good deal?

Gwen: Don't you know what I mean?

Mrs Ardsley: I haven't an idea.

Gwen: I'm very relieved to hear it.

Mrs Ardsley: Won't you explain?

Gwen: You won't be angry with me?

Mrs Ardsley: I shouldn't think so.

Gwen: He's been paying a lot of attention to your Lois.

Mrs Ardsley (*with a chuckle*): Oh, my dear, don't be so ridiculous.

Gwen: I know he's attracted by her.

Mrs Ardsley: How can you be so silly?

Gwen: They're together all the time.

Mrs Ardsley: Nonsense. They play tennis and golf together. They're playing golf now. There are very few men for your husband to play with during the week. It's been nice for both of them. You don't mean to say you're jealous of that?

Gwen: But you see, I know he's madly in love with her.

Mrs Ardsley: Oh, my dear, that's only fancy.

Gwen: How do you know that she isn't in love with him?

Mrs Ardsley: He's old enough to be her father.

Gwen: What does that matter?

Mrs Ardsley: A lot, I should say. I don't want to hurt your feelings, but you know, a girl of Lois's age looks upon you and me, your husband and mine, as older than God.

Gwen: It isn't as if there were a lot of men here. A girl can't pick and choose in a place like this.

Mrs Ardsley: Now I'm afraid I think you're not being very polite.

Gwen: I'm sorry. I don't mean to be rude. I'm so utterly miserable.

Mrs Ardsley (*with kindness*): You poor dear. I'm sure you're mistaken. And in any case you're going away soon and that'll end it.

Gwen (*quickly*): Then you think there's something to end?

Mrs Ardsley: No, no. End your fear, I mean. I know very little about men like your husband. I dare say men of that age are often rather taken by bright young things. I think a sensible wife just shrugs her shoulders and laughs. Her safety is that the bright young things look upon her husband as an old fogey.

Gwen: Oh, I hope you're right. If you only knew the agony I've been through since I found out.

Mrs Ardsley: I'm sure I'm right. And if there is any truth in what you think, I'm convinced that a fortnight after you've left here he'll have forgotten all about her.

> *She gets up to put an end to the conversation.*
> **Gwen** *rises too. She glances out of the window and sees a car stopping at the door.*

Gwen: Here they are.

Mrs Ardsley (*looking out of the window*): Who? Oh, your husband and Lois.

Gwen: He's coming in.

Mrs Ardsley: He promised Sydney to play bridge. You don't object to that, do you?

Gwen: I don't want him to see me. He'll think I'm spying on him. He'll be furious.

Mrs Ardsley: He won't come in here. He'll go into the drawing-room.

Gwen: You won't say anything to Lois, will you? I don't want to put her back up.

Mrs Ardsley: Of course I won't say anything. I'm sure she's absolutely unconscious of what you've been talking about. It would only make her shy and uncomfortable.

Gwen: I'll slip away the moment the coast is clear.

> *The door is burst open and* **Lois** *comes in. She is radiant with health and spirits.*

Lois: Hulloa! Are you here, Gwen?

Gwen: Yes, your mother wanted to see me about the sale of work. I'm just going.

Lois: Wilfred is here.

Gwen: Is he? Give him my love and tell him not to be late for dinner. You're going to play bridge, aren't you?

Lois: Yes. Collie and Howard are coming. They'll have a man's four.

Gwen: Wilfred says your brother plays just as well as if he could see.

Lois: Yes, it's rather marvellous. Of course we have special cards.

Gwen (*catching sight of a pearl necklace Lois has on*): Pretty chain that is you're wearing. I've never seen it before.

Lois (*instinctively putting her hand to her neck and fingering the beads*): I bought it the other day when I went into Stanbury.

Gwen: How extravagant of you. I didn't know any one could afford to buy pearls now.

Lois: It only cost a pound.

Gwen: Aren't they real?

Lois: Of course not. How could they be?

Gwen (*going up to* **Lois** *and feeling the pearls*): I think I know something about pearls. I would have sworn they were real.

Lois: I wish they were.

Gwen: It's the most wonderful imitation I've ever seen.

Lois: They do make them marvellously now. I wonder any one bothers to have real pearls at all.

> **Gwen** *is taken aback. She still looks at the pearls doubtfully, then she makes an effort over herself.*

Gwen: Good-bye, Mrs Ardsley. I'll have everything ready in good time.

Mrs Ardsley: Good-bye, me dear, Lois will see you out.

> **Gwen** *and* **Lois** *go out.* **Mrs Ardsley** *is left reflective. She is a little puzzled.* **Lois** *comes in again.*

Mrs Ardsley: Lois dear. I've been thinking you looked rather peaked. Don't you think it would be a good idea if you went to stay at Aunt Emily's for a week or two?

Lois: I should hate it.

Mrs Ardsley: She does love having you there.

Lois: It's so incredibly boring.

Mrs Ardsley: You'll have to go before the end of the year. Much better go now and get it over.

Lois: I loathe the idea.

Mrs Ardsley: Think about it a little. I can't have you not looking your best, you know, or I shall never get you off my hands. (*She goes out. Her voice is*

heard through the still open door) Oh, here's
Collie. You'll find Sydney in the drawing-room.

As **Collie** *passes the door he sees* **Lois.**

Collie: Hulloa, Lois.
Lois: You're early.

He pauses at the door.

Collie: I had an appointment with your father, but
he's had to go out. I've left a message with the
clerk to say I'm here when I'm wanted.
Lois: Oh, good.
Collie: I'll go along to the drawing-room.
Lois: Right-ho.

He passes on. **Lois** *goes to the looking-glass
and looks again at the little string round her
neck. She feels the pearls.* **Wilfred's** *voice is
heard: 'Lois.'*

Lois: Hulloa.
Wilfred *(still outside)*: Where are you?
Lois: In the dining-room.

He comes to the door.

Wilfred: As Collie's here why shouldn't we start?
Lois: Howard's coming.
Wilfred: I know. But there's no reason why you
shouldn't play a rubber or two before he does.
Lois: Come in a minute, will you.
Wilfred: Why?
Lois: Shut the door.
Wilfred *(closing the door behind him)*: It's shut.
Lois: These pearls you gave me, they are false, aren't
they?
Wilfred: Of course.
Lois: How much did they cost?
Wilfred: I told you. A pound.
Lois: Gwen's just been here.
Wilfred: Why?

Lois: Oh, I don't know. She came to see mother about the sale of work.

Wilfred: Oh, is that all? She's been very funny lately.

Lois: She says they're real.

Wilfred: What does she know about it?

Lois: She says she knows a great deal. She has pearls of her own.

Wilfred: And a pretty packet they cost me.

Lois: Is she right?

Wilfred (*smiling*): I wouldn't swear she wasn't.

Lois: Why did you say they were false?

Wilfred: I didn't think you'd take them if you thought they were real.

Lois: Naturally. (*She puts her fingers to the clasp.*)

Wilfred: What are you going to do?

Lois: I'm going to give them back to you.

Wilfred: You can't do that now. You'll give the whole show away.

Lois: There's nothing to give away.

Wilfred: Oh, isn't there? You don't know Gwen. She's got the tongue of a serpent.

Lois: I can't accept a valuable pearl necklace from you.

Wilfred: At all events you must go on wearing it till we go away.

Lois: How much did you pay for it?

Wilfred: My dear, it's not very good manners to ask what a present costs.

Lois: Several hundred pounds?

Wilfred: I shouldn't wonder.

Lois: D'you know, I've never had a valuable thing in my life. I shall be scared stiff of losing it.

Wilfred: Don't give it a thought. I'm not a very poor man, and if you do I shall survive it.

Lois: But I might never have known. I might have worn it for years under the impression it was worth nothing.

Wilfred: That's what I hoped.

Lois (*with a smile*): You know, that's rather sweet of
you. I would never have thought you capable of
that.

Wilfred: Why?

Lois: Well, I've always looked upon you as rather a
show-off. I should have thought you the sort of man
who, when he gave a present that cost a lot of
money, made pretty sure that you knew it.

Wilfred: That's not very flattering.

Lois: You couldn't expect me to be so awfully
grateful. I mean, a string of false pearls. Howard
might have bought me that when he'd won a fiver
on a horse.

Wilfred: I liked to think of you wearing pearls I'd
given you. It gave me rather a thrill to think of them
round your pretty neck.

Lois: It seems a lot to pay for it.

Wilfred: You see, I'm so terribly in love with you.
Give me a kiss, Lois. (*He puts his arm round her
waist. He tries to kiss her lips, but she turns her
face away, and he kisses her cheek*) You do like
me a little, don't you?

Lois (*coolly*): Yes.

Wilfred: D'you think you could ever love me?

Lois: It wouldn't be much use, would it?

Wilfred: I'd do anything in the world for you. You
know Gwen and I don't get on. We'd be much
happier apart. I know I could make you happy. After
all you don't want to stay in this deadly little place
all your life.

Lois: What are you asking me to do now? Run away
with you?

Wilfred: Why not?

Lois: And be chucked the moment you were sick of
me? Thank you.

Wilfred: I'll settle twenty thousand pounds on you
to-morrow, and if you don't like to run away with
me you needn't.

Lois: Don't be such a donkey.

Wilfred: Gwen would divorce me if I made it worth her while and then we'd be married.

Lois: I've always understood that when the gay seducer had worked his wicked will on the village maiden he screamed like a hyena at the thought of making an honest woman of her.

Wilfred: Oh, Lois, don't laugh at me. I love you with all my heart. Oh, I know I'm as old as the hills. I wish to God I was twenty years younger. I want you so awfully. I want you for keeps.

    Lois *looks at him for a moment seriously*.

Lois: Let's go and play bridge.

    Ethel *comes in*.

Ethel: Sydney's getting impatient. (*to* **Wilfred**, *humorously*) And Howard says, if you don't come along at once you'll have to marry the girl.

Lois: I didn't know you were here.

Ethel: We've only just come.

Lois: Oh, well, if Howard's here you don't want me.

Wilfred: All right, we'll start a rubber. But come and cut in later, won't you.

Lois: I must go and powder my nose.

    Wilfred *goes out*.

Ethel: I hear Evie's been making a scene.

Lois: Has she? What about?

Ethel: Oh, I don't know. Nerves. She ought to get married.

Lois: Who can she marry, poor dear?

Ethel: Collie. They're just about the same age. I think it would be very suitable.

Lois: Wilfred says he's going smash.

Ethel: They could manage. Nobody's got any money nowadays, but one gets along somehow. Even a marriage that isn't quite satisfactory is better than not being married at all.

Lois: Is that your experience?

Ethel: I wasn't talking of myself. I haven't got anything to grumble at.

Lois: Wilfred wants me to run away with him.

Ethel: Wilfred? What do you mean? Why?

Lois: He says he's in love with me.

Ethel: The dirty old man. I don't understand. What does he suggest?

Lois: Well, I suppose his idea is to keep me till he gets his divorce and then I suppose his idea is to marry me.

Ethel: The beast.

Lois: I'm getting on, you know. I'm twenty-six.

Ethel (*aghast*): Lois.

Lois: What have I got to look forward to exactly? Getting jumpy like Eva or making the best of a bad job like you.

Ethel: I have my children. Howard has his faults like everybody else. But he's fond of me. He looks up to me.

Lois: My dear, you've got a wonderful character. I haven't. D'you think I haven't seen what a strain it is on you sometimes?

Ethel: Of course it's a hard life. I ought to have known it would be when I married a tenant farmer.

Lois: But you didn't expect he'd drink.

Ethel: I don't suppose he drinks any more than most men of his class.

Lois: Have you ever really quite got used to him?

Ethel (*defiantly*): I don't know what you mean?

Lois: Well, he's common, isn't he?

Ethel (*smiling*): Are you quite sure that you and I are any great shakes?

Lois: At all events we do talk the King's English. We have decent table manners and we wash.

Ethel: I don't believe you'd wash much if you had to get up at six and milk the cows. All that's convention. One oughtn't to let oneself be upset by things like that.

Lois: But aren't you?

Ethel: Sometimes. I blame myself.

Lois: What have you got in common with him really?

Ethel: A recollection. That first year or two when I loved him so madly. He was gallant and young. He was MANLY! I loved him because he was of the soil and his strength had its roots in it. Nothing mattered then. Nothing that he did offended me.

Lois: My dear, you're so romantic. I'm not. Romance doesn't last. When it's dead what is left but dust and ashes?

Ethel: And the consciousness that you've done your best.

Lois: Oh, that.

Ethel: It's something. I've made my bed and I'm ready to lie on it. Have you ever heard me complain?

Lois: Never.

Ethel: I've carried my head high. I've tried to make Howard a good wife. I've tried to be a good mother to my children. Sometimes I'm inclined to be a little proud of myself.

Lois: I suppose it's never occurred to you that it would have been better for Howard really if he'd married someone in his own class?

Ethel: Oh yes, often. That's why I feel I must always have patience with him. I ought to have known. I oughtn't to have been carried away.

Lois: My dear, you're so noble it makes me positively sick.

Ethel: I'm not noble at all. I merely have a good deal of common sense . . . Lois, you're not really thinking of going away with that man?

Lois: No, not really. It's only that it's rather exciting to have the chance.

Ethel: Oh, I'm so glad.

For Services Rendered

Leonard Ardsley *comes in.*

Ardsley: What are you two girls doing in here? Discussing frocks and frills, I'll be bound.

Ethel (*kissing him*): How are you, father?

Ardsley: Chatter, chatter, chatter all day long. I know you. It's a marvel to me that you never get tired of talking about clothes. Collie's here, isn't he?

Lois: Yes, he's playing bridge.

Ardsley: Well, run along both of you and send him in here. I want to see him.

Lois: All right.

Ardsley: Kiddies well?

Ethel: Oh yes. They always are.

Ardsley: Fine thing for them living on a farm like that. Grand thing a country life.

Ethel: They've gone back to school now.

Ardsley: Of course. I remember. Best thing in the world for them. Happiest time in their lives. (*The two girls go out.* **Ardsley** *catches sight of a ladies' paper and takes it up*) I knew it. (*He gives a complacent smile at his own perspicacity. The door opens and* **Collie** *comes in.* **Ardsley** *at the sight of him assumes his professional air*) How d'you do?

Collie: You weren't in when I turned up at the office just now.

Ardsley: No. I've got someone waiting that I thought you'd better not meet, and I wanted to see you before I saw him. So I came through my private door.

Collie: I'm just as glad. I'm not used to solicitors' offices and I'm always rather intimidated.

Ardsley: I'm afraid I've got something very serious to say to you.

Collie: Oh, Lord.

Ardsley: In the three years you've been here we've seen a good deal of you. We all liked you.

Collie: It's been a snip for me having this house to

46

come to. Except for all of you I should have had a pretty thin time.

Ardsley: I'm sure you'll realize that it's not very pleasant for me to find myself in my present position.

Collie: I suppose that means the game's up. I've made a damned good fight for it. Have I got to file my petition?

Ardsley: The bank wrote to you last month telling you that you were overdrawn and that they wouldn't cash any further cheques you drew until your account was put in order.

Collie: Yes.

Ardsley: And after that you gave several post-dated cheques in payment of various accounts.

Collie: I was being pestered for money all over the shop. I couldn't help myself.

Ardsley: You were hopelessly insolvent. How did you expect to meet them?

Collie: I thought something would turn up.

Ardsley: Don't you know that's a criminal offence?

Collie: Oh, what rot. It's the sort of thing any one might do when he was up against it.

Ardsley: Not without going to gaol.

Collie: Good God, you don't mean to say they're going to prosecute?

Ardsley: You can't expect the injured parties to take it lying down.

Collie: But it's absurd. They know I didn't mean any harm.

Ardsley: It's almost incredible that you should be so un-businesslike.

Collie: What should I know about business? I'm a sailor. I was in the navy for twenty years.

Ardsley: I'm afraid you've been very unwise.

Collie: Then what's going to happen?

Ardsley: The bank-manager is in my office now. You

must be prepared for the worst, Collie. A warrant
will be applied for.

Collie: Does that mean I shall be arrested?

Ardsley: Of course you'll be released on bail. I'll
arrange that. If you elect to be tried by a jury the
justices will refer the case to quarter sessions. It's
early days yet to decide, we'll see what counsel
has to say. My own opinion at the moment is that
the best thing you can do is to plead guilty and
throw yourself on the mercy of the court.

Collie: But I'm not guilty.

Ardsley: Don't be such a fool. You're just as guilty
as the thief who sneaks ten bob from your till
when no one is looking.

Collie: What will they do to me?

Ardsley: In consideration of your previous good
character and your record in the navy, I have little
doubt that the judge will be lenient. I should be
very disappointed if you got more than from three
to six months in the second division.

Collie (*with a flash of anger at the casual way he
takes it*): You don't care, do you?

Ardsley: My dear boy, don't think I'm happy about
it. In my profession one often finds oneself in very
disagreeable situations, but I don't remember ever
having found myself in a more painful one than
this.

Collie: Fortunately most people get over seeing the
other fellow come a cropper.

Ardsley: It's not only the pleasant social relations
we've always had with you, but that you should
have got the D.S.O. and been in command of a
destroyer – it all makes your fall so much more
distressing. I'm afraid it makes it also much more
disgraceful.

Collie: They'll take my D.S.O. away from me.

Ardsley: I suppose so.

Collie: I suppose it doesn't occur to you that when a

fellow has served the country for twenty years in a job that's unfitted him for anything else, it's rather distressing and rather disgraceful that he should be shoved out into the world with no means of earning his living and nothing between him and starvation but a bonus of a thousand pounds or so?

Ardsley: I can't go into that. Though of course it's a good point to take up at the trial. I'll make a note of that. Of course the answer is that the country was up against it and had to economize and if a certain number of individuals had to suffer it can't be helped.

Collie: When I was torpedoed during the war and they fished me out, God, what a bit of luck I said. I never knew.

Ardsley: Do me the justice to admit that I begged you six months ago to file your petition. You wouldn't take my advice.

Collie: I'd had it drummed into me for so many years that nothing is impossible in the British Navy. It was hard to give in while I still had some fight in me.

Ardsley: You mustn't despair.

Collie: There's not much of a future for an ex-naval officer, forty years of age, after six months in gaol.

Ardsley: I've been a hunting man. It's a very good plan not to take your fences before you come to them. Now look here, I must be off. There's whisky and soda on the sideboard. You help yourself to a drink. I'm sure you want it.

Collie: Thank you.

Ardsley (*giving him his hand*): Good-bye, my boy. I'll let you know about things as soon as I hear.

Collie: Good-bye.

> **Ardsley** *goes out.* **Collie**, *sinking into a chair, buries his face in his hands; but hearing the*

*door open he looks up and pulls himself
together.* **Eva** *comes in.*

Eva: Oh, I beg your pardon. I was looking for my bag.
I didn't know any one was here.

Collie: I was just going.

Eva: Please don't. I won't disturb you.

Collie: What are you talking about? Surely you can
come into your own dining-room.

Eva: I wasn't speaking the truth. I knew you were
here and my bag's upstairs. I heard father go. I
wanted to see you. I'm so frightfully anxious.

Collie: What about?

Eva: Every one knows you're in difficulties. Father
let fall a hint at luncheon. I knew he was seeing
you this afternoon.

Collie: It's kind of you to bother, Evie. I've had rather
a rough passage, but at all events I know where I
am now.

Eva: Can nothing be done?

Collie: Not very much, I'm afraid.

Eva: Won't you let me help you?

Collie (*with a smile*): My dear, how can you?

Eva: It's only a matter of money, isn't it?

Collie: Only is good.

Eva: I've got a thousand pounds that my godmother
left me. It's invested and I've always dressed myself
on the interest. I could let you have that.

Collie: I couldn't possibly take money from you. It's
out of the question.

Eva: Why? If I want to give it you.

Collie: It's awfully generous of you, but . . .

Eva (*interrupting*): You must know how frightfully
fond I am of you.

Collie: It's very nice of you, Evie. Besides, your father
would never hear of it.

Eva: It's my own money. I'm not a child.

Collie: Can't be done, my dear.

Eva: Why shouldn't I buy an interest in your garage?
   I mean, then it would be just an investment.

Collie: Can you see your father's face when you
   suggested it? It looked all right when I bought it.
   Things were booming then. But the slump has
   killed it. It isn't worth a bob.

Eva: But surely if you can get more capital you can
   afford to wait till times get better?

Collie: Your father doesn't think much of me as it
   is. He'd think me a pretty mean skunk if he
   thought I'd induced you to put your money into an
   insolvent business.

Eva: You keep on talking of father. It's nothing to do
   with him. It's you and I that are concerned.

Collie: I know you're a damned good sort and you're
   always going out of your way to do things for people,
   but there are limits. Perhaps you'll want to get
   married one of these days and then you'll find your
   thousand pounds devilish useful.

Eva: I shall never have a better use for it than to
   give it to someone who means so much to me as
   you do.

Collie: I'm awfully sorry. God knows I want the
   money, but I really can't take it from any one
   like you.

Eva: I thought you liked me.

Collie: I like you very much. You're a jolly good
   friend.

Eva: I thought perhaps some day we might be more
   than friends. (*There is a moment's silence. She is
   very nervous, but forces herself to go on*) After all,
   if we were engaged, it would be very natural that
   I should come to the rescue when you were in a
   hole.

Collie: But we're not engaged.

Eva: Why shouldn't we pretend to be? Just for a little
   while, I mean. Then I could lend you the money
   and father would help you to get straight.

Collie: Oh, my dear, that's absurd. That's the sort of thing they do in novels. You mustn't be so romantic.

Eva: You could always break if off when you got straight.

Collie: That's not a very pretty rôle you're asking me to play.

Eva (*in a husky voice*): Perhaps when you got used to the idea you wouldn't want to break it off.

Collie: My dear, what on earth ever put such an idea in your head?

Eva: You're alone and I'm alone. There's no one in the world that cares twopence for either of us.

Collie: Oh, what nonsense. Your family's devoted to you. They depend on you so enormously. Why, the whole house centres round you.

Eva: I want to get away. I'm so unhappy here.

Collie: I can't believe that. You're just nervous and run down. I dare say you want a bit of a change.

Eva: You won't understand. How can you be so cruel?

Collie: I'm not cruel. I'm awfully grateful to you.

Eva: I can't say any more than I have. It's so humiliating.

Collie: I'm dreadfully sorry. I don't want to hurt your feelings.

Eva: After all, I'm not so old as all that. Plenty of men have wanted to marry me.

Collie: I don't doubt that for a minute. I'm quite convinced that one of these days you'll find someone that you really like and I'm sure you'll make him a perfectly grand wife. (*She begins to cry and he looks at her with troubled eyes*) I'm sorry.

> *She does not answer and quietly he leaves the room. She sobs. But she hears the door open and starts to her feet, turning her face away so*

*that her tears should not be seen. The new-
comer is* **Howard**. *He is quite sober.*

Howard: Where's Collie?

Eva: How should I know?

Howard: We want him for bridge.

Eva: Well, you can see he isn't here, can't you?

Howard: He was here.

Eva (*stamping her foot*): Well, he isn't here now.

Howard: Temper, temper. What price the angel of mercy now?

Eva: You're very funny, aren't you? Terribly amusing.

Howard: I know what you've been doing. You've been asking him to marry you.

Eva (*furiously*): You drunken brute. Damn you. Blast you.

> *She flings out of the room.* **Howard** *purses his lips and grins. Then he goes over to the sideboard and helps himself to a whisky and soda. While he is sipping it* **Lois** *comes in.*

Lois: Hulloa, I thought you were playing bridge.

Howard: No. Your father wanted to see Collie, and Sydney and Wilfred are having a game of piquet.

Lois: So you seized the opportunity to have a drink on the quiet.

Howard: My dear girl, I had to have something to pull myself together. Evie's been swearing at me. Such language, my dear. Called me a drunken brute. I mean, it shakes a chap's morale when a properly brought-up young lady forgets herself like that.

Lois: Are you obliged to drink?

Howard: Well, in a manner of speaking I am. My poor old father died of drink and his poor old father died of drink. So it's in the family. See?

Lois: It is rotten for Ethel.

Howard: She has a lot to put up with, poor girl. You

don't have to tell me. I know it. Fact is, she's too
good for me.

Lois: Much.

Howard: That's what I say. She's a lady. I mean you
only have to look at her to know that. And mind
you, she never lets up. I can be a gentleman when
I want to, but I don't want to all the time. I mean
to say, I like to have a good old laugh now and
again. She never does. Truth is, between you and
me, she has no sense of humour.

Lois: I dare say after being married to you for fifteen
years it's worn rather thin.

Howard: I like a girl as has a bit of fun in her. Let's
have a good time while we're alive, I say; we can
do all the sitting quiet we want when we're dead
and buried.

Lois: There's something in that.

Howard: Mind you, I'm not complaining of Ethel.
Too much of a gentleman to do that. She's class. I
know that. And I'm only a common farmer. Only,
you know what I mean, you don't always want to
be looking up to your wife, do you?

Lois: No one asked you to marry Ethel.

Howard: Pity you wasn't old enough then. I'd have
married you instead.

Lois: Complimentary, aren't you?

Howard: You're not half the lady what Ethel is. And
you're a bit of a devil, I shouldn't wonder. You and
me'd get on like a house on fire.

Lois: You're drunk.

Howard: No, I'm not. I'm cold stone sober.

Lois: Then I like you better drunk.

Howard: Give me a kiss, honey.

Lois: D'you want your face slapped?

Howard: I don't mind.

Lois: The nerve of it.

Howard: Come on. Be a sport.

Lois: Go to hell.

Howard: I would with you.

> *With a sudden movement he catches hold of
> her and gives her a kiss full on the lips. She
> tears herself away from him.*

Lois: How dare you?

Howard: Oh, come off it. You don't mind. You
liked it.

Lois: It almost made me sick. You stink of cows.

Howard: A lot of girls like that. Makes them go all
funny.

Lois: You filthy beast.

Howard: Want another?

Lois: If it weren't for Ethel I'd go straight to father.

Howard: Don't make me laugh. D'you think I don't
know about girls? And if you don't know about
men it's high time you did. A good-looking girl like
you. You ought to be ashamed of yourself. I mean,
think what you're missing.

Lois: You've got a pretty good opinion of yourself
haven't you?

Howard: And not without cause. Of course I don't
say it's like the war. God, I wish it had gone on
for ever. Those were the days. If you liked the look
of a girl you just walked her up the garden path.
Of course the uniform had a lot to do with it, and
being a blasted hero.

Lois: Brute.

Howard (*confidentially*): Look here, why don't you
come up to the farm for a few days? We could
have a grand old time.

Lois: I don't know what you take me for, Howard.

Howard: Don't talk that sort of rot to me. You're
human, same as I am, aren't you? What's the good
of mouldering away without having a bit of fun in
your life? You come up to the farm. Now the kids
have gone to boarding-school their room's empty.

Lois: If you're not drunk you're crazy.

Howard: No, I'm not. You'll come, my girl.

Lois (*contemptuously*): And what makes you think that?

Howard: I'll tell you. Because I want you and you know I want you and there isn't a thing that takes a girl like that. By God, I want you.

> *He looks at her and the violence of his desire seems heavy in the room.* **Lois** *instinctively puts her hand to her breast. Her breathing is oppressed. There is a silence.* **Mrs Ardsley** *comes in.*

Lois (*recovering herself*): Oh, mother.

Howard: I've just been telling this young woman she ought to come up to the farm for a few days. She looks to me as if she wanted a change.

Mrs Ardsley: I'm glad you agree with me. Only a little while ago I was suggesting that she should go and stay with Aunt Emily for two or three weeks.

Lois: I've been thinking it over, mother. I dare say you're quite right. When d'you think I'd better go?

Mrs Ardsley: The sooner the better. To-morrow.

Lois: All right. I'll send the old girl a wire and tell her I'm coming.

Mrs Ardsley: You needn't do that. I've just written to her to say that you'll arrive in time for dinner.

Lois: Have you? You domineering old lady.

Mrs Ardsley: You're a very good girl, Lois. I didn't think you'd disregard my wishes.

Lois: I don't think I'm a very good girl. But you're a darling old mother.

> *She kisses her tenderly.* **Mrs Ardsley** *smiling, pats her hand.*

CURTAIN

Act III

*The drawing-room at the Ardsleys' house. It is a large
low room, with french windows leading on to the
terrace that was the scene of the first act. It is
furnished in an old-fashioned, common-place and
comfortable way. Nothing much has been added
since it was all new when the Ardsleys married. The
walls are over-crowded with framed engravings and
water-colours, copies of Florentine bas-reliefs,
weapons on wooden shields and plates in old English
china. The occasional tables are laden with knick-
knacks. The arm-chairs and sofas are covered with
loose-covers of faded cretonne. It is a rainy, windy
day, and there is a fire burning on the hearth. The
light is falling. It is about half-past four.* **Wilfred** *is
standing at the fire warming his hands.* **Lois** *comes
in. She is wearing a coat and skirt.*

Lois (*coming towards him with outstretched hand*):
How d'you do? Mother's out. She'll be back to tea.
She's gone to Stanbury.

Wilfred: I know. I asked the maid if I could see you.
Is it true you're going away to-day?

Lois: Yes, I'm spending a fortnight with an aunt near
Canterbury.

Wilfred: But in a fortnight I shall be gone.

Lois: Will you?

Wilfred: Were you going without saying good-bye to
me?

Lois: I thought mother would say it for me.

Wilfred (*in a husky, agitated tone*): Don't go, Lois.

Lois (*indifferently*): Why not?

Wilfred: Why are you going?

57

Lois: Mother thought I wanted a change. I generally spend a fortnight with Aunt Emily once or twice a year. She's my godmother and she says she's going to leave me something in her will.

Wilfred: I was going up to London to-morrow to settle that money on you.

Lois: Don't be silly. As if I wanted that. If I ran away with you I wouldn't take it. I'd rather have my independence.

Wilfred: You might have given me the last fortnight. It means nothing to you. And so much to me.

Lois: How did you know I was going?

Wilfred: Gwen told me.

Lois: How did she know?

Wilfred: Your mother rang up.

Lois: Oh!

Wilfred: Are you quite sure it was about the sale of work that Gwen came to see your mother yesterday?

Lois: She wouldn't have dared. You don't know mother. She'd never let any one say a word against any of us. You've only seen her when she's being nice. She can be as stiff as a poker if one tries to take a liberty with her.

Wilfred: Gwen spotted the pearls all right.

Lois (*beginning to unclasp them*): Oh, I forgot. I can give them back to you now.

Wilfred: Won't you keep them? Please. It can't hurt you and it'll give me so much pleasure.

Lois: I don't see how. The chances are that we shall never see one another again. As far as you're concerned it's just throwing money away.

Wilfred: I want to be able to think that you're wearing something I gave you. I've held them in my hands. I want to think that they have the warmth of your body and they touch the softness of your neck.

Lois (*tempted*): I've never had anything so valuable. I suppose I'm half a strumpet.

Wilfred: They only cost a pound, Lois.

Lois: Oh, you liar. Does Gwen know you gave them to me?

Wilfred: She hasn't said so. She knows there's no one else who could.

Lois: Has she been making a scene?

Wilfred: Oh, no, she's been holding herself in. She's afraid.

Lois: Why? Are you so terrifying?

Wilfred: I don't think you'd find me so.

Lois: Are you awfully in love with me?

Wilfred: Awfully.

Lois: Strange, isn't it? I wonder why.

Wilfred: I'm broken-hearted, Lois. I know you don't love me. There's no reason why you should. But you might. If I were very kind to you. And patient. I'd do anything in the world to make you happy.

Lois: It's curious, it does give one rather a funny feeling to know someone's in love with you.

Wilfred: When Gwen told me you were going, the whole world went black. She tried to say it casually, but she knew she was thrusting a dagger in my heart and she watched my face to see me writhe.

Lois: Poor Gwen. I suppose people can be rather foul when they're jealous.

Wilfred: Oh, damn Gwen. I can only think of myself. You're everything in the world to me, and every one else can go to hell. It's my last chance, Lois.

She slowly shakes her head. He looks at her for a moment with despair.

Wilfred: Is there nothing I can say to persuade you?

Lois: Nothing.

Wilfred: I'm done. I'm finished.

Lois: I don't think so. You'll get over it. When are you going to the Riviera?

Wilfred: It's only a joke to you. (*Violently*) Oh, I hate being old.

> **Eva** *comes in.*

Eva: Why haven't the curtains been drawn? Oh, Wilfred!

Wilfred (*trying to seem naturally casual*): How are you to-day?

Eva: I'll turn on the lights.

> *She switches on the electricity while* **Lois** *draws the curtains.*

Lois: It is a foul day.

Wilfred: I'll be getting along.

Eva: Oh, aren't you going to stay to tea? Sydney's just coming. He'd love to play piquet with you.

Wilfred: I'm sorry, I must be off. I only came to say good-bye to Lois.

Eva: We shall be seeing you again soon, I suppose?

Wilfred: I expect so.

> *They shake hands.* **Lois** *gives him her hand.*

Lois: Good-bye. Give my love to Gwen.

Wilfred: Good-bye. (*He goes out quickly.*)

Eva: What's the matter with him? He seems all funny to-day.

Lois: I didn't notice that he was any different.

Eva: Are you all packed up and everything?

Lois: Yes.

Eva: Are you taking the five-fifty?

Lois: Yes.

Eva: That gives you nice time to have tea. Ethel's coming in.

Lois: I know. She wants me to take some partridges to Aunt Emily.

> **Sydney** *comes in.*

Sydney: Tea ready?

Eva: It's not five yet.

Sydney: Thank God for the fire. I hate that gas-stove in my room. Mother's not back yet, I suppose?

Eva: No. She said she'd be in to tea.

Lois: Howard says he's expecting a very hard winter.

Sydney: Cheerful.

Lois: Oh, I hate the winter.

Eva: If it weren't for the winter we shouldn't enjoy the spring.

Sydney: Are you obliged to say things like that, Evie?

Eva: It happens to be true.

Sydney: It happens to be true that two and two are four, but one needn't make a song and dance about it.

Lois: I'll put on a record, shall I?

Eva: Oh, for goodness' sake don't, it drives me mad.

Lois: Oh, all right. (*They both give her a little look of surprise.*)

Eva: I'm rather jumpy to-day. I suppose it's the east wind.

Sydney: Give me my tatting, Lois, will you?

Lois: I will.

> *She gives it to him and while he talks he proceeds mechanically with his work.*

Sydney: I wonder if Collie will turn up?

Eva: I rang up to ask him to come in to tea. He hasn't been at the garage all day.

> **Ethel** *and* **Howard** *come in.*

Ethel: How's everybody?

Sydney: Hulloa.

Howard: We've brought the partridges. They'd better be hung for a couple of days. They were only shot yesterday.

Sydney: Got many birds this year, Howard?

Howard: A few. What's that you're doing?

Sydney: Tatting.

Eva: Put on the gramophone if you want to.

For Services Rendered

Howard: I'll put it on.

He goes over, gives the machine a wind and starts a record.

Ethel: I'm afraid it won't be very amusing for you at Aunt Emily's.

Lois: I shall read a lot.

Sydney: Let's hope she'll die soon and leave you a packet.

Lois: She's got very little to leave.

Suddenly **Mr Ardsley** *bursts into the room.*

Ethel: Oh, father.

Ardsley: Turn off the gramophone.

Eva: What's the matter?

Howard *who is still at the gramophone stops the record.*

Ardsley: Something dreadful's happened. I thought I'd better come in and tell you at once.

Eva (*with a cry*): Collie.

Ardsley: How d'you know?

Sydney: What is it, father?

Ardsley: They've just telephoned to me from the police station. There's been an accident. Collie's been shot.

Howard: Shot? Who by?

Ardsley: I'm afraid he shot himself.

Howard: Good God!

Eva: He isn't dead?

Ardsley: Yes.

Eva gives a loud, long shriek. It is a sound that is only just human.

Ethel: Evie!

Eva goes up to her father with arms raised high in the air and clenched hands.

Eva: You killed him, you fiend.

Ardsley: I? What *are* you talking about?

Eva: You fiend! You beast!

Ethel (*putting a restraining hand on her*): Evie!

Eva (*shaking her off angrily*): Leave me alone. (*To Ardsley*) You could have saved him. You devil! I hate you!

Ardsley: Are you mad, Eva?

Eva: You hounded him to his death. You never gave him a chance.

Ardsley: Good heavens, we all gave him chance after chance.

Eva: It's a lie. He begged for money. He begged for time. And not one of you would help him. Not one of you remembered that he'd risked his life for you a hundred times. You brutes.

Ardsley: Oh, what rubbish.

Eva: I hope you're shamed before the whole world. Let every one know that a brave and gallant gentleman went to his death because there wasn't a soul in this bloody place who would lend him two hundred pounds.

Ardsley: Pretty language, Eva. In point of fact two hundred pounds wouldn't have helped him. It would have saved him from going to gaol, but that's all.

Eva: Gaol?

Ardsley: Yes, a warrant for his arrest was issued this morning.

Eva (*with anguish*): Poor Collie. I can't bear it. Cruel. Cruel. (*She begins to sob desperately.*)

Ardsley: Now, my dear, don't take it so much to heart. Go and lie down in your room. Ethel will come and bathe your forehead with eau-de-Cologne. Of course the whole thing is very unfortunate. No one regrets it more than I do. The poor fellow was in a hopeless mess and perhaps he took the best way out of a situation that could only have thrown discredit on the uniform he'd worn.

For Services Rendered

While he says this **Eva** *raises her head and looks at him with eyes of horror.*

Eva: But he was alive and he's dead. He's gone from us for ever. He's been robbed of all the years that were before him. Haven't you any pity for him? He used to come here almost every day.

Ardsley: He was a very nice fellow and a gentleman. Unfortunately he wasn't a very good business man.

Eva: As if I cared if he was a good business man.

Ardsley: There's no reason why you should. But his creditors did.

Eva: He was everything in the world to me.

Ardsley: My dear, what an exaggerated way to speak. You ought to have more sense at your age.

Eva: He loved me and I loved him.

Ardsley: Don't talk such nonsense.

Eva: We were engaged to be married.

Ardsley (*with astonishment*): What's that? Since when?

Eva: Since ages.

Ardsley: Well, my dear, you're out of that. He was in no position to marry.

Eva (*with anguish*): It was my only chance.

Ardsley: You have a good home. You'd much better stay here.

Eva: And make myself useful?

Ardsley: There's no harm in that.

Eva: I've got just as much right to life and happiness as any one else.

Ardsley: Of course you have.

Eva: You've done everything you could to prevent me from marrying.

Ardsley: Rubbish.

Eva: Why should I be sacrificed all the time? Why should I be at everybody's beck and call? Why should I have to do everything? I'm sick of being put upon. I'm sick of you, I'm sick of Sydney, I'm sick of Lois. I'm sick of you all.

> *During the speech her agitation has become quite uncontrolled. There is a table covered with ornaments by her, and now with a violent gesture she throws it over so that everything is scattered on the floor.*

Ethel: Evie.

Eva: Damn you. Damn you. Damn you.

> *Shrieking she throws herself down and hysterically beats upon the floor with her fists.*

Ardsley: Stop it. Stop it.

Howard: Better get her out of here.

> *He picks her up and carries her out of the room. **Ardsley** opens the door. He and **Ethel** follow her out. **Lois** and **Sydney** are left alone. **Lois**, pale and trembling, has watched the scene with terror.*

Lois: What's the matter with her?

Sydney: Hysterics. Upset you?

Lois: I'm frightened.

Sydney: I'll telephone for Uncle Charlie. I think she wants a doctor.

> *He makes his way out of the room. **Lois** stands stock still. She cannot control the nervous trembling that seizes her. **Howard** comes in.*

Howard: I've put her on the dining-room sofa.

Lois: Are Ethel and father with her?

Howard: Yes. (*He looks at her and sees the condition she is in. He puts his arm round her shoulders*) Poor old girl, gave you quite a turn, didn't it?

Lois (*unconscious of his touch*): I'm frightened.

Howard: It's not serious, you know. Do her good to let off steam like that. You mustn't take it to heart. (*He bends down and kisses her on the cheek.*)

65

For Services Rendered

Lois: Why do you do that?

Howard: I don't like to see you miserable.

She turns round a little and gives him a thoughtful look. He smiles rather charmingly.

Howard: I'm quite sober.

Lois: You'd better take your arm away. Ethel can come in any minute.

Howard: I'm terribly fond of you, Lois. Don't you like me?

Lois (*miserably*): Not much.

Howard: Shall I come over and see you when you're staying at Aunt Emily's?

Lois: Why should you?

Howard (*in a low passionate whisper*): Lois.

She looks at him curiously and with a cold hostility.

Lois: Isn't human nature funny? I know with my mind that you're a rotter. And I despise you. Isn't it lucky you can't see into my heart?

Howard: Why, what should I see there?

Lois: Desire.

Howard: What for? I don't know what you mean.

Lois: I didn't think you would or I shouldn't have told you. How shameful and ugly. I see that all right. It's funny, it doesn't seem to make any difference.

Howard: Oh, I see what you mean now. That's quite O.K. Give it time, girlie, I'll wait.

Lois (*coolly, indifferently*): You swine.

Sydney comes in.

Sydney: Uncle Charlie's on his way round now.

Lois: Mother will be back in a minute.

Sydney: How are you going to get to the station?

Howard: I'll drive you if you like.

Lois: Oh, it's all arranged.

Ardsley comes in.

Ardsley: Prentice has come. They're putting Evie to bed.

Lois: I'll go and see if I can do anything. (*She goes out.*)

Ardsley (to **Sydney**): Sydney, did you know anything about her being engaged to Collie?

Sydney: I don't believe she was.

Ardsley: D'you mean to say you think it was pure invention?

Sydney: I shouldn't wonder. But I think she'll stick to it. After all no one can now prove she wasn't.

Ardsley: It's a terrible thing about poor Collie. No one can be more distressed than I.

Sydney: It seems a bit hard that after going through the war and getting a D.S.O., he should have come to this end.

Ardsley: He may have been a very good naval officer. He was a very poor business man. That's all there is to it.

Sydney: We might put that on his tombstone. It would make a damned good epitaph.

Ardsley: If that's a joke, Sydney, I must say I think it in very bad taste.

Sydney (*with bitter calm*): You see, I feel I have a certain right to speak. I know how dead keen we all were when the war started. Every sacrifice was worth it. We didn't say much about it because we were rather shy, but honour did mean something to us and patriotism wasn't just a word. And then, when it was all over, we did think that those of us who'd died hadn't died in vain, and those of us who were broken and shattered and knew they wouldn't be any more good in the world were buoyed up by the thought that if they'd given everything they'd given it in a great cause.

Ardsley: And they had.

Sydney: Do you still think that? I don't. I know that we were the dupes of the incompetent fools who

67

ruled the nations. I know that we were sacrificed to their vanity, their greed, and their stupidity. And the worst of it is that as far as I can tell they haven't learnt a thing. They're just as vain, they're just as greedy, they're just as stupid as they ever were. They muddle on, muddle on, and one of these days they'll muddle us all into another war. When that happens I'll tell you what I'm going to do. I'm going out into the streets and cry: 'Look at me, don't be a lot of damned fools; it's all bunk what they're saying to you, about honour and patriotism and glory. Bunk, bunk, bunk.'

Howard: Who cares if it is bunk? I had the time of my life in the war. No responsibility and plenty of money. More than I'd ever had before or ever since. All the girls you wanted and all the whisky. Excitement. A roughish time in the trenches, but a grand lark afterwards. I tell you it was a bitter day for me when they signed the armistice. What have I got now? Just the same old thing day after day, working my guts out to keep body and soul together. The very day war is declared I join up and the sooner the better, if you ask me. That's the life for me. By God!

Ardsley (*to his son*): You've had a lot to put up with, Sydney. I know that. But don't think you're the only one. It's been a great blow to me that you haven't been able to follow me in my business as I followed my father. Three generations, that would have been. But it wasn't to be. No one wants another war less than I do, but if it comes I'm convinced that you'll do your duty, so far as in you lies, as you did it before. It was a great grief to me that when the call came I was too old to answer. But I did what I could. I was enrolled as a special constable. And if I'm wanted again I shall be ready again.

Sydney (*between his teeth*): God give me patience.

Howard: You have a whisky and soda, old boy, and you'll feel better.

Sydney: Will a whisky and soda make me forget poor Evie half crazy, Collie doing away with himself rather than go to gaol, and my lost sight?

Ardsley: But, my dear boy, that's just our immediate circle. Of course we suffered, perhaps we've had more than our share, but we're not every one.

Sydney: Don't you know that all over England there are families like ours, all over Germany, and all over France? We were quite content to go our peaceful way, jogging along obscurely, and happy enough. All we asked was to be left alone. Oh, it's no good talking.

Ardsley: The fact is, Sydney, you think too much.

Sydney (*smiling*): I dare say you're right, father. You see, I have little else to do. I'm thinking of collecting stamps.

Ardsley: That's a very good idea, my boy. If you go about it cleverly there's no reason why it shouldn't be a very sound investment.

> **Mrs Ardsley** *comes in. She is still wearing her hat and coat.*

Sydney: Hulloa, mother.

> *As she sits down, a trifle wearily, her eye catches the litter on the floor of all the things* **Eva** *threw over when she upset the table.*

Mrs Ardsley: Been having a picnic?

Ardsley: Evie upset the table.

Mrs Ardsley: In play or anger?

Howard: I'd better pick the things up.

Mrs Ardsley: It does look rather untidy.

> *He picks up one piece after the other and sets the table straight.*

Ardsley: Poor Collie's killed himself.

Mrs Ardsley: Yes, I've heard. I'm sorry.

Ardsley: Evie's in rather a state about it.

Mrs Ardsley: Poor thing, I'll go to her.

Ardsley: Charlie Prentice is with her.

Sydney: Why don't you wait till you've had a cup of tea, mother? You sound tired.

Mrs Ardsley: I am rather. (**Dr Prentice** *comes in and she gives him a smile*) Oh, Charlie. I was just coming upstairs.

Prentice: I wouldn't. I've given Evie a hypodermic. I'd rather she were left alone.

Ardsley: Take a pew, Charlie. I'm going back to my office. One or two things I want to finish up. I'll be along for tea in a quarter of an hour.

Mrs Ardsley: Very well. (*He goes out.*)

Howard (*having finished*): There. That's all right, I think. I say, I think I'll just go along to Collie's garage. There are one or two bits and pieces that I've got my eye on. I'd just as soon make sure that nobody sneaks them.

Sydney: Oh, yeah.

Howard: Tell Ethel I'll come back for her. I shan't be long. (*He goes out.*)

Sydney: What did the specialist say, mother?

Mrs Ardsley: What specialist, Sydney?

Sydney: Come off it, darling. You don't generally favour your family with a very detailed account of your movements. When you took such pains to tell us exactly why you were going into Stanbury this afternoon, I guessed that you were going to see a specialist.

Mrs Ardsley: I never believe a word doctors say to me.

Prentice: Don't mind me.

Mrs Ardsley: Tell me about Evie.

Prentice: I hardly know yet. It may be it would be better if she went into a home for a few weeks.

Mrs Ardsley: She isn't mad?

Prentice: She's very unbalanced . . . I was just coming

round when Sydney telephoned. Murray rang me
up after he'd seen you.

Mrs Ardsley: Why didn't he mind his own business?

Prentice: It was his business.

Sydney: Would you like me to leave you?

Mrs Ardsley *gives him a little, thoughtful look.*

Mrs Ardsley: No, stay if you like. But go on with
your tatting and pretend you don't hear.

Sydney: All right. (*He takes his work and goes on as
though absorbed in it.*)

Mrs Ardsley: Don't interrupt.

Prentice: I'm afraid Murray could only confirm my
diagnosis, Charlotte.

Mrs Ardsley (*cheerfully*): I had an idea he would, you
know. You stick together, you doctors.

Prentice: He agrees with me that an immediate
operation is necessary.

Mrs Ardsley: I believe he does.

Prentice: When I spoke to him on the telephone he
said you were – hesitating a little.

Mrs Ardsley: Not at all. I didn't hesitate for a minute.

Prentice: I'm delighted to hear it. I know your
courage. I was confident in your good sense.

Mrs Ardsley: I'm glad.

Prentice: I'll make all the arrangements and we'll
have it done as soon as possible.

Mrs Ardsley: I'm not going to be operated on,
Charlie.

Prentice: My dear, I must be frank with you. It's the
only chance we have of saving your life.

Mrs Ardsley: That's not true, Charlie. It's the only
chance you have of prolonging my life. For a few
months or a year perhaps. And then it'll start all
over again. Do you think it's worth it? I don't.

Prentice: You have your husband and your children
to think of.

Mrs Ardsley: I know. It would be a frightful expense.

If I got over the operation I should always be an
invalid. I should have to have a nurse. I should be
much more bother than I was worth.

Prentice: That's unkind, Charlotte. And it's untrue.

Mrs Ardsley: You've known me a great many years,
Charlie. Haven't you noticed that when once I
make up my mind I don't change it?

Prentice: Don't be a damned fool, Charlotte.

Mrs Ardsley: I have nothing to complain of. I haven't
had an unhappy life. I'm prepared to call it a day.

Prentice: I don't know if Murray made himself quite
clear.

Mrs Ardsley: I asked him to.

Prentice: Listen to me. I mean every word I say. If
you won't consent to an operation, I'm afraid you
have only a few months to live.

Mrs Ardsley (*coolly*): How odd! Those were his very
words.

Prentice: Well?

Mrs Ardsley: I've often wondered in the past how I
should take it when I was told that I was going to
die. I've wondered if I'd scream or faint. You know,
I didn't do either. It gave me a funny sort of thrill.
I felt as if I'd drunk a glass of port on an empty
stomach. I had some shopping to do at Stanbury
afterwards. I'm afraid I was rather extravagant. I felt
so gay and light-hearted.

Prentice: That's more than I do.

Mrs Ardsley: It shows how right Leonard is when he
says it's silly to take your jumps before you come
to them.

Prentice: Oh, damn Leonard!

Mrs Ardsley: I'm free. Nothing matters very much
any more. It's a very comfortable feeling.

Prentice: And the rest?

Mrs Ardsley: Oh, the rest, my dear, is between me
and the pale, distant shadow that is all you clever
people have left me of God.

Prentice (*after a moment's reflection*): If you take that view of it, if you know the facts and are prepared to take the consequences, I have no more to say. Perhaps you're right. I admire your courage. I should like to think that I should have enough to follow your example.

Mrs Ardsley: There is one thing I'm going to ask you to do for me.

Prentice: My dear, anything in the world.

Mrs Ardsley: I don't want to suffer more than I need. We've always had a great deal of affection for one another, Charlie.

Prentice: I suppose we have.

Mrs Ardsley: You doctors are a brutal lot and there's no end to the amount of pain you can bear in other people.

Prentice: I will do everything medical practice permits me to save you from suffering.

Mrs Ardsley: But I'm going to ask you to do something more.

A long, intent look passes between them.

Prentice: I'll do even that.

Mrs Ardsley (*with a change of manner, cheerfully*): Then that's all right. And now let's forget that I have anything the matter with me.

> **Sydney** *gets up, and, coming over to his mother, bends down and kisses her on the forehead.*

Mrs Ardsley: As you're up you might ring the bell, Sydney. I'm simply dying for a cup of tea.

As he rings **Ethel** *comes in.*

Ethel: I didn't know you were back, mother.

Mrs Ardsley: Yes, I got in a few minutes ago. (**Ethel** *kisses her*) I was going up to see Evie, but Uncle Charlie thought I'd better wait.

Ethel: She's quite comfortable.

73

Mrs Ardsley: Asleep?

Ethel: No, but resting.

Mrs Ardsley: Where's Lois?

Ethel: She's in her room. She's just coming.

> **The Maid** *comes in with a tray, which she puts on a little table.*

Mrs Ardsley *(to her):* Oh, Gertrude, if any one calls I'm not at home.

Gertrude: Very good, ma'am.

Mrs Ardsley: I don't feel inclined to cope with visitors this afternoon.

Prentice: I'll take myself off.

Mrs Ardsley: Don't be stupid. You're going to stay and have a cup of tea.

Prentice: I have other patients, you know.

Mrs Ardsley: They can wait.

> **Lois** *comes in.*

Mrs Ardsley: You ought to be starting soon, Lois, oughtn't you?

Lois: I've got time yet. It won't take me five minutes to get to the station.

Ethel: You won't forget the partridges?

Lois: No.

Mrs Ardsley: Give Aunt Emily my love.

Prentice: You might remember me to her, Lois.

Lois: I will.

Mrs Ardsley: Her chrysanthemums ought to be coming on just now.

> **Gertrude** *has gone out of the room after bringing in the tray, and now comes back.*

Gertrude: Mrs Cedar has called, ma'am.

Mrs Ardsley: I told you to say I wasn't at home.

Gertrude: I said you wasn't, ma'am, but she says it's very important.

Mrs Ardsley: Tiresome woman. Tell her I've just come back from Stanbury and I'm very tired. Say,

will she forgive me, but I don't feel up to seeing
anybody to-day.

Gertrude: Very good, ma'am.

*She is about to go, when the door bursts open
and* **Gwen** *comes in. She is wrought up.*

Gwen: I'm sorry to force myself on you. It's a matter
of life and death. I must see you.

Mrs Ardsley: I'm not very well, Gwen, don't you
think you can wait till to-morrow?

Gwen: No, no, no, to-morrow it'll be too late. Oh,
God, what shall I do?

Mrs Ardsley: Well, since you're here, perhaps the
best thing would be sit down and have a cup of tea.

Gwen (*in a strangled voice*): Lois and Wilfred are
going to elope.

Mrs Ardsley: Oh, my dear, don't be so silly. You're
making a perfect nuisance of yourself.

Gwen: It's true, I tell you, it's true.

Mrs Ardsley: Lois is going to spend a fortnight with
my sister-in-law. I didn't think there was anything
in what you said to me, but I didn't want any
unpleasantness, so I arranged that she should be
away till after you'd gone.

Gwen: She's not going to your sister-in-law's.
Wilfred's meeting her at Stanbury. They're going
to London.

Lois: What are you talking about, Gwen?

Gwen: I heard every word you said on the 'phone.

Lois (*trying to hide that she is startled*): When?

Gwen: Just now. Ten minutes ago. You didn't know
I'd had an extension put up into my room. I'm not
such a perfect fool as you thought me. Can you
deny that you spoke to Wilfred?

Lois: No.

Gwen: You said, Wilfred, it's a go. And he said, what
d'you mean? And you said, I'm trusting myself to

75

your tender mercies. You're for it, my boy. I'm
going to elope with you.

Ethel: She was joking with him.

Gwen: A funny joke. He said, my God, you don't
mean it. And she said, I'll get out of the train at
Stanbury. Meet me in the car and we'll talk it over
on the way to London.

Mrs Ardsley: Is it true, Lois?

Lois: Yes.

Sydney: You damned fool, Lois.

Gwen: Oh, Lois, I've never done you any harm. I've
been a good friend to you – you can't take my
husband from me.

Lois: I'm not taking him from you. You lost him
years ago.

Gwen: You're young, you'll have plenty of chances
before you're through. I'm old and he's all I've got.
If he leaves me I swear to you that I'll kill myself.

Mrs Ardsley: But why have you come here? Why
didn't you go to your husband?

Gwen: He won't listen to me. Oh, what a fool I've
been. I ought to have known when I saw the pearls.

Mrs Ardsley: What pearls?

Gwen: She's wearing them now. She pretends they're
false, but they're real, and he gave them to her.

Mrs Ardsley: Take them off, Lois, and give them to
Gwen.

Without a word **Lois** *undoes the clasp and
throws the string on the table.*

Gwen: Do you think I'd touch them? He hates me.
Oh, it's so awful to love someone with all your
heart and to know that the very sight of you
maddens him beyond endurance. I went down on
my knees to him. I begged him not to leave me. He
said he was sick to death of me. He pushed me
over. I heard the door slam. He's gone. He's gone

to join her. (*She falls to her knees and bursts into a passion of tears.*)

Mrs Ardsley: Gwen, Gwen, don't give way like that.

Gwen, *still on her knees, drags herself up to* **Mrs Ardsley.**

Gwen: Don't let her go to him. You know what it feels like to be old. You know how defenceless one is. She'll regret it. You don't know what he's like. He'll throw her aside when he's tired of her as he's thrown all the others aside. He's hard and cruel and selfish. He's made me so miserable.

Mrs Ardsley: If that's true, if he's all you say I should have thought you were well rid of him.

Gwen: I'm too old to start fresh. I'm too old to be left alone. (*She struggles up to her feet*) He's mine. I went through the divorce court to get him. I won't let him go. (*Turning on* **Lois**) I swear to you before God that you shall never marry him. He forced his first wife to divorce him because she hadn't money, but I've got money of my own. I'll never divorce him.

Lois: Nothing would induce me to marry him.

Gwen: Take him if you want to. He'll come back to me. He's old. He tries to keep up. It's all sham. I know the effort it is. He's tired to death and he won't give in. What good can he be to you? How can you be so stupid? You ought to be ashamed.

Mrs Ardsley: Gwen, Gwen.

Gwen: Money. Oh, curse the money. He's a rich man and you haven't got a bob between you. You're all in it. All of you. You all want to get something out of it. You brutes. You beasts.

Dr Prentice *gets up and takes her by the arm.*

Prentice: Come, Mrs Cedar, we've had enough of this. You go too far. You must get out of this.

Gwen: I won't go.

For Services Rendered

Prentice: If you don't, I shall put you out. (*He urges her towards the door.*)

Gwen: I'll make such a scandal that you'll never be able to hold up your heads again.

Prentice: That's enough now. Get out.

Gwen: Leave me alone, damn you.

Prentice: I'm going to take you home. Come on.

> *They both go out. There is a moment's awkward silence when the door is closed on them.*

Lois: I'm sorry to have exposed you to this disgusting scene, mother.

Sydney: You may well be.

Ethel: You're not really going off with that man, Lois?

Lois: I am.

Ethel: You can't be in love with him.

Lois: Of course not. If I were, d'you think I'd be such a fool as to go?

Ethel (*aghast*): Lois.

Lois: If I loved him I'd be afraid.

Ethel: You don't know what you're doing. It would be awful and unnatural if you loved him, but there would be an excuse for you.

Lois: Has love done very much for you, Ethel?

Ethel: Me? I don't know what you mean. I married Howard. I took him for better, for worse.

Lois: You've been a good wife and a good mother. A virtuous woman. And a lot of good it's done you. I've seen you grow old and tired and hopeless. I'm frightened, Ethel, frightened.

Ethel: I wasn't obliged to marry. Mother and father were against it.

Lois: You could have stayed on at home like Evie. So can I. I'm frightened, Ethel. I'm frightened. I don't want to become like Evie.

Ethel: Mother, can't you do something? It's so awful.
It's such madness.

Mrs Ardsley: I'm listening to what Lois has to say.

Ethel (*with a catch in her breath*): You're not running
away from anybody here?

Lois (*smiling*): Oh, my dear, that isn't at all in my
character.

Ethel (*ashamed and awkward*): I thought that
perhaps someone had been trying to make love
to you.

Lois: Oh, Ethel, don't be so silly. Who is there to
make love to me in this God-forsaken place?

Ethel: I didn't know. Perhaps it was only my fancy.
It's just the money?

Lois: Yes, and what money brings. Freedom and
opportunity.

Ethel: Those are mere words.

Lois: I'm sick of waiting for something to turn up.
Time is flying and soon it'll be too late.

Mrs Ardsley: When did you decide, Lois?

Lois: Half an hour ago.

Mrs Ardsley: Have you considered all the
consequences?

Lois: Oh, mother dear, if I did that I should stay here
twiddling my thumbs till my dying day.

Mrs Ardsley: It's not a very nice thing that you're
doing.

Lois: I know.

Mrs Ardsley: It's cruel to Gwen.

Lois (*with a shrug*): I or another.

Mrs Ardsley: It'll be a dreadful blow to your father.

Lois: I'm sorry.

Mrs Ardsley: And the scandal won't be very nice
for us.

Lois: I can't help it.

Ethel: It would be bad enough if you were going to
be married. Gwen says she won't divorce.

Lois: I don't want to marry him.

Ethel: What's to happen to you if he chucks you?

Lois: Darling, you're years older than I am and a married woman. How can you be so innocent? Has it never occurred to you what power it gives a woman when a man is madly in love with her and she doesn't care a row of pins for him?

> **Gertrude** *comes in with the teapot and the hot water on a tray.*

Mrs Ardsley (*to* **Ethel**): Go and tell your father tea is ready, Ethel.

> *With a disheartened gesture* **Ethel** *goes out.*

Lois: I'll go and put on my hat. (**Gertrude** *goes out*) I'm sorry to disappoint you, mother. I don't want to cause you pain.

Mrs Ardsley: Have you quite made up your mind, Lois?

Lois: Quite.

Mrs Ardsley: That is what I thought. Then perhaps you *had* better go and put on your hat.

Lois: What about father? I don't want him to make a scene.

Mrs Ardsley: I'll tell him after you've gone.

Lois: Thank you.

> *She goes out.* **Mrs Ardsley** *and* **Sydney** *are left alone.*

Sydney: Are you going to let her go, mother?

Mrs Ardsley: How can I stop her?

Sydney: You can tell her what the surgeon told you this afternoon.

Mrs Ardsley: Oh, my dear, with one foot in the grave it's rather late to start blackmail.

Sydney: She wouldn't go, you know.

Mrs Ardsley: I don't think she would. I can't do that, Sydney. I shouldn't like to think of her waiting for my death. I should feel like apologizing for every day I lingered on.

Sydney: She might change her mind.

Mrs Ardsley: She's young, she has her life before her, she must do what she thinks best with it. I don't belong to life any longer. I don't think I have the right to influence her.

Sydney: Aren't you afraid she'll come an awful cropper.

Mrs Ardsley: She's hard and selfish. I don't think she's stupid. She can take care of herself.

Sydney: She might be a stranger, to hear you speak.

Mrs Ardsley: Does it sound unkind? You see, I feel as if nothing mattered very much any more. I've had my day. I've done what I could. Now those who come after me must shift for themselves.

Sydney: You're not frightened at all?

Mrs Ardsley: Not a bit. I'm strangely happy. I'm rather relieved to think it's over. I'm not at home in this world of to-day. I'm pre-war. Everything's so changed now. I don't understand the new ways. To me life is like a party that was very nice to start with, but has become rather rowdy as time went on, and I'm not at all sorry to go home.

Ethel comes back.

Ethel: I've told father. He's just coming.

Mrs Ardsley: I'm afraid we've let the tea stand rather a long time.

Sydney: Father likes nothing better than a good strong cup.

Lois comes in. She has her hat on.

Lois (*startled and anxious*): Mother, Evie is coming down the stairs.

Mrs Ardsley: Isn't she asleep?

Sydney: Uncle Charlie said he'd given her something.

The door is opened and Eva comes in. Her eyes are bright from the drug the doctor has given

81

*her. She has a queer, fixed smile on her face.
She has changed into her best frock.*

Mrs Ardsley: I thought you were lying down, Evie.
They told me you didn't feel quite up to the mark.

Eva: I had to come down to tea. Collie's coming.

Lois (*shocked*): Collie!

Eva: He'd have been so disappointed if I hadn't come.

Mrs Ardsley: You've put on your best dress.

Eva: It is rather an occasion, isn't it? You see, I'm
engaged to be married.

Ethel: Evie, what do you mean?

Eva: I'm telling you beforehand so that you should
be prepared. Collie's coming here this afternoon
to talk to father about it. Don't say anything about
it till he comes.

*There is a moment's awkward pause. They
none of them know what to say or do.*

Mrs Ardsley: Let me give you your tea, darling.

Eva: I don't want any tea. I'm too excited. (*She
catches sight of the string pearls that Lois had put
on the table*) What are these pearls doing here?

Lois: You can have them if you like.

Mrs Ardsley: Lois.

Lois: They're mine.

Eva: Can I really? It'll be an engagement present. Oh,
Lois, that is sweet of you. (*She goes up to her and
kisses her, then, standing in front of the glass puts
them on*) Collie always says I have such a pretty
neck.

Mr Ardsley *and* **Howard** *come in.*

Ardsley: Now what about this cup of tea?

Howard: Hulloa, Evie. All right again?

Eva: Oh, yes. There's nothing the matter with me.

Ardsley: All ready to start, Lois?

Lois: Yes.

Ardsley: Don't cut it too fine.

Howard: I may look you up one of these days, Lois. I've got to go over to Canterbury to see a man on business. I don't suppose I shall be able to get back for the night, Ethel.

Ethel: No?

Howard: I'll come over and fetch you in the car, Lois, and we'll do a picture together.

Lois (*mocking him*): That would be grand.

Ardsley: Well, I must say it's very nice to have a cup of tea by one's own fireside and surrounded by one's family. If you come to think of it we none of us have anything very much to worry about. Of course we none of us have more money than we know what to do with, but we have our health and we have our happiness. I don't think we've got very much to complain of. Things haven't been going too well lately, but I think the world is turning the corner and we can all look forward to better times in future. This old England of ours isn't done yet, and I for one believe in it and all it stands for.

       Eva *begins to sing in a thin cracked voice.*

Eva: God save our gracious King!
                Long live our noble King!
                God save our King!

       The others look at her, petrified, in horror-struck surprise. When she stops **Lois** *gives a little cry and hurries from the room.*

CURTAIN

The Letter

A PLAY IN THREE ACTS

Characters

Robert Crosbie
Howard Joyce
Geoffrey Hammond
John Withers
Ong Chi Seng
Chung Hi
Leslie
Mrs Joyce
Mrs Parker
A Sikh Sergeant of Police, a Chinese Woman, Chinese
   Boys and Malay Servants

*The action takes place on a plantation in the Malay
Peninsula and at Singapore.*

The Letter was first produced at the Playhouse
Theatre, London, on 24 February 1927, with the
following cast:

Robert Crosbie	Nigel Bruce
Howard Joyce	Leslie Faber
Geoffrey Hammond	S. J. Warmington
John Withers	James Raglan
Ong Chi Seng	Geroge Carr
Chung Hi	A. G. Poulton
Leslie	Gladys Cooper
Mrs Joyce	Clare Harris
Mrs Parker	Marion Lind

The play produced by Gerald du Maurier

Act I

The scene is the sitting room of the **Crosbies'**
bungalow. Along the whole back of the scene runs
a verandah, which is approached by steps from the
garden. The room is comfortably but quite simply
furnished with rattan chairs, in which are cushions;
there are tables with bowls of flowers on them and
pieces of Malay silver. On the walls are water-colour
pictures, and here and there an arrangement of
krises and parangs; there are horns of sladang and a
couple of tigers' heads. Rattan mats on the floor. On
the cottage piano a piece of music stands open. The
room is lit by one lamp and this stands by a little
table on which is **Leslie's** pillow lace. Another lamp
hangs in the centre of the verandah.

When the curtain rises the sound of a shot is heard
and a cry from **Hammond**. He is seen staggering
towards the verandah. **Leslie** fires again.

Hammond: Oh, my God!

> He falls in a heap on the ground. **Leslie** follows
> him, firing, and then, standing over him, fires
> two or three more shots in rapid succession
> into the prostrate body. There is a little click
> as she mechanically pulls the trigger. The six
> chambers are empty. She looks at the revolver
> and lets it drop from her hand; then her eyes
> fall on the body, they grow enormous, as
> though they would start out of her head, and
> a look of horror comes into her face. She gives
> a shudder as she looks at the dead man and
> then, her gaze still fixed on the dreadful sight,
> backs into the room. There is an excited
> jabbering from the garden and **Leslie** gives a
> start as she hears it. It is immediately followed
> by the appearance of the **Head-Boy** and
> another, and then while they are speaking, two
> or three more appear. These are Chinese and

87

wear white trousers and singlets, the others are Malays in sarongs. The **Head-Boy** *is a small fat Chinaman of about forty.*

Head-Boy: Missy! Missy! Watchee matter? I hear gun fire. (*He catches sight of the body.*) Oh!

The **Boy** with him speaks to him excitedly in Chinese.

Leslie: Is he dead?

Head-Boy: Missy! Missy! Who kill him? (*He bends over and looks at the corpse.*) That Mr Hammond.

Leslie: Is he dead?

The **Head-Boy** *kneels down and feels the man's face. The others stand round and chatter among themselves.*

Head-Boy: Yes, I think him dead.

Leslie: Oh, my God!

Head-Boy (*getting up*): Missy, what for you do that?

Leslie: Do you know where the Assistant District Officer lives?

Head-Boy: Mr Withers, Missy? Yes, I savvy. He live jolly long way from here.

Leslie: Fetch him.

Head-Boy: More better we wait until daylight, Missy.

Leslie: There's nothing to be frightened of. Hassan will drive you over in the car. Is Hassan there?

Head-Boy: Yes, Missy. (*He points to one of the Malays.*)

Leslie: Wake Mr Withers and tell him to come here at once. Say there's been an accident and Mr Hammond's dead.

Head-Boy: Yes, Missy.

Leslie: Go at once.

The **Head-Boy** *turns to* **Hassan** *the chauffeur and gives him instructions in Malay to get the car.* **Hassan** *goes down the verandah steps.*

Head-Boy: I think more better we bring body in, Missy, and put him on bed in spare room.

Leslie (*with a broken cry of anguish*): No.

Head-Boy: No can leave him there, Missy.

Leslie: Don't touch it. When Mr Withers comes he'll say what's to be done.

Head-Boy: All light, Missy. I tell Ah Sing to wait here maybe.

Leslie: If you like . . . I want Mr Crosbie sent for.

Head-Boy: Post office all closed up, Missy, no can telephone till tomorrow morning.

Leslie: What's the time.

Head-Boy: I think, maybe, twelve o'clock.

Leslie: You must wake the man up at the post office as you go through the village, and he must get on to Singapore somehow or other. Or try at the police station. Perhaps they can get on.

Head-Boy: All light, Missy. I try.

Leslie: Give the man two or three dollars. Whatever happens they must get on to him at once.

Head-Boy: If I catchee speak master, what thing I say, Missy?

Leslie: I'll write the message down for you.

Head-Boy: All light, Missy. You write.

She sits down at a table and takes a sheet of paper and tries to write.

Leslie: Oh, my hand! I can't hold the pencil. (*She beats with her fist on the table in anger with herself, and takes the pencil again. She writes a few words and then gets up, paper in hand.*) Here's the message. That's the telephone number. Master is spending the night at Mr Joyce's house.

Head-Boy: I savvy. The lawyer.

Leslie: They must ring and ring till they get an answer. They can give the message in Malay if they like. Read it and see if you understand.

Head-Boy: Yes, Missy, I understand.

The Letter

Leslie (*reading*): Come at once. There's been a terrible accident. Hammond is dead.

Head-Boy: All light, Missy.

There is the sound of a car being started

Leslie: There's the car. Be quick now.

Head-Boy: Yes, Missy.

He goes out by the verandah

Leslie *stands for a moment looking down at the floor. One or two* **Malay Women** *come softly up the steps. They look at the corpse and in whispers talk excitedly to one another.* **Leslie** *becomes conscious of their presence.*

Leslie: What do you want? Go away. All of you.

They fade away silently and only **Ah Sing***, a Chinese boy, is left.* **Leslie** *gives the body a long look, then she goes into a room at the side, her own bedroom, and you hear the door locked.* **Ah Sing** *comes into the room, takes a cigarette out of a box on the table and lights it; he sits down on the armchair, with one leg crossed over the other, and blows the smoke into the air.*

THE CURTAIN FALLS

There is an interval of one minute to mark the passage of three hours. The scene is the same as before. When the curtain rises, **John Withers** *is walking up and down the room. The body has been removed. The* **Head-Boy** *comes in.*

Head-Boy: My believe I hear motor car on road.

Withers *goes to the verandah and listens.*

Withers: I don't. (*Irritably*) I can't imagine why he's so long. (*There is the faint toot of a motor horn.*)

Yes, by George! That's the car. Thank the Lord for that.

> John Withers *is a young man, neatly dressed in a white duck suit. His topee is on a table. He goes to the door of* Leslie's *room and knocks.*

Withers: Mrs Crosbie. (*There is no answer and he knocks again.*) Mrs Crosbie.

Leslie: Yes?

Withers: There's a car on the road. That must be your husband. (*There is no reply to this. He listens for a moment and then with a gesture of impatience moves over to the verandah. The sound is heard of a car arriving. It stops.*) Is that you, Crosbie?

Crosbie: Yes.

Withers: Thank God. I thought you were never coming.

> Crosbie *comes up the verandah steps. He is a man of powerful build, forty years old, with a large, sun-burned face; he is dressed in khaki coat and a broad-brimmed hat.*

Crosbie: Where's Leslie?

Withers: She's in her room. She's locked herself in. She wouldn't see me till you came.

Crosbie: What's happened? (*He goes to the door of* Leslie's *room and knocks urgently.*) Leslie! Leslie!

> *There is a moment's pause.* Joyce *comes up the steps. He is a thin, spare, clean-shaven man of about five and forty. He wears ducks and a topee. He holds out his hand to* Withers.

Joyce: My name is Joyce. Are you the ADO?

Withers: Yes. Withers.

Joyce: Crosbie was spending the night with us. I thought I'd better come along with him.

Crosbie: Leslie! It's me! Open the door!

Withers (*to* Joyce): Oh, are you the lawyer?

Joyce: Yes. Joyce and Simpson.

Withers: I know.

> *The door of* **Leslie's** *room is unlocked and slowly opened. She comes out, and, closing it behind her, stands against it.*

Crosbie (*stretching out his hands as though to take her in his arms*): Leslie.

Leslie (*warding him off with a gesture*): Oh, don't touch me.

Crosbie: What's happened? What's happened?

Leslie: Didn't they tell you over the telephone?

Crosbie: They said Hammond was killed.

Leslie (*looking towards the verandah*): Is he there still?

Withers: No. I had the body taken away.

> *She looks at the three men with haggard eyes and then throws back her head.*

Leslie: He tried to rape me and I shot him.

Crosbie: Leslie!

Withers: My God!

Leslie: Oh, Robert, I'm so glad you've come.

Crosbie: Darling! Darling!

> *She throws herself in his arms and he clasps her to his heart. Now at last she breaks down and sobs convulsively.*

Leslie: Hold me tight. Don't let me go. I'm so frightened. Oh, Robert, Robert.

Crosbie: It'll be all right. There's nothing to be frightened about. Don't let yourself go to pieces.

Leslie: I've got you, haven't I? Oh, Robert, what shall I do? I'm so unhappy.

Crosbie: Sweetheart!

Leslie: Hold me close to you.

Withers: Do you think you could tell us exactly what happened?

Leslie: Now?

Crosbie: Come and sit down, dear heart. You're all in. (*He leads her to a chair and she sinks into it with exhaustion.*)

Withers: I'm afraid it sounds awfully brutal, but my duty is . . .

Leslie: Oh, I know, of course. I'll tell you everything I can. I'll try to pull myself together. (*To* **Crosbie**) Give me your hankie. (*She takes a handkerchief out of his pocket and dries her eyes.*)

Crosbie: Don't hurry yourself, darling. Take your time.

Leslie (*forcing a smile to her lips*): It's so good to have your here.

Crosbie: It's lucky Howard came along.

Leslie: Oh, Mr Joyce, how nice of you! (*She stretches out her hand.*) Fancy your coming all this way at this time of night!

Joyce: Oh, that's all right.

Leslie: How's Dorothy?

Joyce: Oh, she's very well, thank you.

Leslie: I feel so dreadfully faint.

Crosbie: Would you like a drop of whisky?

Leslie (*closing her eyes*): It's on the table.

> **Crosbie** *goes and mixes her a small whisky and seltzer. She is lying on a long chair with her eyes closed, her face pale and wan.*

Joyce (*in an undertone to* **Withers**): How long have you been here?

Withers: Oh, an hour or more. I was fast asleep. My boy woke me up and said the Crosbie's head-boy was there and wanted to see me at once.

Joyce: Yes.

Withers: Of course I jumped up. He was on the verandah. He told me Hammond had been shot, and asked me to come at once.

Joyce: Did he tell you she'd shot him?

Withers: Yes. When I got here Mrs Crosbie had locked

herself in her room and refused to come out till
her husband came.

Joyce: Was Hammond dead?

Withers: Oh, yes, he was just riddled with bullets.

Joyce (*in a tone of faint surprise*): Oh!

Withers (*taking it out of his pocket*): Here's the
revolver. All six chambers are empty.

> **Leslie** *slowly opens her eyes and looks at the
> two men talking.* **Joyce** *takes the revolver in
> his hands at looks at it.*

Joyce (*to* **Crosbie** *as he comes across the room with
the whisky*): Is this yours, Bob?

Crosbie: Yes. (*He goes up to* **Leslie** *and supports her
while she sips.*)

Joyce: Have you questioned the boys?

Withers: Yes, they know nothing. They were asleep
in their own quarters. They were awakened by the
firing, and when they came here they found
Hammond lying on the floor.

Joyce: Where exactly?

Withers (*pointing*): There. On the verandah under the
lamp.

Leslie: Thank you. I shall feel better in a minute. I'm
sorry to be so tiresome.

Joyce: Do you feel well enough to talk now?

Leslie: I think so.

Crosbie: You needn't be in such a devil of a hurry.
She's in no condition to make a long statement now.

Joyce: It'll have to be made sooner or later.

Leslie: It's all right, Robert, really. I feel perfectly well
now.

Joyce: I think we ought to be put in possession of the
facts as soon as possible.

Withers: Take your time, Mrs Crosbie. After all, we're
all friends here.

Leslie: What do you want me to do? If you've got any
questions to ask, I'll do my best to answer them.

Joyce: Perhaps it would be better if you told us the whole story in your own way. Do you think you can manage that?

Leslie: I'll try. (*She gets up from the long chair.*)

Crosbie: What do you want to do?

Leslie: I want to sit upright. (*She sits down and for a moment hesitates.* **Crosbie** *and* **Withers** *are standing up.* **Joyce** *is seated opposite to her. The eyes of all of them on her face. Addressing* **Withers**.) Robert was spending the night in Singapore, you know.

Withers: Yes, your boy told me that.

Leslie: I was going in with him, but I wasn't feeling very well and I thought I'd stay here. I never mind being alone. (*With a half smile at* **Crosbie**) A planter's wife gets used to that, you know.

Crosbie: That's true.

Leslie: I had dinner rather late, and then I started working on my lace. (*She points to the pillow on which a piece of lace half made is pinned with little pins.*)

Crosbie: My wife is rather a dab at lace-making.

Withers: Yes, I know. I've heard that.

Leslie: I don't know how long I'd been working. It fascinates me, you know, and I lose all sense of time. Suddenly I heard a footstep outside and someone came up the steps of the verandah and said: 'Good evening. Can I come in?' I was startled, because I hadn't heard a car drive up.

Withers: Hammond left his car about a quarter of a mile down the road. It's parked under the trees. Your chauffeur noticed it as we were driving back.

Joyce: I wonder why Hammond left his car there.

Withers: Presumably he did not want anyone to hear him drive up.

Joyce: Go on, Mrs Crosbie.

Leslie: At first I couldn't see who it was. I work in spectacles, you know, and in the half-darkness of

the verandah it was impossible for me to recognize
anybody. 'Who is it?' I said. 'Geoff Hammond.'
'Oh, of course, come in and have a drink,' I said.
And I took off my spectacles. I got up and shook
hands with him.

Joyce: Were you surprised to see him?

Leslie: I was rather. He hadn't been up to the house
for ages, had he, Robert?

Crosbie: Three months at least, I should think.

Leslie: I told him Robert was away. He'd had to go to
Singapore on business.

Withers: What did he say to that?

Leslie: He said: 'Oh, I'm sorry. I felt rather lonely
tonight, so I thought I'd just come along and see
how you were getting on.' I asked him how he'd
come, as I hadn't heard a car, and he said he'd left
it on the road because he thought we might be in
bed asleep and he didn't want to wake us up.

Joyce: I see.

Leslie: As Robert was away there wasn't any whisky
in the room, but I thought the boys would be
asleep, so I didn't call them; I just went and fetched
it myself. Hammond mixed himself a drink and
lit his pipe.

Joyce: Was he quite sober?

Leslie: I never thought about it. I suppose he had been
drinking, but just then it didn't occur to me.

Joyce: What happened?

Leslie: Well, nothing very much; I put on my
spectacles again and went on with my work. We
chatted about one thing and another. He asked me
if Robert had heard that a tiger had been seen on
the road two or three days ago. It had killed a couple
of goats and the villagers were in a state about it.
He said he thought he'd try to get it over the
weekend.

Crosbie: Oh, yes, I know about that. Don't you

remember I spoke to you about it at tiffin
yesterday?

Leslie: Did you? I believe you did.

Withers: Fire away, Mrs Crosbie.

Leslie: Well, we were just chatting. Then suddenly he
said something rather silly.

Joyce: What?

Leslie: It's hardly worth repeating. He paid me a little
compliment.

Joyce: I think perhaps you'd better tell us exactly
what he said.

Leslie: He said: 'I don't know how you can bear to
disfigure yourself with those horrible spectacles.
You've got very pretty eyes indeed, you know, and
it's too bad of you to hide them.'

Joyce: Had he ever said anything of the sort to you
before?

Leslie: No, never. I was a little taken aback, but I
thought it best to take it quite lightly. 'I make no
pretensions to being a raving beauty, you know,' I
said. 'But you are,' he said. It sounds awfully silly
to repeat things like this.

Joyce: Never mind. Please let us have his exact words.

Leslie: Well, he said: 'It's too bad of you to try to
make yourself look plain, but thank God you don't
succeed.' (*She gives the two strangers a faintly
deprecating look.*) I shrugged my shoulders. I
thought it rather impertinent of him to talk to me
like that.

Crosbie: I don't wonder.

Joyce: Did you say anything?

Leslie: Yes, I said: 'If you ask me point blank I'm
bound to tell you that I don't care a row of pins what
you think about me.' I was trying to snub him, but
he only laughed. 'I'm going to tell you all the
same,' he said. 'I think you're the prettiest thing
I've seen for many a long year.' 'Sweet of you,' I
said, 'but in that case I can only think you half-

witted.' He laughed again. He'd been sitting over there, and he got up and drew up a chair near the table I was working at. 'You're not going to have the face to deny that you have the prettiest hands in the world,' he said. That rather put my back up. In point of fact, my hands are not very good, and I'd just as soon people didn't talk about them. It's only an awful fool of a woman who wants to be flattered on her worst point.

Crosbie: Leslie darling. (*He takes one of her hands and kisses it.*)

Leslie: Oh, Robert, you silly old thing.

Joyce: Well, when Hammond was talking in that strain, did he just sit still with his arms crossed?

Leslie: Oh, no. He tried to take one of my hands. But I gave him a little tap. I wasn't particularly annoyed, I merely thought he was rather silly. I said to him: 'Don't be an idiot. Sit down where you were before and talk sensibly, or else I shall send you home.'

Withers: But, Mrs Crosbie, I wonder you didn't kick him out there and then.

Leslie: I didn't want to make a fuss. You know, there are men who think it's their duty to flirt with a woman when they get the chance. I believe they think women expect it of them, and for all I know a good many do. But I'm not one of them, am I, Robert?

Crosbie: Far from it.

Leslie: A woman only makes a perfect fool of herself if she makes a scene every time a man pays her one or two compliments. She doesn't need much experience of the world to discover that it means rather less than nothing. I didn't suspect for an instant that Hammond was serious.

Joyce: When did you suspect?

Leslie: Then. What he said next. You see, he didn't move. He just looked at me straight in the face, and said: 'Don't you know that I'm awfully in love with you?'

Crosbie: The cad.

Leslie: 'I don't,' I answered. You see, it meant so little to me that I hadn't the smallest difficulty in keeping perfectly cool. 'I don't believe it for a minute,' I said, 'and even if it were true I don't want you to say it.'

Joyce: Were you surprised?

Leslie: Of course I was surprised. Why, we've known him for seven years, Robert.

Crosbie: Yes, he came here after the war.

Leslie: And he's never paid me the smallest attention. I didn't suppose he even knew what colour my eyes were. If you'd asked me, I should have said I didn't begin to exist for him.

Crosbie (to Joyce): You must remember that we never saw very much of him.

Leslie: When he first came here he was ill and I got Robert to go over and fetch him; he was all alone in his bungalow.

Joyce: Where was his bungalow?

Crosbie: About six or seven miles from here.

Leslie: I couldn't bear the idea of his lying there without anyone to look after him, so we brought him here and took care of him till he was fit again. We saw a certain amount of him after that, but we had nothing much in common, and we never became very intimate.

Crosbie: For the last two years we've hardly seen him at all. To tell the truth, after all that Leslie had done for him when he was ill I thought he was almost too casual.

Leslie: He used to come over now and then to play tennis, and we used to meet him at other people's houses now and again. But I don't think I'd set eyes on him for a month.

Joyce: I see.

The Letter

Leslie: He helped himself to another whisky and soda. I began to wonder if he'd been drinking. Anyhow, I thought he'd had enough. 'I wouldn't drink any more if I were you,' I said. I was quite friendly about it. I wasn't the least frightened or anything like that. I never occurred to me that I couldn't manage him. He didn't pay any attention to what I said. He emptied his glass and put it down. 'Do you think I'm talking to you like this because I'm drunk?' he asked in a funny abrupt way. 'That's the most obvious explanation, isn't it?' I said. It's awful having to tell you all this. I'm so ashamed. It's disgraceful.

Joyce: I know it's hard. But for your own sake. I beg you to tell us the whole story now.

Withers: If Mrs Crosbie would like to wait a little, I don't see any great harm in that.

Leslie: No, if I've got to tell it I'll tell it now. What's the good of waiting? My head's simply throbbing.

Crosbie: Don't be too hard on her, Howard.

Leslie: He's being as kind as he can be.

Joyce: I hope so. 'That's the most obvious explanation,' you said.

Leslie: 'Well, it's a lie,' he said. 'I've loved you ever since I first knew you. I've held my tongue as long as I could, and now it's got to come out. I love you. I love you. I love you.' He repeated it just like that.

Crosbie (*between his teeth*): The swine.

Leslie (*rising from her seat and standing*): I got up and I put away the pillow with my lace. I held out my hand. 'Good-night,' I said. He didn't take it. He just stood and looked at me and his eyes were all funny. 'I'm not going now,' he said. Then I began to lose my temper. I think I'd kept it too long. I think I'm a very even-tempered woman, but when I'm roused I don't care very much what I say. 'But, you poor fool,' I cried at him, 'don't you know that

I've never loved anyone but Robert, and even if I
didn't love Robert you're the last man I should care
for.' 'What do I care?' he said. 'Robert's away.'

Crosbie: The cur. The filthy cur. Oh, my God . . .

Joyce: Be quiet, Bob.

Leslie: That was the last straw. I was beside myself.
Even then I wasn't frightened. It never occurred
to me he'd dare – he'd dare . . . I was just angry. I
thought he was just a filthy swine to talk to me
like that because he knew Robert was safely out of
the way. 'If you don't go away this minute,' I said,
'I shall call the boys and have you thrown out.' He
gave me a filthy look. 'They're out of earshot,' he
said. I walked past him quickly. I wanted to get out
on to the verandah, so that I could give the boys
a call. I knew they'd hear me from there. But he
took hold of my arm and swung me back. 'Let me
go,' I screamed. I was furious. 'Not much,' he said.
'Not much. I've got you now.' I opened my mouth
and I shouted as loud as I could: 'Boy! boy!' But he
put his hand over it. . . . Oh, it's horrible. I can't
go on. It's asking too much of me. It's so shameful,
shameful.

Crosbie: Oh, Leslie, my darling. I wish to God I'd
never left you.

Leslie: Oh, it was awful. (*She sobs broken-heartedly.*)

Joyce: I beseech you to control yourself. You've been
wonderful up to now. I know it's very hard, but
you must tell us everything.

Leslie: I didn't know what he was doing. He flung his
arms round me. He began to kiss me. I struggled.
His lips were burning, and I turned my mouth
away. 'No, no, no!' I screamed. 'Leave me alone. I
won't!' I began to cry. I tried to tear myself away
from him. He seemed like a madman.

Crosbie: I can't bear much more of this.

Joyce: Be quiet, Bob.

Leslie: I don't known what happened. I was all

confused. I was so frightened. He seemed to be talking, talking. He kept on saying that he loved me and wanted me. Oh, the misery! He held me so tight that I couldn't move. I never knew how strong he was. I felt as weak as a rat. It was awful to feel so helpless. I'm trying to tell you everything, but it's all in a blur. I felt myself growing weaker and weaker, and I thought I'd faint. His breath was hot on my face, and it made me feel desperately sick.

Withers: The brute.

Leslie: He kissed me. He kissed my neck. Oh, the horror! And he held me so tight that I felt I couldn't breathe. Then he lifted me right off my feet. I tried to kick him. He only held me tighter. Then I felt he was carrying me. He didn't say anything. I didn't look at him, but somehow I saw his face and it was as white as a sheet and his eyes were burning. He wasn't a man any more, he was a savage; I felt my heart pounding against my ribs . . . Don't look at me. I don't want any of you to look at me. It flashed across me that he was carrying me to the bedroom. Oh!

Crosbie: If he weren't dead I'd strangle him with my own hands.

Leslie: It all happened in a moment. He stumbled and fell. I don't know why. I don't know if he caught his foot on something or if it was just an accident. I fell with him. It gave me a chance. Somehow his hold on me loosened and I snatched myself away from him. It was all instinctive; it was the affair of a moment; I didn't know what I was doing. I jumped up and I ran round the sofa. He was a little slow at getting up.

Withers: He had a game leg.

Crosbie: Yes. He had his kneecap smashed in the war.

Leslie: Then he made a dash at me. There was a revolver on the table and I snatched it. I didn't

even know I'd fired. I heard a report. I saw him
stagger. He cried out. He said something. I don't
know what it was, I was beside myself. I was in a
frenzy. He lurched out of the room on to the
verandah and I followed him. I don't remember
anything. I heard the reports one after the other. I
don't ask you to believe me, but I didn't even know
I was pulling the trigger. I saw Hammond fall
down. Suddenly I heard a funny little click and it
flashed through my mind that I'd fired all the
cartridges and the revolver was empty. It was only
then that I knew what I'd done. It was as if scales
dropped from my eyes, and all at once I caught sight
of Hammond, and he was lying there in a heap.

Crosbie (*taking her in his arms*): My poor child.

Leslie: Oh, Robert, what have I done?

Crosbie: You've done what any woman would have
done in your place, only nine-tenths of them
wouldn't have had the nerve.

Joyce: How did the revolver happen to be there?

Crosbie: I don't very often leave Leslie alone for the
night, but when I do I feel safer if she's got a
weapon handy. I saw that all the barrels were loaded
before I left, and thank God I did.

Leslie: That's all, Mr Withers. You must forgive me
if I wouldn't see you when you came. But I wanted
my husband.

Withers: Of course. May I say that I think you
behaved magnificently. I'm fearfully sorry we had
to put you to the ordeal of telling us all this. But I
think Mr Joyce was right. It was much better that
we should be in possession of all the facts
immediately.

Leslie: Oh, I know.

Withers: It's quite obvious the man was drunk, and
he only got what he deserved.

Leslie: And yet I'd give almost anything if I could

bring him back to life. It's so awful to think that I killed him.

Crosbie: It was an easy death for him. By God, if ever I've wanted to torture anyone . . .

Leslie: No, don't, Robert, don't. The man's dead.

Joyce: Could I see the body for a minute?

Withers: Yes, I'll take you to where it it.

Leslie (*with a little shudder*): You don't want me to come?

Joyce: No, of course not. You stay here with Bob. We shall only be a minute.

Joyce *and* **Withers** *go out.*

Leslie: I'm so tired. I'm so desperately tired.

Crosbie: I know you are darling, I'd do anything to help you, and there doesn't seem to be a thing I can do.

Leslie: You can love me.

Crosbie: I've always loved you with all my heart.

Leslie: Yes, but now.

Crosbie: If I could love you any more I would now.

Leslie: You don't blame me?

Crosbie: Blame you? I think you've been splendid. By God, you're a plucky little woman.

Leslie (*tenderly*): This is going to give you an awful lot of anxiety, my dear.

Crosbie: Don't think about me. I don't matter. Only think about yourself.

Leslie: What will they do to me?

Crosbie: Do? I'd like to see anyone talk of doing anything to you. Why, there isn't a man or woman in the colony who won't be proud to know you.

Leslie: I so hate the idea of everyone talking about me.

Crosbie: I know, darling.

Leslie: Whatever people say you'll never believe anything against me, will you?

Crosbie: Of course not. What should they say?

Leslie: How can I tell? People are so unkind. They might easily say that he would never have made advances at me if I hadn't led him on.

Crosbie: I think that's the last thing anyone who's ever seen you would dream of saying.

Leslie: Do you love me very much, Robert?

Crosbie: I can never tell you how much.

Leslie: We have been happy together all these years, haven't we?

Crosbie: By George, yes! We've been married for ten years and it hardly seems a day. Do you know that we've never even had a quarrel?

Leslie (*with a smile*): Who could quarrel with anyone as kind and as good-natured as you are?

Crosbie: You know, Leslie, it makes me feel stupid and awkward to say some things. I'm not one of those fellows with the gift of the gab. But I do want you to know how awfully grateful I am to you for all you've done for me.

Leslie: Oh, my dear, what are you talking about?

Crosbie: You see, I'm not in the least clever. And I'm a great ugly hulking devil. I'm not fit to clean your boots really. I never knew at the beginning why you ever thought of me. You've been the best wife a man ever had.

Leslie: Oh, what nonsense!

Crosbie: Oh, no, it isn't. Because I don't say much you mustn't fancy I don't think a lot. I don't know how I've deserved all the luck I've had.

Leslie: Darling! It's so good to hear you say that.

> (*He takes her in his arms and lingeringly kisses her mouth.* **Joyce** *and* **Withers** *return.*
> *Without self-consciousness* **Leslie** *releases herself from her husband's embrace and turns to the two men.*) Wouldn't you like something to eat? You must be perfectly ravenous.

Withers: Oh, no, don't bother, Mrs Crosbie.

Leslie: It's no bother at all. I expect the boys are about still, and if they're not I can easily make you a little something myself on the chafing-dish.

Joyce: Personally, I'm not at all hungry.

Leslie: Robert?

Crosbie: No, dear.

Joyce: In point of fact, I think it's about time we started for Singapore.

Leslie (*a trifle startled*): Now?

Joyce: It'll be dawn when we get there. By the time you've had a bath and some breakfast it'll be eight o'clock. We'll ring up the Attorney-General and find out when we can see him. Don't you think that's the best thing we can do, Withers?

Withers: Yes. I suppose so.

Joyce: You'll come with us, of course?

Withers: I think I'd better, don't you?

Leslie: Shall I be arrested?

Joyce (*with a glance at* **Withers**): I think you're by way of being under arrest now.

Withers: It's purely a matter of form, Mrs Crosbie. Mr Joyce's idea is that you should go to the Attorney-General and give yourself up . . . Of course, all this is entirely out of my line. I don't exactly know what I ought to do.

Leslie: Poor Mrs Withers, I'm so sorry to give you all this trouble.

Withers: Oh, don't bother about me. The worst that can happen to me is that I shall get hauled over the coals for doing the wrong thing.

Leslie (*with a faint smile*): And you've lost a good night's rest, too.

Joyce: Well, we'll start when you're ready, my dear.

Leslie: Shall I be imprisoned?

Joyce: That is for the Attorney-General to decide. I hope that after you've told him your story we shall be able to get him to accept bail. It depends on what the charge is.

Crosbie: He's a very good fellow. I'm sure he'll do everything he can.

Joyce: He must do his duty.

Crosbie: What do you mean by that?

Joyce: I think it not unlikely that he'll say only one charge is possible, and in that case I'm afraid that an application for bail would be useless.

Leslie: What charge?

Joyce: Murder.

> *There is a moment's pause. The only sign that* **Leslie** *gives that the word startles her is the clenching of one of her hands. But it requires quite an effort for her to keep her voice level and calm.*

Leslie: I'll just go and change into a jumper. I won't be a minute. And I'll get a hat.

Joyce: Oh, very well. You'd better go and give her a hand, Bob. She'll want someone to do her up.

Leslie: Oh, no, don't bother. I can manage quite well by myself. A jumper doesn't have to be done up, my poor friend.

Joyce: Doesn't it? I forgot. I think you'd better go along all the same, old man.

Leslie: I'm not thinking of committing suicide, you know.

Joyce: I should hope not. The idea never occurred to me. I thought I'd like to have a word or two with Withers.

Leslie: Come along, Robert.

> *They go into her bedroom, leaving the door open.* **Joyce** *goes over and closes it.*

Withers: By George! That woman's a marvel.

Joyce (*good-humouredly*): In what way?

Withers: I never saw anyone so calm in my life. Her self-control is absolutely amazing. She must have a nerve of iron.

Joyce: She has a great deal more character than I ever suspected.

Withers: You've known her a good many years, haven't you?

Joyce: Ever since she married Crosbie. He's my oldest pal in the colony. But I've never known her very well. She hardly ever came in to Singapore. I always found her very reserved and I supposed she was shy. But my wife has been down here a good deal and she raves about her. She says that when you really get to know her she's a very nice woman.

Withers: Of course she's a very nice woman.

Joyce (*with the faintest irony*): She's certainly a very pretty one.

Withers: I was very much impressed by the way in which she told that terrible story.

Joyce: I wish she could have been a little more explicit here and there. It was rather confused towards the end.

Withers: My dear fellow, what do you expect? You could see that she was just holding on to herself like grim death. It seemed to me a marvel that she was so coherent. I say, what a swine that man was!

Joyce: By the way, did you know Hammond?

Withers: Yes, I knew him a little. I've only been here three months, you know.

Joyce: Is this your first job as ADO?

Withers: Yes.

Joyce: Was Hammond a heavy drinker?

Withers: I don't know that he was. He could take his whack, but I never saw him actually drunk.

Joyce: Of course I've heard of him, but I never met him myself. He was by way of being rather a favourite with the ladies, wasn't he?

Withers: He was a very good-looking chap. You know the sort, very breezy and devil-may-care and generous with his money.

Joyce: Yes, that is the sort they fall for.

Withers: I've always understood he was one of the most popular men in the colony. Before he hurt his leg in the war he held the tennis championship, and I believe he had the reputation of being the best dancer between Penang and Singapore.

Joyce: Did you like him?

Withers: He was the sort of chap you couldn't help liking. I should have said he was a man who hadn't an enemy in the world.

Joyce: Was he the sort of chap you'd expect to do a think like this?

Withers: How should I know? How can you tell what a man will do when he's drunk?

Joyce: My own opinion is that if a man's a blackguard when he's drunk he's a blackguard when he's sober.

Withers: What are you going to do, then?

Joyce: Well, it's quite evident that we must find out about him.

> **Leslie** comes in, followed by her husband. She carries a hat in her hand.

Leslie: Well, I haven't been long, have I?

Joyce: I shall hold you up as an example to my Dorothy.

Leslie: She's probably not half as slow as you are. I can always dress in a quarter of the time that Robert can.

Crosbie: I'll just go and start her up.

Withers: Is there room for me, or shall I come along in the other car?

Leslie: Oh, there'll be plenty of room.

> **Crosbie** and **Withers** go out. **Leslie** is about to follow.

Joyce: There's just one question I'd like to ask you.

Leslie: Yes, what is it?

Joyce: Just now, when I was looking at Hammond's

body, it seemed to me that some of the shots must
have been fired when he was actually lying on the
ground. It gives me the impression that you must
have stood over him and fired and fired.

Leslie (*putting her hand wearily on her forehead*): I
was trying to forget for a minute.

Joyce: Why did you do that?

Leslie: I didn't know I did.

Joyce: It's a question you must expect to be asked.

Leslie: I'm afraid you think I'm more cold-blooded
than I am. I lost my head. After a certain time
everything is all blurred and confused. I'm awfully
sorry.

Joyce: Don't let it worry you, then. I daresay it's very
natural. I'm sorry to make a nuisance of myself.

Leslie: Shall we go?

Joyce: Come on.

> *They go out. The* **Head-Boy** *comes in and
> draws down the blinds that lead on to the
> verandah. He puts out the light and slips out.
> The room is in darkness.*

> *CURTAIN*

Act II

*The scene is the visitors' room in the gaol at
Singapore. A bare room with whitewashed walls, on
one of which hangs a large map of the Malay
Peninsula; on another is a framed photograph of
King George V. The window is barred. The only
furniture consists of a table in polished pitch pine
and half a dozen chairs. There are doors right and
left. Through the window you see the green,
luxuriant leaves of some tropical plants and the blue
sky.*

When the curtain rises, **Robert Crosbie** *is seen*

*standing at the window. He wears an air of profound
dejection. He has on the clothes in which he is
accustomed to walk over the estate, shorts and a
khaki shirt; he holds his shabby old hat in his hand.
He sighs deeply. The door on the left is opened and
Joyce comes in. He is followed by **Ong Chi Seng** with
a wallet. **Ong Chi Seng** is a Cantonese, small but
trimly built; he is very neatly dressed in white ducks,
patent leather shoes and gay silk socks. He wears a
gold wrist watch and invisible pince-nez. From his
breast pocket protrudes a rolled-gold fountain pen.*

Crosbie: Howard.

Joyce: I heard you were here.

Crosbie: I'm waiting to see Leslie.

Joyce: I've come to see her too.

Crosbie: Do you want me to clear out?

Joyce: No, of course not. You go along and see her
when they send for you, and then she can come
here.

Crosbie: I wish they'd let me see her here. It's awful
having to see her in a cell with that damned
matron always there.

Joyce: I thought you'd probably look in at the office
this morning.

Crosbie: I couldn't get away. After all, the work on
the estate has got to go on, and if I'm not there to
look after it everything goes to blazes. I came into
Singapore the moment I could. Oh, how I hate
that damned estate!

Joyce: In point of fact, I don't think it's been a bad
thing for you during these last few weeks to have
some work that you were obliged to do.

Crosbie: I daresay not. Sometimes I've thought I
should go mad.

Joyce: You know you must pull yourself together, old
man. You mustn't let yourself go to pieces.

Crosbie: Oh, I'm all right.

The Letter

Joyce: You look as if you hadn't had a bath for a week.

Crosbie: Oh, I've had a bath all right. I know my kit's rather grubby, but it's all right for tramping over the estate. I came just as I was. I hadn't the heart to change.

Joyce: It's funny that you should have taken it all so much harder than your missus. She hasn't turned a hair.

Crosbie: She's worth ten of me. I know that. I don't mind confessing it, I'm all in. I'm like a lost sheep without Leslie. It's the first time we've been separated for more than a day since we were married. I'm so lonely without her. (*He catches sight of* **Ong Chi Seng**) Who's that?

Joyce: Oh, that's my confidential clerk, Ong Chi Seng.

> **Ong Chi Seng** *gives a little bow and smiles with a flash of white teeth.*

Crosbie: What's he come here for?

Joyce: I brought him with me in case I wanted him. Ong Chi Seng is as good a lawyer as I am. He took his degree in the University of Hong Kong, and as soon as he's learnt the ins and outs of my business he's going to set up in opposition.

Ong Chi Seng: Hi, hi.

Joyce: Perhaps you'd better wait outside, Ong. I'll call you if I want you.

Ong Chi Seng: Very good, sir. I shall be within earshot.

Joyce: It'll do if you're within call.

> **Ong Chi Seng** *goes out.*

Crosbie: Oh, Howard, I wouldn't wish my worst enemy the agony that I've gone through during these horrible weeks.

Joyce: You look as if you hadn't had much sleep lately, old thing.

Crosbie: I haven't. I don't think I've closed my eyes the last three nights.

Joyce: Well, thank God it'll be over tomorrow. By the way, you'll clean yourself up a bit for the trial, won't you?

Crosbie: Oh, yes, rather. I'm staying with you tonight.

Joyce: Oh, are you? I'm glad. And you'll both come back to my house after the trial. Dorothy's determined to celebrate.

Crosbie: I think it's monstrous that they should have kept Leslie in this filthy prison.

Joyce: I think they had to do that.

Crosbie: Why couldn't they let her out on bail?

Joyce: It's a very serious charge, I'm afraid.

Crosbie: Oh, this red tape. She did what any decent woman would do in her place. Leslie's the best girl in the world. She wouldn't hurt a fly. Why, hang it all, man, I've been married to her for ten years; do you think I don't know her? God, if I'd got hold of that man I'd have wrung his neck, I'd have killed him without a moment's hesitation. So would you.

Joyce: My dear fellow, everybody's on your side.

Crosbie: Thank God nobody's got a good word to say for Hammond.

Joyce: I don't suppose a single member of the jury will go into the box without having already made up his mind to bring in a verdict of Not Guilty.

Crosbie: Then the whole thing's a farce. She ought never to have been arrested in the first place; and then it's cruel, after all the poor girl's gone through, to subject her to the ordeal of a trial. There's not a soul I've met in Singapore, man or woman, who hasn't told me that Leslie was absolutely justified.

Joyce: The Law is the Law. She admits that she killed the man. It is terrible, and I'm dreadfully sorry both for you and for her.

Crosbie: I don't matter two straws.

Joyce: But the fact remains that murder has been committed, and in a civilized community a trial is inevitable.

The Letter

Crosbie: Is it murder to exterminate noxious vermin? She shot him as she would have shot a mad dog.

Joyce: I should be wanting in my duty as your legal adviser if I didn't tell you that there is one point which causes me a little anxiety. If your wife had only shot Hammond once the whole thing would have been absolutely plain sailing. Unfortunately she fired six times.

Crosbie: Her explanation is perfectly simple. Under the circumstances anyone would have done the same.

Joyce: I daresay, and, of course, I think the explanation is very reasonable.

Crosbie: Then what are you making a fuss about?

Joyce: It's no good closing your eyes to the facts. It's always a good plan to put yourself in another man's place, and I can't deny that if I were prosecuting for the Crown that is the point on which I would centre my enquiry.

Crosbie: Why?

Joyce: It suggests not so much panic as uncontrollable fury. Under the circumstances which your wife has described one would expect a woman to be frightened out of her wits, but hardly beside herself with rage.

Crosbie: Oh, isn't that rather far-fetched?

Joyce: I daresay. I just thought it was a point worth mentioning.

Crosbie: I should have thought the really important thing was Hammond's character, and, by heaven! we've found out enough about him.

Joyce: We've found out that he was living with a Chinese woman, if that's what you mean.

Crosbie: Well, isn't that enough?

Joyce: I daresay it is. It was certainly an awful shock to his friends.

Crosbie: She's been actually living in his bungalow for the last eight months.

Joyce: It's strange how angry that's made people. It's turned public opinion against him more than anything.

Crosbie: I can tell you this, if I'd known it I'd never have dreamed of letting him come to my place.

Joyce: I wonder how he managed to keep it so dark.

Crosbie: Will she be one of the witnesses?

Joyce: I shan't call her. I shall produce evidence that he was living with her, and, public feeling being what it is, I think the jury will accept that as proof that Hammond was a man of notorious character.

> A **Sikh Sergeant of Police** *comes into the room. He is tall, bearded, dark, and dressed in blue.*

Sikh (*to* **Crosbie**): You come now, Sahib.

Crosbie: At last.

Joyce: You haven't got very long to wait now. In another twenty-four hours she'll be a free woman. Why don't you take her somewhere for a trip? Even though we're almost dead certain to get an acquittal, a trial of this sort is anxious work, and you'll both of you want a rest.

Crosbie: I think I shall want it more than Leslie. She's been a brick. Why, d'you know, when I've been to see her it wasn't I who cheered her up, it was she who cheered me up. By God! there's a plucky little woman for you, Howard.

Joyce: I agree. Her self-control is amazing.

Crosbie: I won't keep her long. I know you're busy.

Joyce: Thanks. (**Crosbie** *goes out with the* **Sikh Policeman.**) Is my clerk outside, sergeant? (*He has hardly spoken the words before* **Ong Chi Seng** *sidles in.*) Give me those papers you've got there, will you?

Ong Chi Seng: Yes, sir.

> *He takes a bundle of papers from his wallet and gives them to* **Joyce.** **Joyce** *sits down with them at the table.*

The Letter

Joyce: That's all, Ong. If I want you I'll call.

Ong Chi Seng: May I trouble you for a few words private conversation, sir?

> **Ong Chi Seng** *expresses himself with elaborate accuracy; he has learnt English as a foreign language, and speaks it perfectly; but he has trouble with his R's, he always turns them into L's, and this gives his careful speech every now and then a faintly absurd air.*

Joyce (*with a slight smile*): It's no trouble, Ong.

Ong Chi Seng: The matter upon which I desire to speak to you sir, is delicate and confidential.

Joyce: Mrs Crosbie will be here in five minutes. Don't you think we might find a more suitable occasion for a heart-to-heart talk.

Ong Chi Seng: The matter on which I desire to speak with you, sir, has to do with the case of *R*. v *Crosbie*.

Joyce: Oh?

Ong Chi Seng: Yes, sir.

Joyce: I have a great regard for your intelligence, Ong. I am sure I can trust you not to tell me anything that, as Mrs Crosbie's counsel, it is improper that I should be advised of.

Ong Chi Seng: I think, sir, that you may rest assured of my discretion. I am a graduate of the University of Hong Kong, and I won the Chancellor's Prize for English composition.

Joyce: Fire away, then.

Ong Chi Seng: A circumstances has come to my knowledge, sir, which seems to me to put a different complexion on this case.

Joyce: What circumstance?

Ong Chi Seng: It has come to my knowledge, sir, that there is a letter in existence from the defendant to the unfortunate victim of the tragedy.

Joyce: I should not be at all surprised. In the course of the last seven years I have no doubt that Mrs

Crosbie often had occasion to write to Mr
Hammond.

Ong Chi Seng: That is very probable, sir. Mrs Crosbie
must have communicated with the deceased
frequently, to invite him to dine with her, for
example, or to propose a tennis game. That was
my first idea when the matter was brought to my
notice. This letter, however, was written on the
day of the late Mr Hammond's death.

> *There was an instant's pause.* **Joyce,** *a faint
> smile of amusement in his eyes, continues to
> look intently at* **Ong Chi Seng.**

Joyce: Who told you this?

Ong Chi Seng: The circumstances were brought to
my notice, sir, by a friend of mine.

Joyce: I have always known that your discretion was
beyond praise, Ong Chi Seng.

Ong Chi Seng: You will no doubt recall, sir, that Mrs
Crosbie has stated that until the fatal night she
had had no communication with the deceased for
several weeks.

Joyce: Yes, I do.

Ong Chi Seng: This letter indicates in my opinion
that her statement was not in every respect accurate.

Joyce (*stretching out his hand as though to take it*):
Have you got the letter?

Ong Chi Seng: No, sir.

Joyce: Oh! I suppose you know its contents.

Ong Chi Seng: My friend very kindly gave me a copy.
Would you like to peruse it, sir?

Joyce: I should.

> **Ong Chi Seng** *takes from an inside pocket a
> bulky wallet. It is filled with papers, Singapore
> dollars and cigarette cards.*

Joyce: Ah, I see you collect cigarette cards.

Ong Chi Seng: Yes, sir. I am happy to say that I have

a collection which is almost unique and very comprehensive.

From the confusion he extracts a half-sheet of notepaper and places it before Joyce.

Joyce (*reading it slowly, as though he could hardly believe his eyes*): 'Robert will be away for the night. I absolutely must see you. I shall expect you at eleven. I am desperate, and if you don't come I won't answer for the consequences . . . Don't drive up, Leslie . . .' What the devil does it mean?

Ong Chi Seng: That is for you to say, sir.

Joyce: What makes you think that this letter was written by Mrs Crosbie?

Ong Chi Seng: I have every confidence in the veracity of my informant, sir.

Joyce: That's more than I have.

Ong Chi Seng: The matter can very easily be put to the proof. Mrs Crosbie will no doubt be able to tell you at once whether she wrote such a letter or not.

Joyce gets up and walks once or twice up and down the room. Then he stops and faces Ong Chi Seng.

Joyce: It is inconceivable that Mrs Crosbie should have written such a letter.

Ong Chi Seng: If that is your opinion, sir, the matter is, of course, ended. My friend spoke to me on the subject only because he thought, as I was in your office, you might like to know of the existence of this letter before a communication was made to the Police Prosecutor.

Joyce: Who has the original?

Ong Chi Seng: You will remember, sir, no doubt, that after the death of Mr Hammond it was discovered that he had had relations with a Chinese woman. The letter is at present in her possession.

They face each other for a moment silently.

Joyce: I am obliged to you, Ong. I will give the matter my consideration.

Ong Chi Seng: Very good, sir. Do you wish me to make a communication to that effect to my friend?

Joyce: I daresay it would be as well if you kept in touch with him.

Ong Chi Seng: Yes, sir.

> *He leaves the room.* **Joyce** *reads through the letter once more with knitted brows; he hears a sound and realizes that* **Leslie** *is coming. He places the copy of the letter among the papers on the table.* **Leslie** *comes in with the* **Matron**. *This is a stout middle-aged English-woman in a white dress.* **Leslie** *is very simply and neatly dressed; her hair is done with her habitual care; she is cool and self-possessed.*

Joyce: Good morning, Mrs Crosbie.

> **Leslie** *comes forward graciously. She holds out her hand as calmly as though she were receiving him in her drawing-room.*

Leslie: How do you do? I wasn't expecting you so early.

Joyce: How are you today?

Leslie: I'm in the best of health, thank you. This is a wonderful place for a rest cure. And Mrs Parker looks after me like a mother.

Joyce: How do you do, Mrs Parker?

Mrs Parker: Very well, thank you, sir. This I can't help saying, Mrs Crosbie, no one could be less trouble than what you are. I shall be sorry to lose you, and that's a fact.

Leslie (*with a gracious smile*): You've been very kind to me, Mrs Parker.

Mrs Parker: Well, I've been company for you. When you're not used to it, it's lonely like in a place like this. It's a shame they ever put you here, if you want to know what I think about it.

Joyce: Well, Mrs Parker, I daresay you won't mind leaving us. Mrs Crosbie and I have got business to talk about.

Mrs Parker: Very good, sir.

She goes out.

Leslie: Sometimes she drives me nearly mad, she's so chatty, poor dear. Isn't it strange how few people there are who can ever realize that you may be perfectly satisfied with your own company?

Joyce: You must have had plenty of that lately.

Leslie: I've read a great deal, you know, and I've worked at my lace.

Joyce: I need hardly ask if you've slept well.

Leslie: I've slept like a top. The time has really passed very quickly.

Joyce: It's evidently agreed with you. You're looking very much better and stronger than a few weeks ago.

Leslie: That's more than poor Robert is. He's a wreck, poor darling. I'm thankful for his sake that it'll all be over tomorrow. I think he's just about at the end of his tether.

Joyce: He's very much more anxious about you than you appear to be about yourself.

Leslie: Won't you sit down?

Joyce: Thank you.

They seat themselves. **Joyce** *at the table, with his papers in front of him.*

Leslie: I'm not exactly looking forward to the trial, you know.

Joyce: One of the things that has impressed me is that each time you've told your story you've told it in exactly the same words. You've never varied a hair's breadth.

Leslie (*gently chaffing him*): What does that suggest to your legal mind?

Joyce: Well, it suggests either that you have an extraordinary memory or that you're telling the plain, unvarnished truth.

Leslie: I'm afraid I have a very poor memory.

Joyce: I suppose I'm right in thinking that you had no communication with Hammond for several weeks before the catastrophe.

Leslie (*with a friendly little smile*): Oh, quite. I'm positive of that. The last time we met was at a tennis party at the McFarrens'. I don't think I said more than two words to him. They have two courts, you know, and we didn't happen to be in the same sets.

Joyce: And you hadn't written to him?

Leslie: Oh, no.

Joyce: Are you perfectly certain of that?

Leslie: Oh, perfectly. There was nothing I should write to him for except to ask him to dine or play tennis, and I hadn't done either for months.

Joyce: At one time you'd been on fairly intimate terms with him. How did it happen that you stopped asking him to anything?

Leslie (*with a little shrug of her shoulders*): One gets tired of people. We hadn't anything very much in common. Of course, when he was ill Robert and I did everything we could for him, but the last year or two he's been quite well. And he was very popular. He had a good many calls on his time and there didn't seem to be any need to shower invitations on him.

Joyce: Are you quite certain that was all?

> **Leslie** *hesitates for a moment and reflectively looks down.*

Leslie: Well, of course, I knew about the Chinese woman. I'd actually seen her.

Joyce: Oh! You never mentioned that.

Leslie: It wasn't a very pleasant thing to talk about. And I knew you'd find out for yourselves soon enough. Under the circumstances I didn't think it would be very nice of me to be the first to tell you about his private life?

Joyce: What was she like?

> **Leslie** *gives a slight start and a hard look suddenly crosses her face.*

Leslie: Oh, horrible. Stout and painted and powdered. Covered with gold chains and bangles and pins. Not even young. She's older than I am.

Joyce: And it was after you knew about her that you ceased having anything to do with Hammond?

Leslie: Yes.

Joyce: But you said nothing about it to your husband.

Leslie: It wasn't the sort of thing I cared to talk to Robert about.

> **Joyce** *watches her for a moment. Any suggestion of emotion that showed itself on her face when she spoke of the Chinese woman has left it and she is now once more cool and self-possessed.*

Joyce: I think I should tell you that there is in existence a letter in your handwriting from you to Geoff Hammond.

Leslie: In the past I've often sent him little notes to ask him to something or other or to get me something when I knew he was going into Singapore.

Joyce: This letter asks him to come and see you because Robert was going to Singapore.

Leslie (*smiling*): That's impossible. I never did anything of the kind.

Joyce: You'd better read it for yourself.

> *He takes it from the papers in front of him and*

hands it to her. She gives it a moment's glance and hands it back.

Leslie: That's not my handwriting.

Joyce: I know. It's said to be an exact copy of the original.

She takes the letter again and now reads the words. And as she reads a horrible change comes over her. Her colourless face grows dreadful to look at. The flesh seems on a sudden to fall away and her skin is tightly stretched over the bones. She stares at Joyce with eyes that start from their sockets.

Leslie (*in a whisper*): What does it mean?

Joyce: That is for you to say.

Leslie: I didn't write it. I swear I didn't write it.

Joyce: Be very careful what you say. If the original is in your handwriting, it would be useless to deny it.

Leslie: It would be forgery.

Joyce: It would be difficult to prove that. It would be easy to prove that it was genuine.

A shiver passes through her body. She takes out a handkerchief and wipes the palms of her hands. She looks at the letter again.

Leslie: It's not dated. If I had written it and forgotten all about it, it might have been written years ago. If you'll give me time I'll try to remember the circumstances.

Joyce: I noticed there was no date. If this letter were in the hands of the prosecution they would cross-examine your house-boys. They would soon find out whether someone took a letter to Hammond on the day of his death.

She clasps her hands violently and sways on her chair so that you might think she would faint.

The Letter

Leslie: I swear to you that I did not write that letter.

Joyce: In that case we need not go into the matter further. If the person who possesses this letter sees fit to place it in the hands of the prosecution you will be prepared. (*There is a long pause,* **Joyce** *waits for* **Leslie** *to speak, but she stares straight in front of her*) If you have nothing more to say to me, I think I'll be getting back to my office.

Leslie (*still not looking at him*): What would anyone who read the letter be inclined to think that it meant?

Joyce: He'd know that you had told a deliberate lie.

Leslie: When?

Joyce: When you stated definitely that you had had no communication with Hammond for at least six weeks.

Leslie: The whole thing has been a terrible shock to me. The events of that horrible night have been a nightmare. It's not very strange if one detail has escaped my memory.

Joyce: Your memory has reproduced very exactly every particular of your interview with Hammond. It is very strange that you should have forgotten so important a point as that he came to the bungalow on the night of his death at your express desire.

Leslie: I hadn't forgotten.

Joyce: Then why didn't you mention it?

Leslie: I was afraid to. I thought you'd none of you believe my story if I admitted that he'd come at my invitation. I daresay it was very stupid of me. I lost my head, and after I'd once said that I'd had no communication with Hammond I was obliged to stick to it.

Joyce: You will be required to explain, then, why you asked Hammond to come to you when Robert was away for the night.

Leslie (*with a break in her voice*): It was a surprise I was preparing for Robert's birthday. I knew he wanted a gun, and, you know, I'm dreadfully stupid about sporting things. I wanted to talk to Geoff about it. I thought I'd get him to order it for me.

Joyce: Perhaps the terms of the letter are not very clear to your recollection. Will you have another look at it?

Leslie (*quickly drawing back*): No, I don't want to.

Joyce: Then I must read it to you. *Robert will be away for the night. I absolutely must see you. I shall expect you at eleven, I am desperate, and if you don't come I won't answer for the consequences. Don't drive up. – Leslie.* Does it seem to you the sort of letter a woman would write to a rather distant acquaintance because she wanted to consult him about buying a gun?

Leslie: I daresay it's rather extravagant and emotional. I do express myself like that, you know. I'm quite prepared to admit it's rather silly.

Joyce: I must have been very much mistaken. I always thought you a very reserved and self-possessed woman.

Leslie: And after all, Geoff Hammond wasn't quite a distant acquaintance. When he was ill I nursed him like a mother.

Joyce: By the way, did you call him Geoff?

Leslie: Everybody did. He wasn't the kind of man anyone would think of calling Mr Hammond.

Joyce: Why did you ask him to come at so late an hour?

Leslie (*recovering of self-possession*): Is eleven very late? He was always dining somewhere or other. I thought he'd look in on his way home.

Joyce: And why did you ask him not to drive up?

Leslie (*with a shrug of the shoulder*): You know how Chinese boys gossip. If they'd heard him come, the last thing they'd have ever thought was that he was there for a perfectly innocent purpose.

The Letter

Joyce gets up and walks once or twice up and down the room. Then, leaning over the back of his chair, he speaks in a tone of deep gravity.

Joyce: Mrs Crosbie, I want to talk to you very, very seriously. This case was comparatively plain sailing. There was only one point that seemed to me to require explanation. So far as I could judge, you had fired no less than four shots into Hammond when he was lying on the ground. It was hard to accept the possibility that a delicate, frightened woman, of gentle nurture and refined instincts, should have surrendered to an absolutely uncontrollable frenzy. But, of course, it was admissible. Although Geoffrey Hammond was much liked, and on the whole thought highly of, I was prepared to prove that he was the sort of man who might be guilty of the crime which in justification of your act you accused him of. The fact, which was discovered after his death, that he had been living with a Chinese woman gave us something very definite to go on. That robbed him of any sympathy that might have been felt for him. We made up our minds to make every use of the odium that such a connection cast upon him in the minds of all respectable people. I told your husband just now that I was certain of an acquittal, and I wasn't just telling him that to cheer him up. I do not believe the jury would have left the box. (*They look into each other's eyes. Leslie is strangely still. She is like a bird paralyzed by the fascination of a snake.*) But this letter has thrown an entirely different complexion on the case. I am your legal adviser. I shall represent you in court. I take your story as you tell it to me, and I shall conduct your defence according to its terms. It may be that I believe your statements, or it may be that I doubt them. The duty of counsel is to

persuade the jury that the evidence placed before
them is not such as to justify them in bringing a
verdict of guilty, and any private opinion he may
have of the innocence or guilt of his client is
entirely beside the point.

Leslie: I don't know what you're driving at.

Joyce: You're not going to deny that Hammond came
to your house at your urgent and, I may even say,
hysterical invitation?

> **Leslie** *does not answer for a moment. She*
> *seems to consider.*

Leslie: They can prove that the letter was taken to
his bungalow by one of the house-boys. He rode
over on his bicycle.

Joyce: You mustn't expect other people to be stupider
than you. The letter will put them on the track of
suspicions that have entered nobody's head. I will
not tell you what I personally thought when I read
it. I do not wish you to tell me anything but what
is needed to save your neck.

> **Leslie** *crumples up suddenly. She falls to the*
> *floor in a dead faint before* **Joyce** *can catch*
> *her. He looks round the room for water, but*
> *can find none. He glances at the door, but*
> *will not call for help. He does not wish to be*
> *disturbed. He kneels down beside her,*
> *waiting for her to recover, and at last she opens*
> *her eyes.*

Joyce: Keep quite still. You'll be better in a minute.

Leslie: Don't let anyone come.

Joyce: No. No.

Leslie: Mr Joyce, you won't let them hang me.

> *She begins to cry hysterically: he tries in*
> *undertones to calm her.*

Joyce: Sh! Sh! Don't make a noise. Sh! Sh! It's all

right. Don't, don't, don't! For goodness' sake pull
yourself together.

Leslie: Give me a minute.

> *You see the effort she makes to regain her self-
> control and soon she is once more calm.*

Joyce (*with almost unwilling admiration*): You've got
pluck. I think no one could deny that.

Leslie: Let me get up now. It was silly of me to faint.

> *He gives her his hand and helps her to her feet.
> He leads her to a chair and she sinks down
> wearily.*

Joyce: Do you feel a little better?

Leslie (*with her eyes closed*): Don't talk to me for a
moment or two.

Joyce: Very well.

Leslie (*at last, with a little sigh*): I'm afraid I've made
rather a mess of things.

Joyce: I'm sorry.

Leslie: For Robert, not for me. You distrusted me from
the beginning.

Joyce: That's neither here nor there.

> *She gives him a glance and then looks down.*

Leslie: Isn't it possible to get hold of the letter?

Joyce (*with a frown to conceal his embarrassment*):
I don't think anything would have been said to me
about it if the person in whose possession it is was
not prepared to sell it.

Leslie: Who's got it?

Joyce: The Chinese woman who was living in
Hammond's house.

> **Leslie** *instinctively clenches her hands; but
> again controls herself.*

Leslie: Does she want an awful lot for it?

Joyce: I imagine that she has a pretty shrewd idea of
its value. I doubt if it would be possible to get hold
of it except for a very large sum.

Leslie (*hoarsely*): Are you going to let me be hanged?

Joyce (*with some irritation*): Do you think it's so simple as all that to secure possession of an unwelcome piece of evidence?

Leslie: You say the woman is prepared to sell it.

Joyce: But I don't know that I'm prepared to buy it.

Leslie: Why not?

Joyce: I don't think you know what you're asking me. Heaven knows, I don't wish to make phrases, but I've always thought I was by way of being an honest man. You're asking me to do something that is no different from suborning a witness.

Leslie (*her voice rising*): Do you mean to say you can save me and you won't? What harm have I ever done to you? You can't be so cruel.

Joyce: I'm sorry it sounds cruel. I want to do my best for you, Mrs Crosbie. A lawyer has a duty not only to his client, but also to his profession.

Leslie (*with dismay*): Then what is going to happen to me?

Joyce (*very gravely*): Justice must take its course.

> **Leslie** *grows very pale. A little shudder passes through her body. When she answers her voice is low and quiet.*

Leslie: I put myself in your hands. Of course, I have no right to ask you to do anything that isn't proper. I was asking more for Robert's sake than mine. But if you knew everything, I believe you'd think I was deserving of your pity.

Joyce: Poor old Bob, it'll nearly kill him. He's utterly unprepared.

Leslie: If I'm hanged it certainly won't bring Geoff Hammond back to life again.

> *There is a moment's silence while* **Joyce** *reflects upon the situation.*

Joyce (*almost to himself*): Sometimes I think that when we say our honour prevents us from doing this or that we deceive ourselves, and our real motive is vanity. I ask myself, what really is the explanation of that letter? I daren't ask you. It's not fair to you to conclude from it that you killed Hammond without provocation. (*With emotion*) It's absurd how fond I am of Bob. You see, I've known him so long. His life may very well be ruined, too.

Leslie: I know I have no right to ask you to do anything for me, but Robert is so kind and simple and good. I think he's never done anyone any harm in his life. Can't you save him from this bitter pain and this disgrace?

Joyce: You mean everything in the world to him, don't you?

Leslie: I suppose so. I'm very grateful for the love he's given me.

Joyce (*making his resolution*): I'm going to do what I can for you. (*She gives a little gasp of relief.*) But don't think I don't know I'm doing wrong. I am. I'm doing it with my eyes open.

Leslie: It can't be wrong to save a suffering woman. You're doing no harm to anybody else.

Joyce: You don't understand. It's only natural. Let's not discuss that . . . Do you know anything about Bob's circumstances?

Leslie: He has a good many tin shares and a part interest in two or three rubber estates. I suppose he could raise money.

Joyce: He would have to be told what it was for.

Leslie: Will it be necessary to show him the letter?

Joyce: Don't you want him to see it.

Leslie: No.

Joyce: I shall do everything possible to prevent him from seeing it till after the trial. He will be an important witness. I think it very necessary that he should be as firmly convinced of your innocence as he is now.

Leslie: And afterwards?

Joyce: I'll still do my best for you.

Leslie: Not for my sake – for his. If he loses trust in me he loses everything.

Joyce: It's strange that a man can live with a woman for ten years and not know the first thing about her. It's rather frightening.

Leslie: He knows that he loves me. Nothing else matters.

Joyce (*goes to the door and opens it*): Mrs Parker, I'm just going.

    Mrs Parker *comes in again.*

Mrs Parker: Gracious, how white you look, Mrs Crosbie. Mr Joyce hasn't been upsetting you, has he? You look like a ghost.

Leslie (*graciously smiling, with an instinctive resumption of her social manner*): No, he's been kindness itself. I daresay the strain is beginning to tell on me a little. (*She holds out her hand to Joyce*) Goodbye. It's good of you to take all this trouble for me. I can't begin to tell you how grateful I am.

Joyce: I shan't see you again till just before the trial tomorrow.

Leslie: I've got a lot to do before then. I've been making Mrs Parker a lace collar, and I want to get it done before I leave here.

Mrs Parker: It's so grand, I shall never be able to bring myself to wear it. She makes beautiful lace, you'd be surprised.

Joyce: I know she does.

Leslie: I'm afraid it's my only accomplishment.

Joyce: Good morning, Mrs Parker.

Mrs Parker: Good morning, sir.

    She goes out accompanied by **Leslie**. **Joyce** *gathers his papers together. There is a knock at the door.*

Joyce: Come in.

The Letter

The door is opened and **Ong Chi Seng** *enters.*

Ong Chi Seng: I desire to remind you, sir, that you
have an appointment with Mr Reed, of Reed and
Pollock, at twelve-thirty.

Joyce (*with a glance at his watch*): He'll have to wait.

Ong Chi Seng: Very good sir. (*He goes to the door
and is about to go out, then, as though on an
afterthought, he stops.*) Is there anything further
you wish me to say to my friend, sir?

Joyce: What friend?

Ong Chi Seng: About the letter which Mrs Crosbie
wrote to Hammond, deceased, sir.

Joyce (*very casually*): Oh, I'd forgotten about that. I
mentioned it to Mrs Crosbie and she denies having
written anything of the sort. It's evidently a forgery.

*He takes out the copy from the papers in front
of him, and hands it to* **Ong Chi Seng.** *The
Chinaman ignores the gesture.*

Ong Chi Seng: In that case, sir, I suppose there would
be no objection if my friend delivered the letter to
the Public Prosecutor.

Joyce: None. But I don't quite see what good that
would do your friend.

Ong Chi Seng: My friend thought it was his duty, sir,
in the interests of justice.

Joyce (*grimly*): I am the last man in the world to
interfere with anyone who wishes to do his duty,
Ong.

Ong Chi Seng: I quite understand, sir, but from my
study of the case, *R.* v. *Crosbie*, I am of the opinion
that the production of such a letter would be
damaging to our client.

Joyce: I have always had a high opinion of your legal
acumen, Ong Chi Seng.

Ong Chi Seng: It has occurred to me, sir, that if I
could persuade my friend to induce the Chinese

woman who has the letter to deliver it into our
hands it would save a great deal of trouble.

Joyce: I suppose your friend is a business man. Under
what circumstances do you think he would be
induced to part with the letter?

Ong Chi Seng: He has not got the letter.

Joyce: Oh, has he got a friend, too?

Ong Chi Seng: The Chinese woman has got the letter.
He is only a relation of the Chinese woman. She is
an ignorant woman; she did not know the value of
the letter till my friend told her.

Joyce: What value did he put on it?

Ong Chi Seng: Ten thousand dollars, sir.

Joyce: Good God! Where on earth do you suppose Mrs
Crosbie can get ten thousand dollars? I tell you
the letter's a forgery.

Ong Chi Seng: Mr Crosbie owns an eighth share of
the Bekong Rubber Estate, and a sixth share of the
Kelanton River Rubber Estate. I have a friend who
will lend him the money on the security of his
properties.

Joyce: You have a large circle of acquaintances, Ong.

Ong Chi Seng: Yes, sir.

Joyce: Well, you can tell them all to go to hell. I
would never advise Mr Crosbie to give a penny more
than five thousand for a letter that can be very
easily explained.

Ong Chi Seng: The Chinese woman does not want to
sell the letter, sir. My friend took a long time to
persuade her. It is useless to offer her less than the
sum mentioned.

Joyce: Ten thousand dollars is an awful lot.

Ong Chi Seng: Mr Crosbie will certainly pay it rather
than see his wife hanged by the neck, sir.

Joyce: Why did your friend fix upon that particular
amount?

Ong Chi Seng: I will not attempt to conceal anything
from you, sir. Upon making enquiry, sir, my friend

came to the conclusion that ten thousand dollars was the largest sum Mr Crosbie could possibly get.

Joyce: Ah, that is precisely what occurred to me. Well, I will speak to Mr Crosbie.

Ong Chi Seng: Mr Crosbie is still here, sir.

Joyce: Oh! What's he doing?

Ong Chi Seng: We have only a very short time, sir, and the matter, in my opinion, brooks of no delay.

Joyce: In that case be brief, Ong.

Ong Chi Seng: It occurred to me that you would wish to speak to Mr Crosbie and, therefore, I took the liberty of asking him to wait. If it would be convenient for you to speak to him now, sir, I could impart your decision to my friend when I have my tiffin.

Joyce: Where is the Chinese woman now?

Ong Chi Seng: She is staying in the house of my friend, sir.

Joyce: Will she come to my office?

Ong Chi Seng: I think it more better you go to her, sir. I can take you to the house tonight, and she will give you the letter. She is a very ignorant woman and she does not understand cheques.

Joyce: I wasn't thinking of giving her a cheque. I should bring banknotes with me.

Ong Chi Seng: It would only be waste of time to bring less than ten thousand dollars, sir.

Joyce: I quite understand.

Ong Chi Seng: Shall I tell Mr Crosbie that you wish to see him, sir

Joyce: Ong Chi Seng.

Ong Chi Seng: Yes, sir.

Joyce: Is there anything else you know?

Ong Chi Seng: No, sir. I am of the opinion that a confidential clerk should have no secrets from his employer. May I ask why you make this enquiry, sir?

Joyce: Call Mr Crosbie.

Ong Chi Seng: Very good sir.

He goes out, and in a moment opens the door once more for **Crosbie.**

Joyce: It's good of you to have waited, old man.

Crosbie: Your clerk said that you particularly wished me to.

Joyce (*as casually as he can*): A rather unpleasant thing has happened, Bob. It appears that your wife sent a letter to Hammond asking him to come to the bungalow on the night he was killed.

Crosbie: But that's impossible. She's always stated that she had had no communication with Hammond. I know from my own knowledge that she hadn't set eyes on him for a couple of months.

Joyce: The fact remains that the letter exists. It's in the possession of the Chinese woman Hammond was living with.

Crosbie: What did she write to him for?

Joyce: Your wife meant to give you a present on your birthday, and she wanted Hammond to help her to get it. Your birthday was just about then, wasn't it?

Crosbie: Yes. In point of fact it was a fortnight ago today.

Joyce: In the emotional excitement that she suffered from after the tragedy she forgot that she'd written a letter to him, and having once denied having any communication with Hammond she was afraid to say she'd made a mistake.

Crosbie: Why?

Joyce: My dear fellow. It was, of course, very unfortunate, but I daresay it was not unnatural.

Crosbie: That's unlike Leslie. I've never known her afraid of anything.

Joyce: The circumstances were exceptional.

Crosbie: Does it very much matter? If she's asked about it she can explain.

The Letter

Joyce: It would be very awkward if this letter found its way into the hands of the prosecution. Your wife has lied, and she would be asked some difficult questions.

Crosbie: Leslie would never tell a lie intentionally.

Joyce (*with a shadow of impatience*): My dear Bob, you *must* try to understand. Don't you see that it alters things a good deal if Hammond did not intrude, an unwanted guest, but came to your house by invitation? It would be easy to arouse in the jury a certain indecision of mind.

Crosbie: I may be very stupid, but I don't understand. You lawyers, you seem to take a delight in making mountains out of mole-heaps. After all, Howard, you're not only my lawyer, you're the oldest friend I have in the world.

Joyce: I know. That is why I'm taking a step the gravity of which I can never expect you to realize. I think we must get hold of that letter. I want you to authorize me to buy it.

Crosbie: I'll do whatever you think is right.

Joyce: I don't think it's right, but I think it's expedient. Juries are very stupid. I think it's just as well not to worry them with more evidence than they can conventionally deal with.

Crosbie: Well, I don't pretend to understand, but I'm perfectly prepared to leave myself in your hands. Go ahead and do as you think fit. I'll pay.

Joyce: All right. And now put the matter out of your mind.

Crosbie: That's easy. I could never bring myself to believe that Leslie had ever done anything that wasn't absolutely square and above board.

Joyce: Let's go to the club. I badly want a whisky and soda.

CURTAIN

Act III

Scene I

The scene is a small room in the Chinese quarter of Singapore. The walls are whitewashed, but dirty and bedraggled, on one of them hangs a cheap Chinese oleograph, stained and discoloured; on another, unframed and pinned up, a picture of a nude from one of the illustrated papers. The only furniture consists of a sandalwood box and a low Chinese pallet bed, with a lacquered neck-rest. There is a closed window, which is at the back, and a door on the right. It is night and the room is lit by one electric light, a globe without a shade.

When the curtain rises **Chung Hi** *is lying on the pallet bed, with his opium pipe, his lamp, and the tray on which are the little tin of opium and a couple of long needles. He is reading a Chinese newspaper. He is a fat Chinaman in white trousers and a singlet. On his feet are Chinese slippers. A* **Boy,** *dressed in the same way, is seated on the sandalwood chest idly playing a Chinese flute. He plays a strange Chinese tune,* **Chung Hi** *dips his needle in the opium and heats it over the flame of the lamp, puts it in the pipe, inhales and presently blows out a thick cloud of smoke. There is a scratching at the door,* **Chung Hi** *speaks a few words in Chinese and the* **Boy** *goes to it and just opens it. The* **Boy** *speaks to the person there and still from the door says something to* **Chung Hi. Chung Hi** *makes answer and gets up from the pallet bed, putting his opium things aside. The door is opened wider and* **Ong Chi Seng** *comes in.*

The Letter

Ong Chi Seng: This way, sir, please. Come in.

Joyce enters, wearing his topee.

Joyce: I nearly broke my neck on those stairs.

Ong Chi Seng: This is my friend, sir.

Joyce: Does he speak English?

Chung Hi: Yes, my speakee velly good English. How do you do, sir? I hope you are quite well. Please to come in. ⸎

Joyce: Good evening. I say, the air in here is awful. Couldn't we have the window open?

Chung Hi: Night air velly bad, sir. Him bring fever.

Joyce: We'll risk it.

Ong Chi Seng: Very good, sir. I will open the window. *(He goes to it and does so.)*

Joyce *(taking off his topee and putting it down)*: I see you've been smoking.

Chung Hi: Yes, my suffer velly bad from my belly. Smokee two, thlee pipes make it more better.

Joyce: We'd better get to our business.

Ong Chi Seng: Yes, sir. Business is business, as we say.

Joyce: What is your friend's name, Ong?

Chung Hi: My callee all same Chung Hi. You no see him written on shop? Chung Hi. General dealer.

Joyce: I suppose you know what I've come for?

Chung Hi: Yes, sir. My velly glad to see you in my house. My give you my business card. Yes?

Joyce: I don't think I need it.

Chung Hi: My sell you velly good China tea. All same Suchong. Number one quality. My can sell more cheap than you buy at stores.

Joyce: I don't want any tea.

Chung Hi: My sell you Swatow silk. Velly best quality. No can get more better in China. Make velly good suits. My sell you cheap.

Joyce: I don't want any silk.

Chung Hi: Velly well. You take my business card.

Chung Hi, General Dealer, 264 Victoria Street. Maybe you want some tomorrow or next day.

Joyce: Have you got this letter?

Chung Hi: Chinese woman have got.

Joyce: Where is she?

Chung Hi: She come presently.

Joyce: Why the devil isn't she here?

Chung Hi: She here all right. She come presently. She wait till you come. See?

Ong Chi Seng: More better you tell her to come, I think.

Chung Hi: Yes, I tell her come this minute. (*He speaks to the* **Boy** *in Chinese, who gives a guttural, monosyllabic reply and goes out. To* **Joyce**) You sit down. Yes?

Joyce: I prefer to stand.

Chung Hi (*handing him a green tin of cigarettes*): You smokee cigarette. Velly good cigarette. All same Thlee Castles.

Joyce: I don't want to smoke.

Chung Hi (*to* **Joyce**): You wantchee buy China tea velly cheap. Number one quality.

Joyce: Go to hell.

Chung Hi: All light. My no savee. Maybe you likee Swatow silk. No! You wantchee see jade? Have got string number one quality. My sell you one thousand dollars. Velly nice plesent your missus.

Joyce: Go to hell.

Chung Hi: All light. I smokee cigarette.

The door is opened and the **Boy** *comes in again with a tray on which are bowls of tea. He takes it to* **Joyce**, *who shakes his head and turns away. The others help themselves.*

Joyce: Why the devil doesn't this woman come?

Ong Chi Seng: I think she come now, sir.

There is a scratching at the door.

Joyce: I'm curious to see her.

The Letter

Ong Chi Seng: My fliend say that poor Mr Hammond deceased was completely under her thumb, sir.

Chung Hi: She no speakee English. She speakee Malay and Chinese.

> *Meanwhile the* **Boy** *has gone to the door and opened it. The* **Chinese Woman** *comes in. She wears a silk sarong and a long muslin coat over a blouse. On her arms are heavy gold bangles; she wears a gold chain round her neck and gold pins in her shining, black hair. Her cheeks and mouth are painted, and she is heavily powdered; arched eyebrows make a thin dark line over her eyes. She comes in and walks slowly to the pallet bed and sits on the edge of it with her legs dangling.* **Ong Chi Seng** *makes an observation to her in Chinese, and she briefly answers. She takes no notice of the white man.*

Joyce: Has she got the letter?

Ong Chi Seng: Yes, sir.

Joyce: Where is it?

Ong Chi Seng: She's a very ignorant woman, sir. I think she wants to see the money before she gives the letter.

Joyce: Very well.

> *The* **Chinese Woman** *takes a cigarette from the tin and lights it. She appears to take no notice of what is proceeding.* **Joyce** *counts out the ten thousand dollars and hands them to* **Ong Chi Seng.** **Ong Chi Seng** *counts them for himself, while* **Chung Hi** *watches him. They are all grave, businesslike, and the Chinese are oddly unconcerned.*

Ong Chi Seng: The sum is quite correct, sir.

> *The* **Chinese Woman** *takes the letter from her*

tunic and hands it to **Ong Chi Seng. Ong Chi
Seng** *gives it a glance.*

This is the right document, sir.

> *He hands it to* **Joyce,** *who reads it silently.*

Joyce: There's not very much for the money.

Ong Chi Seng: I am sure you will not regret it, sir.
Considering all the circumstances, it is what you
call dirt cheap.

Joyce (*ironically*): I know that you have too great a
regard for me to allow me to pay more for an
article than the market price.

Ong Chi Seng: Shall you want me for anything else
tonight, please, sir?

Joyce: I don't think so.

Ong Chi Seng: In that case, sir, if it is convenient, I
will stay here and talk to my friend.

Joyce (*sardonically*): I suppose you want to divide the
swag.

Ong Chi Seng: I am sorry, sir, that is a word I have
not come across in my studies.

Joyce: You'd better look it out in the dictionary.

Ong Chi Seng: Yes, sir. I will do it without delay.

Joyce: I have been wondering how much you were
going to get out of this, Ong Chi Seng.

Ong Chi Seng: The labourer is worthy of his hire, as
Our Lord said, sir.

Joyce: I didn't know you were a Christian, Ong.

Ong Chi Seng: I am not, sir, to the best of my belief.

Joyce: In that case he certainly isn't your Lord.

Ong Chi Seng: I was only making use of the common
English idiom, sir. In point of fact, I am a disciple of
the late Herbert Spencer. I have also been much
influenced by Nietzsche, Shaw and Herbert G.
Wells.

Joyce: It is no wonder that I am no match for you.

> *As he goes out the curtain falls quickly.*

Scene II

The scene is the same as in Act I. The sitting-room at the **Crosbies'** *bungalow.*

It is about five o'clock in the afternoon and the light is soft and mellow.

When the curtain rises the stage is empty, but immediately the sound is heard of a car stopping, and **Mrs Joyce** *and* **Withers** *come up the steps of the verandah and enter the room. They are followed in an instant by the* **Head-Boy** *and another Chinese servant, one with a suitcase and the other with a large basket.* **Mrs Joyce** *is a buxom, florid, handsome woman of about forty.*

Mrs Joyce: Good gracious, how desolate the place looks. You can see in the twinkling of a eye that there hasn't been a woman here to look after things.

Withers: I must say it does look a bit dreary.

Mrs Joyce: I knew it. I felt it in my bones. That's why I wanted to get here before Leslie. I thought we might have a chance to do a little something before she came

> *She goes over to the piano, opens it and puts a piece of music on the stand*

Withers: A few flowers would help.

Mrs Joyce: I wonder if these wretched boys will have had the sense to pick some. (*To the* **Head-Boy** *who bears the basket*) Is the ice all right, boy?

Head-Boy: Yes, missy.

Mrs Joyce: Well, put it in some place where it won't melt. Are there any flowers?

Head-Boy: My lookee see.

Mrs Joyce (*to the other boy*): Oh, that's my bag. Put it in the spare room.

Withers: You know, I can't help wondering how Mrs Crosbie can bring herself to come back here.

Mrs Joyce: My poor friend, the Crosbies haven't got half a dozen houses to choose from. When you've only one house I suppose you've got to live in it no matter what's happened.

Withers: At all events I should have liked to wait a bit.

Mrs Joyce: I wanted her to. I'd made all my plans for them both to come back to my house after the trial. I wanted them to stay with me till they were able to get away for a holiday.

Withers: I should have thought that much the most sensible thing to do.

Mrs Joyce: But they wouldn't. Bob said he couldn't leave the estate and Leslie said she couldn't leave Bob. So then I said Howard and I would come down here. I thought it would be easier for them if they had someone with them for a day or two.

Withers (*with a smile*): And I think you were determined not to be robbed of your celebration.

Mrs Joyce (*gaily*): You don't know my million-dollar cocktails, do you? They're celebrated all through the FMS. When Leslie was arrested I made a solemn vow that I wouldn't make another until she was acquitted. I've been waiting for this day and no one is going to deprive me of my treat.

Withers: Hence the ice, I suppose?

Mrs Joyce: Hence the ice, wise young man. As soon as the others come I'll start making them.

Withers: With your own hands?

Mrs Joyce: With my own hands. I don't mind telling you I never knew anyone who could make a better cocktail than I can.

Withers (*with a grin*): We all think the cocktails we

make ourselves better than anybody else's, you know.

Mrs Joyce (*merrily*): Yes, but you're all lamentably mistaken, and I happen to be right.

Withers: The ways of Providence are dark.

> *The two* **Boys** *come in with bowls of flowers. They place them here and there, so that the room looks exactly as it did during the first Act.*

Mrs Joyce: Oh, good. That makes the room look much more habitable.

Withers: They ought to be here in a minute.

Mrs Joyce: We went very fast, you know. And I daresay a good many people wanted to say a word or two to Leslie. I don't suppose they were able to get away as quickly as they expected.

> *The* **Boys** *go out.*

Withers: I'll wait till they come, shall I?

Mrs Joyce: Of course you must wait.

Withers: I thought the Attorney-General was very decent.

Mrs Joyce: I knew he would be. I know his wife, you know. She said she thought Leslie should never be tried at all. But, of course, men are so funny.

Withers: I shall never forget the shout that went up when the jury came in and said: 'Not guilty.'

Mrs Joyce: It was thrilling, wasn't it? And Leslie absolutely impassive, sitting there as though it had nothing to do with her.

Withers: I can't get over the way she gave evidence. By George, she's a marvel.

Mrs Joyce: It was beautiful. I couldn't help crying. It was so modest and so restrained. Howard, who thinks me very hysterical and impulsive, told me the other day he'd never known a woman who had so much self-control as Leslie. And that's real

praise, because I don't think he very much likes
her.

Withers: Why not?

Mrs Joyce: Oh, you know what men are. They never
care very much for the women their particular
friends marry.

*The **Head-Boy** comes in with a pillow covered
by a cloth.*

Withers: Hulloa, what's this?

Head-Boy: Missy pillow lace.

Mrs Joyce (*going to it and taking the cloth off*): Oh,
did you bring that?

Head-Boy: I thought maybe Missy wantchee.

*He puts it down on the table on which it stood
in the first Act.*

Mrs Joyce: I'm sure she will. That was very
thoughtful of you, boy. (*To **Withers** as the **Boy** goes
out*) You know, sometimes you could kill these
Chinese boys, and then all of a sudden they'll do
things that are so kind and so considerate that you
forgive them everything.

Withers (*looking at the lace*): By George, it is
beautiful, isn't it? You know, it's just the sort of
thing you'd expect her to do.

Mrs Joyce: Mr Withers, I want to ask you something
rather horrible. When you came that night, where
exactly was Geoff Hammond's body lying?

Withers: Out on the verandah, just under that lamp.
By God, it gave me a turn when I ran up the steps
and nearly fell over him.

Mrs Joyce: Has it occurred to you that every time
Leslie comes into the house she'll have to step over
the place where the body lay? It's rather grim.

Withers: Perhaps it won't strike her.

Mrs Joyce: Fortunately she's not the sort of hysterical
fool that I am. But I – oh dear, I could never sleep
again.

The Letter

There is the sound of a car driving up.

Withers: There they are. They haven't been so long, after all.

Mrs Joyce (*going over to the verandah*): No, they must have started within ten minutes of us. (*Calling*) Leslie! Leslie!

> **Leslie** *comes on, followed by* **Crosbie** *and* **Joyce. Crosbie** *is wearing a neat suit of ducks.* **Leslie** *wears a silk wrap and a hat.*

Leslie: You haven't been here long, have you?

Mrs Joyce (*taking her in her arms*): Welcome. Welcome back to your home.

Leslie (*releasing herself*): Darling. (*She looks round.*) How nice and cosy it looks. I can hardly realize that I've ever been away.

Mrs Joyce: Are you tired? Would you like to go and lie down?

Leslie: Tied? Why, I've been doing nothing but rest for the last six weeks.

Mrs Joyce: Oh, Bob, aren't you happy to have her back again?

Joyce: Now, Dorothy, don't gush, and if you must gush, gush over me.

Mrs Joyce: I'm not going to gush over you, you old brute. What have you done?

Leslie (*holding out her hand to him, with a charming smile*): He's done everything. I can never thank him enough. You don't know what he's been to me through all this dreary time of waiting.

Mrs Joyce: I don't mind confessing that I thought you made rather a good speech, Howard.

Joyce: Thank you for those kind words.

Mrs Joyce: I think perhaps you might have been a little more impassioned without hurting yourself.

Withers: I don't agree with you, Mrs Joyce. It's just because it was so cold and measured and businesslike that it was so effective.

Joyce: Let's have this drink you've been talking about, Dorothy.

Mrs Joyce: Come and help me, Mr Withers. When I make a cocktail I want a great many assistants.

Leslie (*taking off her hat*): I know what an elaborate business your million-dollar cocktail is, Dorothy.

Mrs Joyce (*as she goes out with* **Withers**): Don't be impatient. I can't hurry it. I must take my time.

Leslie: I'll go and tidy myself up.

Crosbie: You don't need it. You look as if you'd just come out of a bandbox.

Leslie: I shan't be a minute.

Crosbie: There's something I particularly want to say to you.

Joyce: I'll make myself scarce.

Crosbie: No, I want you, old man. I want your legal opinion.

Joyce: Oh, do you? Fire away.

Crosbie: Well, look here, I want to get Leslie away from here as quickly as possible.

Joyce: I think a bit of a holiday would do you both good.

Leslie: Could you get away, Robert? Even if it's only for two or three weeks I'd be thankful.

Crosbie: What's the use of two or three weeks? We must get away for good.

Leslie: But how can we?

Joyce: You can't very well throw up a job like this. You'd never get such a good one again, you know.

Crosbie: That's where you're wrong. I've got something in view that's much better. We can neither of us live here. It would be impossible. We've gone through too much in this bungalow. How can we ever forget . . .

Leslie (*with a shudder*): No, don't, Bob, don't.

Crosbie (*to* **Joyce**): You see. Heaven knows, Leslie has nerves of iron, but there is a limit to human endurance. You know how lonely the life is. I

should never have a moment's peace when I was
out and thought of her sitting in this room by
herself. It's out of the question.

Leslie: Oh, don't think of me, Bob. You've made this
estate, it was nothing when you came here. Why,
it's like your child. It's the apple of your eye.

Crosbie: I hate it now. I hate every tree on it. I must
get away, and so must you. You don't want to
stay?

Leslie: It's all been so miserable. I don't want to make
any more difficulties.

Crosbie: I know our only chance of peace is to get to
some place where we can forget.

Joyce: But could you get another job?

Crosbie: Yes, that's just it. Something has suddenly
cropped up. That's why I wanted to talk to you
about it at once. It's in Sumatra. We'd be right away
from everybody, and the only people round us
would be Dutch. We'd start a new life, with new
friends. The only thing is that you'd be awfully
lonely, darling.

Leslie: Oh, I wouldn't mind that. I'm used to
loneliness. (*With sudden vehemence*) I'd be glad to
go, Robert. I don't want to stay here.

Crosbie: That settles it then. I'll go straight ahead and
we can fix things up at once.

Joyce: Is the money as good as here?

Crosbie: I hope it'll be better. At all events I shall be
working for myself and not for a rotten company
in London.

Joyce (*startled*): What do you mean by that? You're
not buying an estate?

Crosbie: Yes, I am. Why should I go on sweating my
life out for other people? It's a chance in a
thousand. It belongs to a Malacca Chinaman who's
in financial difficulties, and he's willing to let it
go for thirty thousand dollars if he can have the
money the day after tomorrow.

Joyce: But how are you going to raise thirty thousand dollars?

Crosbie: Well, I've saved about ten thousand since I've been in the East, and Charlie Meadows is willing to let me have the balance on mortgage.

> **Leslie** and **Joyce** *exchange a glance of consternation.*

Joyce: It seems rather rash to put all your eggs in one basket.

Leslie: I shouldn't like you to take such a risk on my account, Robert. You needn't worry about me, really. I shall settle down here quite comfortably.

Crosbie: Don't talk nonsense, darling. It's only a moment ago that you said you'd give anything to clear out.

Leslie: I spoke without thinking. I believe it would be a mistake to run away. The sensible thing to do is to sit tight. Everybody's been so kind, there's no reason to suppose they're not going to continue. I'm sure all our friends will do all they can to make things easy for us.

Crosbie: You know, dear, you mustn't be frightened at a little risk. It's only if one takes risks that one can make big money.

Joyce: These Chinese estates are never any good. You know how haphazard and careless the Chinese are.

Crosbie: This is not that sort of thing at all. It belongs to a very progressive Chinaman, and he's had a European manager. It's not a leap in the dark. It's a thoroughly sound proposition, and I reckon that in ten years I can make enough money to allow us to retire. Then we'll settle down in England and live like lords.

Leslie: Honestly, Robert, I'd prefer to stay here. I'm attached to the place, and when I've had time to forget all that has happened . . .

Crosbie: How can you forget?

The Letter

Joyce: Anyhow, it's not a thing that you must enter into without due consideration. You'd naturally want to go over to Sumatra and look for yourself.

Crosbie: That's just it. I've got to make up my mind at once. The offer only holds for thirty-six hours.

Joyce: But my dear fellow, you can't pay thirty thousand dollars for a estate without proper investigation. None of you planters are any too businesslike, but really there are limits.

Crosbie: Don't try and make me out a bigger fool than I am. I've had it examined and it's worth fifty thousand if it's worth a dollar. I've got all the papers in my office. I'll go and get them and you can see for yourself. And I have a couple of photographs of the bungalow to show Leslie.

Leslie: I don't want to see them.

Crosbie: Oh, come, darling. That's just nerves. That shows how necessary it is for you to get away. Darling, in this case you must let me have my own way. I want to go, too. I can't stay here anymore.

Leslie (*with anguish*): Oh, why are you so obstinate?

Crosbie: Come, come, dear, don't be unreasonable. Let me go and get the papers. I shan't be a minute.

> *He goes out. There is a moment's silence.*
> **Leslie** *looks at* **Joyce** *with terrified appeal; he makes a despairing gesture.*

Joyce: I had to pay ten thousand dollars for the letter.

Leslie: What are you going to do?

Joyce (*miserably*): What can I do?

Leslie: Oh, don't tell him now. Give me a little time. I'm at the end of my strength. I can't bear anything more.

Joyce: You heard what he said. He wants the money at once to buy this estate. He can't. He hasn't got it.

Leslie: Give me a little time.

Joyce: *I* can't afford to give you a sum like that.

Leslie: No, I don't expect you to. Perhaps I can get it somehow.

Joyce: How? You know it's impossible. It's money I put by for the education of my boys. I was glad to advance it, and I wouldn't have minded waiting a few weeks . . .

Leslie (*interrupting*): If you'd only give me a month I'd have time to think of something. I could prepare Robert and explain to him by degrees. I'd watch for my opportunity.

Joyce: If he buys this estate the money will be gone. No, no, no. I can't let him do that. I don't want to be unkind to you, but I can't lose my money.

Leslie: Where is the letter?

Joyce: I have it in my pocket.

Leslie: Oh, what shall I do?

Joyce: I'm dreadfully sorry for you.

Leslie: Oh, don't be sorry for me. I don't matter. It's Robert. It'll break his heart.

Joyce: If only there were some other way. I don't know what to do.

Leslie: I suppose you're right. There's only one thing to do. Tell him. Tell him and have done with it. I'm broken.

> **Crosbie** *comes in again with a bundle of papers in his hand and two large photographs.*

Crosbie: Of course if it hadn't been for Leslie I should have run over to Sumatra last week. I'd just like you to have a look first at the report I've had.

Joyce: Look here, Bob, has it struck you that your costs over this affair will be pretty heavy?

Crosbie: I know all your lawyers are robbers. I daresay this will leave me a little short of ready money, but I don't suppose you'll mind if I keep you waiting till I've had time to settle down. You know I can be trusted, and if you like I'll pay you interest.

Joyce: I don't think you have any idea how large the

sum is. Of course, we don't want to press you, but we can't be out of our money indefinitely. I think I should warn you that when you've settled with us, you won't have much money left over to embark in rather hazardous speculations.

Crosbie: You're putting the fear of God into me. How much will the costs come to?

Joyce: I'm not going to charge you anything for my personal services. Whatever I've done has been done out of pure friendship, but there are certain out-of-pocket expenses that I'm afraid you must pay.

Crosbie: Of course. It's awfully good of you not to wish to charge me for anything else. I hardly like to accept. What do the out-of-pocket expenses amount to?

Joyce: You remember that I told you yesterday that there was a letter of Leslie's that I thought we ought to get hold of.

Crosbie: Yes. I really didn't think it mattered very much, but of course I put myself in your hands. I thought you were making a great deal out of something that wasn't very important.

Joyce: You told me to do what I thought fit, and I bought the letter from the person in whose possession it was. I had to pay a great deal of money for it.

Crosbie: What a bore! Still, if you thought it necessary, I'm not going to grouse. How much was it?

Joyce: I'm afraid I had to pay ten thousand dollars for it.

Crosbie (*aghast*): Ten thousand dollars! Why, that's a fortune. I thought you were going to say a couple of hundred. You must have been mad.

Joyce: You may be quite sure that I wouldn't have given it if I could have got it for less.

Crosbie: But that's everything I have in the world. It reduces me to beggary.

Joyce: Not that exactly, but you must understand that you haven't got money to buy an estate with.

Crosbie: But why didn't you let them bring the letter in and tell them to do what they damned well liked?

Joyce: I didn't dare.

Crosbie: Do you mean to say it was absolutely necessary to suppress the letter?

Joyce: If you wanted your wife acquitted.

Crosbie: But ... but ... I don't understand. You're not going to tell me that they could have brought in a verdict of guilty. They couldn't have hanged her for putting a noxious vermin out of the way.

Joyce: Of course, they wouldn't have hanged her. But they might have found her guilty of manslaughter. I daresay she'd have got off with two or three years.

Crosbie: Three years. My Leslie. My little Leslie. It would have killed her ... But what was there in the letter?

Joyce: I told you yesterday.

Leslie: It was very stupid of me. I ...

Crosbie (*interrupting*): I remember now. You wrote to Hammond to ask him to come to the bungalow.

Leslie: Yes.

Crosbie: You wanted him to get something for you, didn't you?

Leslie: Yes, I wanted to get a present for your birthday.

Crosbie: Why should you have asked him?

Leslie: I wanted to get you a gun. He knew all about that sort of thing, and you know how ignorant I am.

Crosbie: Bertie Cameron had a brand new gun he wanted to sell. I went into Singapore on the night of Hammond's death to buy it. Why should you want to make me a present of another?

The Letter

Leslie: How should I know that you were going to buy a gun?

Crosbie (*abruptly*): Because I told you.

Leslie: I'd forgotten. I can't remember everything.

Crosbie: You hadn't forgotten that.

Leslie: What do you mean, Robert? Why are you talking to me like this?

Crosbie (*to* **Joyce**): Wasn't it a criminal offence that you committed in buying that letter?

Joyce (*trying not to take it seriously*): It's not the sort of thing that a respectable lawyer does in the ordinary way of business.

Crosbie (*pressing him*): It was a criminal offence?

Joyce: I've been trying to keep the fact out of my mind. But if you insist on a straight answer I'm afraid I must admit it was.

Crosbie: Then why did you do it? You, you of all people. What were you trying to save me from?

Joyce: Well, I've told you. I felt that . . .

Crosbie (*hard and stern*): No, you haven't.

Joyce: Come, come, Bob, don't be a fool. I don't know what you mean. Juries are very stupid, and you don't want to let them get any silly ideas in their heads.

Crosbie: Who has the letter now? Have you got it?

Joyce: Yes.

Crosbie: Where is it?

Joyce: Why do you want to know?

Crosbie (*violently*): God damn it. I want to see it.

Joyce: I've got no right to show it you.

Crosbie: Is it your money you bought it with, or mine? I've got to pay ten thousand dollars for that letter, and by God I'm going to see it. At least I'd like to know that I've had my money's worth.

Leslie: Let him see it.

Without a word **Joyce** *takes his pocket-book*

*from his pocket and takes out the letter. He
hands it to* **Crosbie**. *He reads it.*

Crosbie (*hoarsely*): What does this mean?

Leslie: It means that Geoff Hammond was my lover.

Crosbie (*covering his face with his hands*): No, no,
no.

Joyce: Why did you kill him?

Leslie: He'd been my lover for years. He became my
lover almost immediately after he came back from
the war.

Crosbie (*in agony*): It's not true.

Leslie: I used to drive out to a place we knew and he
met me, two or three times a week, and when
Robert went to Singapore he used to come to the
bungalow late, when the boys had gone for the
night. We saw one another, constantly, all the time.

Crosbie: I trusted you. I loved you.

Leslie: And then lately, a year ago, he began to change.
I didn't know what was the matter. I couldn't
believe that he didn't care for me any more. I was
frantic. Oh, if you knew what agonies I endured.
I passed through hell. I knew he didn't want me
any more, and I wouldn't let him go. Sometimes
I thought he hated me. Misery! Misery! I loved him.
I didn't want to love him. I couldn't help myself.
I hated myself for loving him, and yet he was
everything in the world to me. He was all my life.

Crosbie: Oh, God! Oh, God!

Leslie: And then I heard he was living with a Chinese
woman. I couldn't believe it. I wouldn't believe it.
At last I saw her, I saw her with my own eyes,
walking in the village, with her gold bracelets and
her necklaces – a Chinese woman. Horrible! They
all knew in the kampong that she was his
mistress. And when I passed her, she looked at me,
and I saw that she knew I was his mistress, too.

Crosbie: Oh, the shame.

Leslie: I sent for him. I told him I must see him. You've read the letter. I was mad to write it. I didn't know what I was doing. I didn't care. I hadn't seen him for ten days. It was a lifetime. And when last we'd parted he held me in his arms and kissed me, and told me not to worry. And he went straight from my arms to hers.

Joyce: He was a rotter. He always was.

Leslie: That letter. We'd always been so careful. He always tore up any word I wrote to him the moment he'd read it. How was I to know he'd leave that one?

Joyce: That doesn't matter now.

Leslie: He came, and I told him I knew about the Chinawoman. He denied it. He said it was only scandal. I was beside myself. I don't know what I said to him. Oh, I hated him then. I hated him because he'd made me despise myself. I tore him limb from limb. I said everything I could to wound him. I insulted him. I could have spat in his face. And at last he turned on me. He told me he was sick and tired of me and never wanted to see me again. He said I bored him to death. And then he acknowledged that it was true about the Chinawoman. He said he'd known her for years, and she was the only woman who really meant anything to him, and the rest was just pastime. And he said he was glad I knew, and now, at last, I'd leave him alone. He said things to me that I thought it impossible a man could ever say to a woman. He couldn't have been more vile if I'd been a harlot on the streets. And then I don't know what happened; I was beside myself; I seized the revolver and fired. He gave a cry and I saw I'd hit him. He staggered and rushed for the verandah. I ran after him and fired again. He fell, and then I stood over him and I fired and fired till there were no more cartridges.

There is a pause and then **Crosbie** *goes up to her.*

Crosbie: Have I deserved this of you, Leslie?

Leslie: No. I've been vile. I have no excuses to offer for myself. I betrayed you.

Crosbie: What do you want to do now?

Leslie: It is for you to say.

Crosbie: It was for your sake I wanted to go away. I only saved that money for you. I shall have to stay here now, but I could manage to give you enough to live on in England.

Leslie: Where am I to go? I have no family left and no friends. I'm quite alone in the world. Oh, I'm so unhappy.

Crosbie: How could you, Leslie? What did I do wrong that I couldn't win your love?

Leslie: What can I say? It wasn't me that deceived you. It wasn't me that loved that other. It was a madness that seized me, and I was as little my own mistress as though I were delirious with fever. It brought me no happiness, that love – it only brought me shame and remorse.

Crosbie: The awful part is that notwithstanding everything – I love you still. Oh, God, how you must despise me! I despise myself.

Leslie shakes her head slowly.

Leslie: I don't know what I've done to deserve your love. I'm worthless. Oh, if only I could blame anybody but myself. I can't. I deserve everything I have to suffer. Oh, Robert, my dear.

He turns aside and buries his head in his hands.

Crosbie: Oh, what shall I do? It's all gone. All gone.

He begins to sob with the great, painful, difficult sobs of a man unused to tears. She sinks on her knees beside him.

The Letter

Leslie: Oh, don't cry. Darling. Darling.

He springs up and pushes her on one side.

Crosbie: I'm a fool. There's no need for me to make an exhibition of myself. I'm sorry.

He goes hastily out of the room. **Leslie** *rises to her feet.*

Joyce: Don't go to him. Give him a moment to get hold of himself.

Leslie: I'm so dreadfully sorry for him.

Joyce: He's going to forgive you. He can't do without you.

Leslie: If only he'd give me another chance.

Joyce: Don't you love him at all?

Leslie: No. I wish to God I did.

Joyce: Then what's to be done?

Leslie: I'll give my life such as it is to him, to him only. I swear to you that I'll do everything in the world to make him happy. I'll make amends. I'll oblige him to forget. He shall never know that I don't love him as he wants to be loved.

Joyce: It's not easy to live with a man you don't love. But you've had the courage and the strength to do evil; perhaps you will have the courage and the strength to do good. That will be your retribution.

Leslie: No, that won't be my retribution. I can do that and do it gladly. He's so kind, he's so tender. My retribution is greater. With all my heart I still love the man I killed.

CURTAIN

Appendix

Since a play is published not only to gratify an author's vanity, but also for the convenience of amateurs, I have thought it well to print here the version acted at the Playhouse. After two or three rehearsals, I replaced Leslie Crosbie's final confession with a 'throwback', because I thought it would bore an audience to listen to two long narratives in one play. I have a notion that an author may prudently take a risk to avoid tediousness.

> *Without a word* **Joyce** *takes his pocket-book from his pocket and takes out the letter. He hands it to* **Crosbie**. *He reads it.*

Crosbie (*hoarsely*): What does it mean?

Leslie: It means that Geoff Hammond was my lover.

Crosbie (*covering his face with his hands*): No, no.

Joyce: Why did you kill him?

Leslie: He'd been my lover for years.

Crosbie (*in agony*): It's not true.

Leslie: For years. And then he changed. I didn't know what was the matter. I couldn't believe that he didn't care for me any more. I loved him; I didn't want to love him. I couldn't help myself. I hated myself for loving him, and yet he was everything in the world to me. He was all my life. And then I heard he was living with a Chinese woman. I couldn't believe it. I wouldn't believe it. At last I saw her, I saw her with my own eyes, walking in the village, with her gold bracelets and her necklaces – a Chinese woman. Horrible! They all knew in the kampong that she was his mistress. And when I passed her, she looked at me, and I saw that she knew I was his mistress, too. I sent for him.

The Letter

The stage darkens for a moment. When the lights go up **Leslie**, *wearing the dress she wore in the first Act, is seated at the table working at her lace.* **Geoffrey Hammond** *comes in. He is a good-looking fellow in the late thirties, with a breezy manner and abundant self-confidence.*

Leslie: Geoff! I thought you were never coming.

Hammond: What's that bold bad husband of yours gone to Singapore for?

Leslie: He's gone to buy a gun that Bertie Cameron wants to sell.

Hammond: I suppose he wants to bag that tiger the natives are talking about. I bet I get him first. What about a little drink?

Leslie: Help yourself.

He goes to a table and pours himself out a whisky and soda.

Hammond: I say, is anything the matter? That note of yours was rather hectic.

Leslie: What have you done with it?

Hammond: I tore it up at once. What do you take me for?

Leslie (*suddenly*): Geoff, I can't go on like this any more. I'm at the end of my tether.

Hammond: Why, what's up?

Leslie: Oh, don't pretend. What's the good of that? Why have you left me all this time without a sign?

Hammond: I've had an awful lot to do.

Leslie: You haven't had so much to do that you couldn't spare a few minutes to write to me.

Hammond: There didn't seem to be any object in taking useless risks. If we don't want a bust-up, we must take certain elementary precautions. We've been very lucky so far. It would be silly to make a mess of things now.

Leslie: Don't treat me like a perfect fool.

160

Hammond: I say, Leslie darling, if you sent for me just to make a scene, I'm going to take myself off. I'm sick of these eternal rows.

Leslie: A scene? Don't you know how I love you?

Hammond: Well, darling, you've got a damned funny way of showing it.

Leslie: You drive me to desperation.

> *He looks at her for a moment reflectively, then, with his hands in his pockets, goes up to her with deliberation.*

Hammond: Leslie, I wonder if you've noticed that we hardly ever meet now without having a row?

Leslie: Is it my fault?

Hammond: I don't say that. I daresay it's mine. But when that happens with two people who are on the sort of terms that we are, it looks very much as though things were wearing a bit thin.

Leslie: What do you mean by that?

Hammond: Well, when that happens, I'm not sure if the commonsense thing is not to say: 'We've had a ripping time, but all good things must come to an end, and the best thing we can do is to make a break while we've still got the chance of keeping friends.'

Leslie (*frightened*): Geoff.

Hammond: I'm all for facing facts.

Leslie (*suddenly flaming up*): Facts! What is that Chinawoman doing in your house?

Hammond: My dear, what are you talking about?

Leslie: Do you think I don't know that you've been living with a Chinawoman for months?

Hammond: Nonsense.

Leslie: What sort of a fool do you take me for? Why, it's the common gossip of the kampong.

Hammond (*with a shrug of the shoulders*): My dear, if you're going to listen to the gossip of the natives . . .

The Letter

Leslie (*interrupting*): Then what is she doing in your bungalow?

Hammond: I didn't know there was a Chinawoman about. I don't bother much about what goes on in my servants' quarters as long as they do their work properly.

Leslie: What does that mean?

Hammond: Well, I shouldn't be surprised if one of the boys had got a girl there. What do I care as long as she keeps out of my way?

Leslie: I've seen her.

Hammond: What is she like?

Leslie: Old and fat.

Hammond: You're not paying me a very pretty compliment. My head-boy's old and fat, too.

Leslie: Your head-boy isn't going to dress a woman in silk at five dollars a yard. She had a couple of hundred pounds' worth of jewellery on her.

Hammond: It sounds as though she were of a thrifty disposition. Perhaps she thinks that the best way to invest her savings.

Leslie: Will you swear she's not your mistress?

Hammond: Certainly.

Leslie: On your honour?

Hammond: On my honour.

Leslie (*violently*): It's a lie.

Hammond: All right then, it's a lie. But in that case, why won't you let me go?

Leslie: Because, in spite of everything, I love you with all my heart. I can't let you go now. You're all I have in the world. If you have no love for me, have pity on me. Without you I'm lost. Oh, Geoff, I love you. No one will ever love you as I've loved you. I know that often I've been beastly to you and horrible, but I've been so unhappy.

Hammond: My dear, I don't want to make you unhappy, but it's no good beating about the bush.

The thing's over and done with. You must let me go now. You really must.

Leslie: Oh, no, Geoff, you don't mean that, you can't mean that.

Hammond: Leslie, dear, I'm terribly sorry, but the facts are there and you've got to face them. This is the end and you've got to make the best of it. I've made up my mind, and there it is.

Leslie: How cruel! How monstrously cruel! You wouldn't treat a dog as you're treating me.

Hammond: Is it my fault if I don't love you? Damn it all, one either loves or one doesn't.

Leslie: Oh, you're of stone. I'd do anything in the world for you, and you won't give me a chance.

Hammond: Oh, my God, why can't you be reasonable? I tell you I'm sick and tired of the whole thing. Do you want me to tell you in so many words that you mean nothing to me? Don't you know that? Haven't you felt it? You must be blind.

Leslie (*desperately*): Yes, I've known it only too well. And I've felt it. I didn't care. It's not love any more that seethes in my heart; it's madness; it's torture to see you, but it's torture ten times worse not to see you. If you leave me now, I'll kill myself. (*She picks up the revolver that is lying on the table.*) I swear to God I'll kill myself.

Hammond (*impatiently*): Oh, don't talk such damned rot!

Leslie: Don't you think I mean it? Don't you think I have the courage?

Hammond (*beside himself with irritation*): I have no patience with you. You're enough to drive anyone out of his senses. If you'd got sick of me, would you have hesitated to send me about my business? Not for a minute. D'you think I don't know women?

Leslie: You've ruined my life, and now you're tired of

me you want to cast me aside like a worn-out
coat. No, no, no!

Hammond: You can do what you like, and say what
you like, but I tell you it's finished.

Leslie: I'll never let you go. Never! Never!

*She flings her arms round his neck, but he
releases himself roughly. The touch of her
exasperates him.*

Hammond: I'm fed up. Fed up. I'm sick of the sight
of you.

Leslie: No, no, no.

Hammond (*violently*): If you want the truth you must
have it. Yes, the Chinawoman is my mistress, and
I don't care who knows it. If you ask me to choose
between you and her, I choose her. Every time.
And now for God's sake leave me alone.

Leslie: You cur!

*She seizes the revolver and fires at him. He
staggers and falls. The lights go out, and the
stage is once more in darkness.*

Leslie: I ran after him and fired again. He fell, and
then I stood over him and I fired and fired till there
were no more cartridges.

The lights go up. **Crosbie** *and* **Joyce** *are
listening to* **Leslie's** *story. She is dressed as at
the beginning of the scene.*

Crosbie: Have I deserved this of you, Leslie?

Leslie: No, I have no excuses to offer for myself. I
betrayed you.

Crosbie: What do you want to do now?

Leslie: It is for you to say.

Crosbie: How could you, Leslie! The awful part is
that, notwithstanding everything – I love you still.
Oh, God, how you must despise me! I despise
myself.

Leslie *shakes her head slowly.*

Leslie: I don't know what I've done to deserve your love. Oh, if only I could blame anybody but myself. I can't. I deserve everything I have to suffer. Oh, Robert, my dear.

He turns aside and buries his head in his hands.

Crosbie: Oh, what shall I do? It's all gone. All gone.

He begins to sob with the great, painful difficult sobs of a man unused to tears. She sinks on her knees beside him.

Leslie: Oh, don't cry. My dear – my dear.

He springs up and pushes her on one side.

Crosbie: I'm a fool. There's no need for me to make an exhibition of myself. I'm sorry.

He goes hastily out of the room. **Leslie** *rises to her feet.*

Joyce: No. Don't go to him. Give him a moment to get hold of himself.

Leslie: I'm so dreadfully sorry for him.

Joyce: He's going to forgive you. He can't do without you.

Leslie: If only he'd give me another chance.

Joyce: Don't you love him at all?

Leslie: No. I wish to God I did.

Joyce: Then what's to be done?

Leslie: I swear to you that I'll do everything in the world to make him happy. I'll make amends. I'll oblige him to forget. He shall never know that I don't love him as he wants to be loved.

Joyce: It's not easy to live with a man you don't love. But you've had the courage and the strength to do evil; perhaps you will have the courage and the strength to do good. That will be your retribution.

Leslie: No, that won't be my retribution. I can do that and do it gladly. He's so kind and good. My retribution is greater. With all my heart I still love the man I killed.

CURTAIN

Home and Beauty

A FARCE IN THREE ACTS

Characters

William, a hero
Frederick, another
Victoria, a dear little thing
Mr Leicester Paton, a wangler
Mr A. B. Raham, a solicitor
Miss Montmorency, a maiden lady
Mrs Shuttleworth, a mother-in-law
Miss Dennis, a manicurist
Mrs Pogson, a respectable woman
Taylor, a parlourmaid
Nannie, a nurse
Clarence, a boy

The action of the play takes place at Victoria's house in Westminster towards the end of November 1918.

Act I

The scene is **Victoria's** *bedroom. It is the kind of
bedroom which is only used to sleep in; and but for
the bed, with its hangings and its beautiful coverlet,
and the great lacquer dressing-table, crowded with
the necessary aids to feminine beauty, might just as
well be a sitting-room. There are graceful pieces of
furniture here and there, attractive pictures on the
walls, flowers: it is all very comfortable, luxurious
and modish. In the fire-place a bright fire is burning.*

Victoria, *a pretty little thing in a lovely
'confection', which is partly tea-gown and partly
dressing-gown, is lying on a sofa having her hands
manicured.* **Miss Dennis,** *the manicurist, is a neat,
trim person of twenty-five. She has a slight cockney
accent.*

Miss Dennis (*evidently ending a long story*): And so
at last I said to him: Oh, very well, 'ave it your
own way.
Victoria: One has to in the end, you know.
Miss Dennis: He'd asked me five times, and I really
got tired of saying no. And then, you see, in my
business you get to know all the ins and outs of
married life, and my impression is that, in the
long run, it don't really matter very much who you
marry.
Victoria: Oh, I do so agree with you there. It all
depends on yourself. When my first husband was
killed, poor darling, I went all to pieces. My bust
simply went to nothing. I couldn't wear a low
dress for months.
Miss Dennis: How dreadful.

Victoria: I simply adored him. But you know, I'm just as fond of my second husband.

Miss Dennis: You must have one of those loving natures.

Victoria: Of course, I should never survive it if anything happened to my present husband, but if anything did – touch wood – you know, I couldn't help myself, I'd just have to marry again, and I know I'd love my third husband just as much as I loved the other two.

Miss Dennis (*sighing*): Love is a wonderful thing.

Victoria: Oh, wonderful. Of course, I'd wait the year. I waited the year when my first was killed.

Miss Dennis: Oh yes, I think one always ought to wait the year.

Victoria: I noticed you had an engagement ring on the moment you came in.

Miss Dennis: I didn't really ought to wear it during business hours, but I like to feel it's there.

Victoria: I know the feeling so well. You turn it round under your glove, and say to yourself: Well, that's settled. Is he nice-looking?

Miss Dennis: Well, he's not what you might call exactly handsome, but he's got a nice face.

Victoria: Both my husbands have been handsome men. You know, people say it doesn't matter what a man looks like, but that's all nonsense. There's nothing shows a woman off like a good-looking man.

Miss Dennis: He's very fair.

Victoria: Of course, it's all a matter of taste, but I don't think I should like that myself. They always say fair men are deceitful. Both my husbands were dark, and they both had the D.S.O.

Miss Dennis: That's funny, isn't it?

Victoria: I flatter myself there are not many women who've been married to two D.S.O.s. I think I've done my bit.

Miss Dennis: I should just think you had. If it's not asking too much, I should like to know which of them you liked best.

Victoria: Well, you know I really can't say.

Miss Dennis: Of course, I haven't the experience, but I should have thought you'd prefer the one who wasn't there. That almost seems like human nature, doesn't it?

Victoria: The fact is, all men have their faults. They're selfish, brutal, and inconsiderate. They don't understand how much everything costs. They can't *see* things, poor dears; they're cat-witted. Of course, Freddie's very unreasonable sometimes, but then so was Bill. And he adores me. He can hardly bear me out of his sight. They both adored me.

Miss Dennis: That makes up for a great deal, I must say.

Victoria: I can't understand the women who complain that they're misunderstood. I don't want to be understood. I want to be loved.

> **Taylor** opens the door and introduces **Mrs Shuttleworth**. This is **Victoria's** mother, an elderly, grey-haired lady in black.

Taylor: Mrs Shuttleworth.

> *Exit.*

Victoria (*gushing*): Darling Mother.

Mrs Shuttleworth: My precious child.

Victoria: This is Miss Dennis. It's the only moment in the day she was able to give me.

Mrs Shuttleworth (*graciously*): How do you do?

Victoria: You don't mind coming up all these stairs, do you darling? You see, we have to be dreadfully economical with our coal. We tried to wangle more, but we couldn't manage it.

Mrs Shuttleworth: Oh, I know. The coal controller was positively rude to me. Red tape, you know.

Victoria: They say we can have only two fires. Of

course, we have to have one in the nursery, and I
must have one in my bedroom. So I have to see
people in here.

Mrs Shuttleworth: And how are the precious darlings?

Victoria: Fred's got a slight cold, and Nannie thought
he'd better stay in bed, but Baby's splendid.
Nannie will bring him in presently.

Miss Dennis: Are they both boys, Mrs Lowndes?

Victoria: Yes. But I'm going to have a girl next time.

Mrs Shuttleworth: Fred will be two next month,
Victoria.

Victoria: I know. I'm beginning to feel so old. Poor
lamb, he wasn't born till three months after his
father was killed.

Miss Dennis: How very sad. You don't like the nails
too red, do you?

Victoria: Not too red.

Mrs Shuttleworth: She looked too sweet in mourning.
I wish you could have seen her, Miss Dennis.

Victoria: Mother, how can you say anything so
heartless? Of course, black does suit me. There's no
denying that.

Mrs Shuttleworth: I insisted on her going to Mathilde.
Mourning *must* be well made, or else it looks
nothing at all.

Miss Dennis: Did you say your little boy's name was
Fred? After his father, I suppose?

Victoria: Oh, no, my first husband was called
William. He particularly wanted the baby to be
called Frederick after Major Lowndes. You see,
Major Lowndes had been my husband's best man,
and they'd always been such great friends.

Miss Dennis: Oh, I see.

Victoria: Then, when I married Major Lowndes, and
my second baby was born, we thought it would be
nice to give it my first husband's name, and so we
called it William.

Mrs Shuttleworth: I was against it myself. I thought

it would always remind the dear child of what
she'd lost.

Victoria: Oh, but, Mother darling. I don't feel a bit
like that about Bill. I shall never forget him. (*To*
Miss Dennis, *pointing to a double photograph
frame*) You see, I have their photographs side by
side.

Miss Dennis: Some men wouldn't like that very
much.

Victoria: Freddie has me now. He can't grudge it if I
give a passing thought to that poor dead hero
who's lying in a nameless grave in France.

Mrs Shuttleworth: Don't upset yourself, darling. You
know how bad it is for your skin. She has such a
soft heart, poor dear.

Victoria: Of course, now the war's over, it's different,
but when Freddie was at the front I always thought
it must be a consolation to him to think that if
anything happened to him and I married again I
should always keep a little corner in my heart for
him.

Miss Dennis: There, I think that's all for today, Mrs
Lowndes. Would you like me to come again on
Friday?

> *She proceeds to put away the various utensils
> she has been using.*

Victoria (*looking at her nails*): Please. You do them
beautifully. There's something very satisfactory in
a well-manicured hand. It gives you a sense of
assurance, doesn't it? If I were a man I would never
want to hold a hand that wasn't nicely manicured.

Miss Dennis: The gentleman I'm going to marry said
to me that the first thing that attracted him was
the way my nails were polished.

Victoria: One never knows what'll take a man's
fancy.

Mrs Shuttleworth: Personally, I am a firm believer in

first impressions. And that is why I say to all the girls I know: Whenever you are being shown into a drawing-room bite both your lips hard, give them a good lick, put your head in the air, and then sail on. There's nothing men like more than a red moist mouth. I'm an old woman now, but I never go into a room without doing it.

Miss Dennis: Fancy, now, I never thought of that. I must try it and see.

Mrs Shuttleworth: It may make all the difference to your life.

Victoria: Miss Dennis is engaged to be married, mother.

Mrs Shuttleworth: Ah, my dear, don't make the common mistake of thinking that because you've got one man safe you need not make yourself attractive to others.

Victoria: On Friday next, then, Miss Dennis.

Miss Dennis: Very well, Mrs Lowndes. Is there anything you're wanting at this moment?

Victoria: Nothing, thanks.

Miss Dennis: I've got a new skin food that they've just sent me over from Paris. I would like you to give it a trial. I think it's just the thing for your complexion.

Victoria: I'm afraid to try anything I don't know. I've got such a delicate skin.

Miss Dennis: It's been specially prepared for skins like yours, Mrs Lowndes. The ordinary skin food is well enough for the ordinary skin, but a really beautiful skin like yours wants something very extra-special in the way of food.

Victoria: I expect it's frightfully expensive, and you know, they say that we must economize. I suppose somebody's got to pay for the war.

Miss Dennis: I'll make special terms for you, Mrs Lowndes. I'll only charge you fifty-nine and six for a three-guinea pot. It's a large pot, as large as that.

(*She measures with her fingers a pot about three inches high.*) I promise you it's not an extravagance. A good skin food is an investment.

Victoria: Oh well, bring it with you next time you come.

Miss Dennis: I'm sure you won't regret it. Good afternoon, Mrs Lowndes. (*To* **Mrs Shuttleworth**) Good afternoon.

She goes out.

Mrs Shuttleworth: I dare say she's right. They pick up a lot of experience, those women. I always say the same thing to girls: Look after your skin, and your bills will look after themselves.

Victoria: She was telling me that the Johnston Blakes are going to divorce.

Mrs Shuttleworth (*without concern*): Really. Why?

Victoria: He's been fighting for the last four years. He says he wants a little peace now.

Mrs Shuttleworth: I'm afraid many of these men who've been away so long will have got out of the habit of being married. I dare say it was a mercy that poor Bill was killed.

Victoria: Mother, darling, how can you say anything so dreadful?

Mrs Shuttleworth: Well, I must say I was thankful when Freddie got a job at the War Office. The difference between men and women is that men are not naturally addicted to matrimony. With patience, firmness, and occasional rewards you can train them to it just as you can train a dog to walk on its hind legs. But a dog would rather walk on all fours and a man would rather be free. Marriage is a habit.

Victoria: And a very good one, mother.

Mrs Shuttleworth: Of course. But the unfortunate thing about this world is that good habits are so much easier to get out of than bad ones.

Victoria: Well, one thing I do know, and that is that Freddie simply adores being married to me.

Mrs Shuttleworth: In your place, I should have married Leicester Paton.

Victoria: Good heavens, why?

Mrs Shuttleworth: Have you never noticed that he wears spats? Men who wear spats always make the best husbands.

Victoria: It probably only means that he has cold feet. I expect he wears bedsocks, and I should hate that.

Mrs Shuttleworth: Nonsense. It means that he has a neat and orderly mind. He likes things just so. Everything in its place and at the proper season. In fact, a creature of habit. I am convinced that after six months of marriage Leicester Paton would forget that he'd ever been a bachelor.

Victoria: I was a soldier's widow. I don't think it would have been very patriotic to marry a civilian.

Mrs Shuttleworth: You girls all talked as though the war would last for ever. Heroism is all very well, but at a party it's not nearly so useful as a faculty for small talk.

Taylor *comes in.*

Taylor: Mr Leicester Paton has called, madam. I said I didn't know if you could see him.

Victoria: Talk of the devil. Oh yes, bring him up here.

Taylor: Very good, madam.

Exit.

Mrs Shuttleworth: I didn't know you were seeing anything of him, Victoria.

Victoria (*with some archness*): He's been rather attentive lately..

Mrs Shuttleworth: I knew I was right. I felt sure you attracted him.

Victoria: Oh, darling, you know I can never think of anyone but Freddie, but of course it's useful to

have someone to run errands for one. And he can
wangle almost anything one wants.

Mrs Shuttleworth: Butter?

Victoria: Everything, my dear, butter, sugar, whisky.

Mrs Shuttleworth: Bite your lips, darling, and give
them a good lick. (**Victoria** *carries out the
suggestion.*) You missed the chance of your life.

Victoria: After all, he never asked me.

Mrs Shuttleworth: Don't be silly, Victoria, you should
have made him.

Victoria: You know that I adored Freddie. Besides,
ration books hadn't come in then.

Mrs Shuttleworth: By the way, where is Freddie?

Victoria: Oh, my dear, I'm perfectly furious with him.
He promised to take me out to luncheon, and he
never turned up. He never telephoned or anything;
not a word. I think it's too bad of him. He may be
dead for all I know.

Mrs Shuttleworth: Optimist.

> **Taylor** *ushers in* **Mr Leicester Paton**, *and then
> goes out. He is a small, fat man, very well
> pleased with the world and with himself,
> beautifully dressed and obviously prosperous.
> You could tell at a mile that he had so much
> money that he did not know what to do with
> it. He is affable, gallant and easy.*

Taylor: Mr Leicester Paton.

Victoria: I hope you don't mind being dragged up all
these stairs. We have to be so dreadfully
economical with our coal. I can only afford to have
a fire in my bedroom.

Paton (*shaking hands with her*): You're not going to
tell me that you have any trouble about getting
coal. Why on earth didn't you let me know?
(*Shaking hands with* **Mrs Shuttleworth**) How do
you do?

Victoria: You don't mean to say you could get me some?

Paton: It's quite out of the question that a pretty woman shouldn't have everything she wants.

Victoria: I told Freddie that I felt sure he could wangle it somehow. What's the use of being at the War Office if you can't have some sort of a pull?

Paton: Leave it to me. I'll see what I can do for you.

Victoria: You're a perfect marvel.

Paton: Now that these men are coming back from the front no one would look at us poor devils who stayed at home if we didn't at least make ourselves useful.

Victoria: You only stayed at home because it was your duty.

Paton: I attested, you know; I didn't wait to be called up. But the Government said to me: You're a shipbuilder: go on building ships. So I built them ships.

Mrs Shuttleworth: I think it was very noble of you.

Paton: And then they bring in a tax on excess profits. As I said to the Prime Minister myself: It's trying one's patriotism rather high. It really is.

Mrs Shuttleworth: A little bird has whispered to me that the Government intends to show its appreciation of your great services in the next Honours List.

Paton: Oh, one doesn't ask for that. One's glad to have been able to do one's bit.

Victoria: How very true that is. That's just what I feel.

Mrs Shuttleworth: Victoria has worked like a dog, you know. It's a marvel to me how her health has stood it.

Victoria: I don't know how many committees I've been on. I've sold at twenty-three bazaars.

Paton: There's nothing that takes it out of one so much.

Victoria: At the beginning of the war I worked in a
canteen, but I had to give that up, because I could
never go out to lunch anywhere. I thought at one
time of working in a hospital, but you know all
the red tape there is in those places – they said I
had no training.

Mrs Shuttleworth: I'm sure you'd have made a
wonderful nurse.

Victoria: I didn't propose to be the ordinary sort of
nurse at all. I was quite content to leave that to
those unfortunate females who make their living
by it. But it doesn't want any particular training
to be nice to those poor, dear, wounded boys, to
shake out their pillows and take them flowers,
and read to them. It only wants sympathy.

Paton: I don't know anyone who has more.

Victoria (*with flash of her eyes*): With people I like.

Mrs Shuttleworth: Have you stopped your teas,
darling?

Victoria: Oh, yes, after the armistice.

Paton: You used to give teas to wounded soldiers?

Victoria: Yes, Tommies, you know. I think it's so
important to cultivate the personal relation. I used
to invite a dozen every Thursday. At first I had
them in the drawing-room, but it made them shy,
poor dears, so I thought it would be nicer for them
if they had it in the servants' hall. I'm the only
woman I know who never had the smallest trouble
with her maids.

Mrs Shuttleworth: Darling, I think I'll go upstairs and
see how my dear little grandson is. I do hope it's
not influenza.

Victoria: Yes, do, mother. He'll be thrilled to see you.

> **Mrs Shuttleworth** *goes out.* **Leicester Paton,**
> *rising as she does, when he sits down again*
> *takes a place on the sofa beside* **Victoria.**

Paton: Is anything the matter with your little boy?

Victoria: Poor darling, he's got a cold.

Paton: I'm so sorry.

Victoria: I dare say it's nothing, but you know what a mother is: she can't help feeling anxious.

Paton: You're a wonderful mother.

Victoria: I adore my children.

Paton (*going on with his sentence*): And a perfect wife.

Victoria: D'you think so?

Paton: Doesn't your husband?

Victoria: Oh, he's only my husband. His opinion doesn't count.

Paton: Does he know what a lucky man he is?

Victoria: If he does he's quite convinced that he deserves to be.

Paton: I envy him.

Victoria (*flashing a glance at him*): You don't think I'm quite detestable then?

Paton: Shall I tell you what I think of you?

Victoria: No, don't, you'll only exaggerate. You know, there are only two qualities that I flatter myself on: I'm not vain and I am unselfish.

> **Frederick** *comes in. He is a tall, soldierly fellow in uniform, with red tabs and a number of ribbons on his tunic. He nods to* **Leicester Paton** *and shakes hands with him.*

Victoria: Freddie, where *have* you been all this time?

Frederick: I've been at the club.

Victoria: But you promised to take me out to luncheon.

Frederick: Did I? I forgot all about it. I'm so sorry.

Victoria: Forgot? I suppose something more amusing turned up.

Frederick: Well, I only said I'd come if I wasn't too busy.

Victoria: Were you busy?

Frederick: I was.

Victoria: Bill was never too busy to give me luncheon when I wanted it.

Frederick: Fancy that.

Paton: I think I'll be getting along. Now the war's over you fellows can take things easily. My work goes on just the same.

Frederick: That's a new car you've got, isn't it?

Paton: I have to get about somehow, you know.

Frederick: So do I, but being only a soldier I manage to do it on my flat feet.

Paton (*shaking hands with* **Victoria**): Goodbye.

Victoria: Goodbye. So nice of you to come and see me.

> **Leicester Paton** *goes out.*

Victoria: I should be glad to know why you threw me over like that.

Frederick: Are you obliged to receive visitors in your bedroom?

Victoria: You don't mean to say you're jealous, darling? I thought you seemed grumpy. Is he put out? Let him come and give his little wife a nice kiss.

Frederick (*irritably*): I'm not in the least jealous.

Victoria: You silly old thing. You know it's the only room in the house that's got a fire.

Frederick: Why the dickens don't you have one in the drawing-room?

Victoria: My poor lamb, have you forgotten that there's been a war and there happens to be a shortage of coal? I will tell you exactly why we don't have a fire in the drawing-room. Patriotism.

Frederick: Patriotism be hanged. The place is like an ice-house.

Victoria: Darling, don't be unreasonable. After spending two winters in the trenches I shouldn't have thought you'd be such a slave to your comfort. I know you don't mean it when you say patriotism be hanged, but you shouldn't say things like that even in jest.

Frederick: I'm dashed if I can see why it would be less patriotic to have a fire in the drawing-room where we could all benefit by it, rather than here where it's no good to anyone but you.

Victoria (*opening her eyes very wide*): Darling, you're not going to ask me to do without a fire in my bedroom? How can you be so selfish? Heaven knows, I don't want to boast about anything I've done, but after having slaved my life out for four years I do think I deserve a little consideration.

Frederick: How's the kid?

Victoria: And it's not as if I grudged you the use of my room. You can come and sit here as much as you like. Besides, a man has his club. He can always go there if he wants to.

Frederick: I apologise. You're quite right. You're always right.

Victoria: I thought you wanted me to be happy.

Frederick: I do, darling.

Victoria: Before we were married, you said you'd make that the chief aim of your life.

Frederick (*smiling*): I can't imagine that a sensible man could want a better one.

Victoria: Confess that you've been a perfect pig.

Frederick: A brute beast, darling.

Victoria (*mollified*): D'you know that I asked you to give me a kiss just now? It's not a request that I'm in the habit of having ignored.

Frederick: I trust it's not one that you're in the habit of making to all and sundry.

He kisses her.

Victoria: Now tell me why you forgot to take me out to luncheon today.

Frederick: I didn't forget. I was prevented. I . . . I

haven't had any luncheon myself. I'll just ring and
ask the cook to send me up something.

Victoria: My poor lamb, the cook left this morning.

Frederick: Again?

Victoria: How d'you mean again? This is the first
time she's left.

Frederick: Hang it all, she's only been here a week.

Victoria: You needn't get cross about it. It's much
more annoying for me than for you.

Frederick (*irritably*): I don't know why on earth you
can't keep your servants.

Victoria: No one can keep servants nowadays.

Frederick: Other people do.

Victoria: Please don't speak to me like that, Freddie.
I'm not used to it.

Frederick: I shall speak to you exactly as I choose.

Victoria: It's so petty to lose your temper just because
you can't have something to eat. I should have
thought after spending two years in the trenches
you'd be accustomed to going without a meal now
and then.

Frederick: For goodness' sake don't make a scene.

Victoria: It's not I who am making a scene. It's you
who are making a scene.

Frederick: Victoria, I beg you to control yourself.

Victoria: I don't know how you can be so unkind to
me. After all the anxiety I suffered on your account
when you were in France, I do think you might
have a little consideration for me.

Frederick: Seeing that for the last year I've had a
perfectly safe, cushy job in the War Office, I think
you might by now have recovered from any anxiety
you felt on my account.

Victoria: Must I remind you that my nerves were
shattered by poor Bill's death

Frederick: No, but I was confident you would.

Victoria: The doctor said I should need the greatest
attention for several years. I don't believe I shall

ever quite get over it. I should have thought even
if you didn't love me any more you'd have a little
human pity for me. That's all I ask, just the tolerant
kindness you'd show to a dog who was fond of
you. (*Working herself up into a passion*) Heaven
knows I'm not exacting. I do everything I can to
make you happy. I'm patience itself. Even my worst
enemy would have to admit that I'm unselfish.
(*As he is about to speak*) You weren't obliged to
marry me. I didn't ask you to. You pretended you
loved me. I would never have married you if it
hadn't been for Bill. You were his greatest friend.
You made me love you because you spoke so
beautifully of him. (*He is just going to say
something, but she goes on implacably*) That's my
mistake. I've loved you too much. You're not big
enough to bear so great a love. Oh, what a fool I've
been. I let myself be taken in by you, and I've been
bitterly punished. (*Heading off the words she sees
he wants to speak*) Bill would never have treated
me like that. Bill wouldn't have taken my poor,
loving heart and thrown it aside like an old hat.
Bill loved me. He would have always loved me. I
adored that man. He waited on me hand and foot.
He was the most unselfish man I ever knew. He
was a hero. He's the only man I ever really cared
for. I was mad ever to think of marrying you, mad,
mad, mad. I shall never be happy again. I would
give anything in the world to have my dear, dear
Bill back again.

Frederick: I'm glad you feel like that about it, because
he'll be here in about three minutes.

Victoria (*brought up short*): What? What on earth
d'you mean by that?

Frederick: He rang me up at the club a little while
ago.

Victoria: Freddie. What are you talking about? Are
you mad?

Frederick: No. Nor drunk.

Victoria: I don't understand. Who talked to you?

Frederick: Bill.

Victoria: Bill, Bill who?

Frederick: Bill Cardew.

Victoria: But, poor darling, he's dead.

Frederick: He showed no sign of it on the telephone.

Victoria: But, Freddie . . . Freddie. Oh, you're pulling my leg. It's too beastly of you. How can you be so heartless?

Frederick: Well, just wait and you'll see for yourself. (*Looking at his wrist watch*) In about two and a half minutes now, I should think.

Victoria (*coaxing him*): Now, Freddie, don't be vindictive. I dare say I was rather catty. I didn't mean it. You know I adore you. You can have a fire in your study, and damn the food controller. I'm sorry for all I said just now. There, now, it's all right, isn't it?

Frederick: Perfectly. But it's not going to prevent Bill from walking into this room in about two minutes and a quarter.

Victoria: I shall scream. It's not true. Oh, Freddie, if you ever loved me, say it's not true.

Frederick: There's no need to take my word for it.

Victoria: But Freddie, darling, do be sensible. Poor Bill was killed at the Battle of Ypres. He was actually seen to fall. He was reported dead by the War Office. You know how distressed I was. I wore mourning and everything. We even had a memorial service.

Frederick: I know. It'll want a devil of a lot of explaining, turning up like this.

Victoria: I shall go stark, staring mad in a minute. How do you know it was Bill who spoke to you on the telephone?

Frederick: He said so.

Victoria: That proves nothing. Lots of people say they're the Kaiser.

Frederick: Yes, but they speak from a lunatic asylum. He spoke from Harwich Station.

Victoria: I dare say it was somebody else of the same name.

Frederick: That's idiotic, Victoria. I recognized his voice.

Victoria: What did he say exactly?

Frederick: Well, he said he was at Harwich Station, and would be in London at 3.13. And would I break it to you?

Victoria: But he must have said more than that.

Frederick: No, not much.

Victoria: For goodness' sake, tell me exactly what he said – exactly.

Frederick: Well, I was just coming along to take you out to luncheon, when I was told I was wanted on the telephone. A long-distance call – Harwich.

Victoria: I know. A seaport town.

Frederick: I strolled along and took up the receiver. I said: 'Is that you, darling?'

Victoria: Why did you say that?

Frederick: That's always a good opening on the telephone. It puts the person at the other end at their ease.

Victoria: Idiot.

Frederick: Somebody said: 'Is that you, Freddie?' I thought I recognized the voice, and I felt all funny. 'Yes,' I said. 'It's me, Bill,' he said, 'Bill Cardew.'

Victoria: For heaven's sake be quick about it.

Frederick: 'Hulloa,' I said. 'I thought you were dead.' 'I thought as much,' he answered. 'How are you?' I said. 'A1,' he said.

Victoria: What an idiotic conversation.

Frederick: Damn it all, I had to say something.

Victoria: You ought to have said a thousand things.

Frederick: We only had three minutes.

Victoria: Well, go on.

Frederick: He said: 'I'm just tootling up to London.'

I'll be up at 3.13. You might go along and break it to Victoria.' 'Right ho,' I said. He said: 'So-long,' and I said, 'So-long.' And we rang off.

Victoria: But that was before luncheon. Why didn't you come at once and tell me?

Frederick: To tell you the truth I was a bit shaken by then. I thought the first thing was to have a double whisky and a small soda.

Victoria: And what did you do then?

Frederick: Well, I sat down to think. I thought steadily for a couple of hours.

Victoria: And what have you thought?

Frederick: Nothing.

Victoria: It seems hardly worth while to have gone without your lunch.

Frederick: It's a devilish awkward position for me.

Victoria: For you? And what about me?

Frederick: After all, Bill was my oldest pal. He may think it rather funny that I've married his wife.

Victoria: Funny!

Frederick: On the other hand, he may not.

Victoria: Why didn't you tell me the moment you came in, instead of talking about heaven knows what?

Frederick: It wasn't a very easy thing to say. I was trying to find an opportunity to slip it in casually, don't you know.

Victoria (*furiously*): Wasting precious time.

Frederick (*blandly*): Darling, you surely don't think making a scene is ever a waste of time.

Victoria: Now we haven't got a chance to decide on anything. I haven't even time to put a frock on.

Frederick: What the deuce do you want to put a frock on for?

Victoria: After all, I am his widow. I think it would be only nice of me to be wearing mourning when he comes. What did he say when you told him?

Frederick: When I told him what?

187

Victoria: How can you be so stupid! When you told him you and I were married.

Frederick: But I didn't tell him.

Victoria: Do you mean to say that he's coming here under the impression that I'm his wife?

Frederick: Why, naturally.

Victoria: But why on earth didn't you tell him at once? It was the only thing to do. Surely you see that.

Frederick: It didn't strike me at the moment. Besides, it's rather a delicate thing to say on the telephone.

Victoria: Well, someone must tell him.

Frederick: I've come to the conclusion that you're quite the best person to do that.

Victoria: I? I? I? Do you think I'm going to do all your dirty work?

Frederick: I must say, I don't think it would come well from me.

Victoria: I'm not going to deal my darling Bill this bitter, bitter blow.

Frederick: By the way, it's – it's jolly he's alive, isn't it?

Victoria: Ripping.

Frederick: I am glad, aren't you?

Victoria: Yes, awfully glad.

Frederick: Then you'll just break the news as gently as you can, Victoria.

Victoria (*as if she were weighing the matter*): I really don't think that's my province.

Frederick (*exercising all his charm*): Darling, you've got so much tact. I never knew anyone who could deal with a delicate situation as you can. You have such a light hand. You're so sympathetic. And you've got such a wonderful tenderness.

Victoria: I don't think you've got hold of the right line at all. There's only one way to manage a thing like this. You just take him by the arm and say: Look here, old man, the fact is . . .

Frederick (*interrupting*): Victoria, you don't mean to say you're willing to give up the chance of making the biggest scene you've ever made in your life?

Victoria: Now look here, Freddie, this is the only thing I've ever asked you to do for me in my life. You know how frail I am. I'm not feeling at all well. You're the only man I have to lean on.

Frederick: It's no good, Victoria. I won't.

Victoria (*furiously*): Damn you.

Frederick: By George, here he is.

Victoria: I've not even powdered my nose. Fortunately I have no personal vanity.

> *She begins to powder herself feverishly. The voice is heard of someone coming up the stairs:* Hulloa! Hulloa! Hulloa! *Then the door is flung open and in bursts* **William**. *He is a well-set-up, jovial fellow, wearing at the moment a very shabby suit.*

William: Here we are again.

Victoria: Bill!

Frederick: Was I right?

Victoria: I can hardly believe my eyes.

William: Give me a kiss, old lady. (*He seizes her in his arms and gives her a hearty kiss. Then he turns to* **Frederick**. *They shake hands*) Well, Freddie, old man, how's life.

Frederick: A1, thanks.

William: Are you surprised to see me?

Frederick: A little.

Victoria: In fact, a good deal.

William: I'm jolly glad to see you here, Freddie, old man. On the way up in the train I cursed myself five times for not having asked you to wait with Victoria till I rolled up. I was afraid you might have some damned feeling of delicacy.

Frederick: I?

William: You see, it struck me you might think

Victoria and I would want to be alone just the first
moment, but I should have been as sick as a dog if
I hadn't seen your ugly old face here to welcome
me. By the way, you've neither of you said you
were glad to see me.

Victoria: Of course we're glad, Bill, darling.

Frederick: Rather.

William: Tactful of me to get old Freddie to come
round and break the news to you, I think, Victoria.

Victoria: Yes, darling, and exactly like you.

William: It's just like old times to hear you call me
darling every other minute.

Frederick: It's one of Victoria's favourite words.

William: You know, I nearly didn't warn you. I
thought it would be rather a lark to break in on
you in the middle of the night.

Frederick *and* **Victoria** *give a little start.*

Victoria: I'm just as glad you didn't do that, Bill.

William: What a scene, my word. The sleeping beauty
on her virtuous couch. Enter a man in a shocking
old suit. Shrieks of the sleeping beauty. It is I, your
husband. Tableau.

Victoria (*to turn the conversation*): You're quite right,
it is a shocking old suit. Where did you get it?

William: I didn't get it. I pinched it. I must say I
wouldn't mind getting into some decent things.

He walks towards a door that leads out of
Victoria's *room.*

Victoria (*hastily*): Where are you going?

William: I was going into my dressing-room. Upon
my soul, I almost forget what I've got. I had a blue
serge suit that was rather dressy.

Victoria: I've put all your clothes away, darling.

William: Where?

Victoria: In camphor. You couldn't put them on until
they've been aired.

William: Hell, said the duchess.

> **Mrs Shuttleworth** *comes in.* **William** *is standing so that at first she does not see him.*

Mrs Shuttleworth: I think the little lamb is going on nicely, Victoria.

Victoria (*swallowing*): Mother.

William: I was just going to ask about the kid.

> **Mrs Shuttleworth** *jumps out of her skin. She turns round and sees* **William**.

Mrs Shuttleworth: Who is that?

William: Who the devil d'you think it is?

Mrs Shuttleworth: The language and the voice – Bill Cardew's. Who is that?

William (*walking towards her*): Well, I may be a bit thinner and it certainly is a shocking old suit.

Mrs Shuttleworth: Don't come near me or I shall scream.

William: You can't escape me. I'm going to kiss you.

Mrs Shuttleworth: Take him away. Don't let him come near me. Victoria, who is that man?

Frederick: Well, Mrs Shuttleworth, it's Bill Cardew.

Mrs Shuttleworth: But he's dead.

Frederick: He doesn't seem to know it.

Mrs Shuttleworth: It's absurd. Will someone wake me up.

William: Shall I pinch her, and if so, where?

Mrs Shuttleworth: It's a horrible dream. Of course he's dead. That man's an imposter.

William: Shall I show you the strawberry mark on my left shoulder?

Mrs Shuttleworth: I tell you Bill Cardew's dead.

William: Prove it.

Mrs Shuttleworth (*indignantly*): Prove it? The War Office announced it officially; Victoria went into mourning.

William: Did she look nice in it?

Mrs Shuttleworth: Sweet. Perfectly sweet. I insisted on her going to Mathilde. Mourning must be well

made or else it looks nothing at all. Why, we had
a memorial service.

Frederick: Fully choral.

William: Did you have a memorial service for me,
Victoria? That was nice of you.

Victoria: It was very well attended.

William: I'm glad it wasn't a frost.

Frederick: I say, old man, we don't want to hurry you,
you know, but we're all waiting for some sort of
explanation.

William: I was coming to that. I was just giving you
time to get over your first raptures at seeing me
again. Have you got over them?

Frederick: I can only speak for myself.

William: Well, you know, I was damned badly
wounded.

Frederick: Yes, at Ypres. A fellow saw you fall. He
said you were shot through the head. He just stopped
a minute, and saw you were killed, and went on.

William: A superficial observer. I wasn't. I was
eventually picked up and taken to Germany.

Victoria: Why didn't you write?

William: Well, I think I must have been rather dotty
for a bit. I don't know exactly how long I was in
hospital, but when I began to sit up and take
nourishment I couldn't remember a damned thing.
My memory had completely gone.

Mrs Shuttleworth: Strange. To my mind very strange.

William: I think my wound must have made me a bit
irritable. When I was being taken along to a camp I
had a difference of opinion with a German officer,
and I laid him out. By George, they nearly shot
me for that. Anyhow, they sentenced me to about
a hundred and fifty years imprisonment, and
prevented me from writing, or making any sign that
I was alive.

Victoria: But your memory came back?

William: Yes, gradually. And, of course, I realized

then that you'd think I was dead. But I had no means of letting you know.

Frederick: You might have wired from Rotterdam.

William: The lines were so congested. They told me I'd arrive before my wire.

Mrs Shuttleworth: It's all quite probable.

William: More or less, I flatter myself. But you can bet your life on one thing: I'm not dead, and, what's more, I propose to live for another forty years, if not fifty.

> **Taylor** *comes in.*

Taylor: If you please, ma'am, where shall I put the gentleman's things? He told me to bring them upstairs.

William: Oh, it's only a few odds and ends for the journey that I got on my way. Put them in the dressing-room.

Victoria: No, leave that for a moment, Taylor. We'll decide presently.

Taylor: Very good, madam.

> *She goes out.*

William: What's the matter with the dressing-room, Victoria?

Victoria: My poor darling, don't forget your arrival is a complete surprise. Nothing is ready.

William: Don't let that worry you. After what I've been used to, I can pig it anywhere. (*Looking at the bed*) By George, a spring mattress. Father will sleep without rocking tonight.

Mrs Shuttleworth (*firmly*): Something's got to be done.

William: How d'you mean?

Victoria (*hurriedly*): We haven't got a cook.

William: Oh, you needn't bother about that. Freddie and I will do the cooking. My speciality is grilled steak. What can you do, Freddie?

Frederick: I can boil an egg.

William: Splendid. They always say that's the one thing a chef can't do. Nothing to worry about. We'll get in some *pâté de fois gras* and a few oysters, and there you are. Now let's have a look at the kid.

Mrs Shuttleworth: He's not very well today. I don't think he should leave his bed.

William: Oh, all right. I'll toddle up and see him. I haven't made his lordship's acquaintance yet. What's his name?

Victoria (*rather nervously*): Don't you remember, just before you went away, you said you'd like him called Frederick if he were a boy.

William: Yes, I know I did, but you said you'd see me damned. You'd quite made up your mind to call him Lancelot.

Victoria: When I thought you were dead I felt I must respect your wishes.

William: It must have been a shock if it took you like that.

Victoria: Of course, I asked Freddie to be godfather.

William: Has the old ruffian been a stand-by to you while I've been away?

Victoria: I . . . I've seen a good deal of him.

William: I felt you were safe with him, you know. He's a brick.

Frederick: I say, you might spare my blushes while you're about it.

Victoria: He was very kind to me during my – bereavement.

William: Dear old chap. I knew you were a tower of strength.

Frederick (*sweating freely*): I . . . I did what I could, you know.

William: Well, don't be so modest about it.

Mrs Shuttleworth (*more firmly*): I tell you something must be done.

William: My dear Victoria, what is the matter with your mother.

Frederick (*trying to change the conversation*): I think we might bust ourselves and have some bubbly tonight, Victoria.

William: And damn the expense.

Frederick: I wonder if it's arrived yet. I told them to send a case in the day before yesterday.

William: Have you been running the cellar? Rash to let him do that, Victoria, very rash.

Victoria: I know nothing about wine.

William: Freddie knows a thing or two. I say, do you remember the last time we went on a bat together? You were blind to the world.

Frederick: Go to blazes! I was nothing of the sort.

William: Pretty little thing that was. Are you as thick with her as you used to be?

> **Victoria** *draws herself up and looks daggers at* **Frederick.**

Frederick (*with dignity*): I haven't any idea who you're referring to.

William: Oh, my dear old boy, don't put any frills on. Victoria's a married woman, and she knows what the lads of the village are when they get out. A very nice little girl indeed, Victoria. If I hadn't been a married man I'd have had a shot at cutting Freddie out.

Victoria (*icily*): He always told me he'd never looked at a woman in his life.

William: You shouldn't encourage the young to lie. That's what they all say. Rapid. These wretched aeroplane fellows have been turning out engine after engine, and they can't keep pace with him. Talk of a lurid past; Mrs Shuttleworth, veil your face.

Frederick: My poor Bill, your memory! When you recovered it, I'm afraid you remembered all sorts of things that had never happened.

William: Past, did I say? Unless I'm very much

mistaken, his present wouldn't bear the closest inspection.

Frederick: By George, I've hit it. The poor fellow thinks he's being funny.

William (*going on*): I don't blame you. Make hay while the sun shines. I admire the way you can make love to three women at a time and make each one believe she's the only one you've ever really cared for.

Mrs Shuttleworth (*with determination*): If someone doesn't do something at once I shall do it myself.

William (*in a whisper to* **Victoria**, *pointing at* **Mrs Shuttleworth**): Air raids?

At that moment a baby's wail is heard outside.

Victoria (*with agitation*): Willie.

William: Hulloa, what's that? Is that the kid? (*He goes swiftly to the door and opens it. The crying is heard more loudly.*) Why, it's coming upstairs. You told me the kid was in the nursery. (*Addressing the nurse*) Bring him along and let me have a look at him.

A nurse, in a neat grey uniform, comes in with a baby in her arms.

Victoria (*desperately*): Freddie, do something, even if it's only something stupid.

Frederick: The only thing that occurs to me is to stand on my head.

William (*jovially*): Hulloa, hulloa, hulloa.

Frederick: That's not the way to talk to a baby, you owl.

William: Not such as baby as all that. Can he speak yet, nurse?

Nurse: Oh no, sir, not yet.

William: Rather backward, isn't he? Not what I should have expected in a son of mine.

The **Nurse** *gives him a look of surprise, and*

> *then with a look at* **Victoria** *assumes an*
> *appearance of extreme primness.*

Nurse: I never knew a baby to talk as young as that, sir.

William: Upon my soul, there's not much of him. Looks to me rather a stumer. I think we've been done, Victoria.

Nurse (*indignantly*): Oh, I don't think you ought to say that, sir. He's a very fine boy. He weighs more than a good many do when they're six months.

William: What's that? How old is he?

Nurse: Four months last Tuesday, sir.

William: You've been busy in my absence, Victoria.

Victoria: Freddie, for goodness' sake speak. Don't stand there like a stuffed tomato.

Mrs Shuttleworth: Leave the room, nannie.

> *The* **Nurse** *pursing her lips, intrigued and*
> *perplexed, goes out.*

Frederick (*trying to take it lightly*): The fact is, you've made rather an absurd mistake. You've been away so long that of course there's a good deal you don't know.

William: I'm a simple creature.

Frederick: Well, to cut a long story short –

William: What story?

Frederick: I wish you wouldn't interrupt me. I'm telling you as quickly as I can. To cut a long story short, the infant that's just gone out of the room is not your son.

William: I had a sort of suspicion he wasn't. I tell you that frankly.

Victoria: Oh, the fool. The blithering nincompoop.

William: Well, who the deuce is his father?

Frederick: In point of fact, I am.

William: You? You don't mean to say you're married?

Frederick: Lots of people are. In fact, marriage has been quite the thing during the war.

William: Why on earth didn't you tell me?

Frederick: Hang it all, man, you've been dead for the last three years. How could I?

William (*seizing his hand*): Well, I'm jolly glad to hear it, old chap. I knew you'd be caught one of these days. You were a wily old bird, but – ah, well, we all come to it. My very best congratulations.

Frederick: That's awfully good of you. I'm – er – I'm staying here, you know.

William: Are you? That's first rate. Is your missus here too?

Frederick: It's rather difficult to explain.

William: Don't tell me she's only got one eye.

Frederick: Can't you guess why I'm staying here?

William: No. (*He looks round the room and his eyes fall on* **Mrs Shuttleworth**.) You don't mean to say you've married Victoria's mother?

Frederick: No, not exactly.

William: What does he mean by *not exactly* I hope you haven't been trifling with the affections of my mother-in-law.

Mrs Shuttleworth: Do I look as if I were the mother of that baby?

William: We live in an age of progress. One should keep an open mind about things.

Frederick: You quite misunderstand me, Bill.

William: Is there nothing between you and Victoria's mother?

Frederick: Certainly not.

William: Well, I'm sorry. I should have liked to be your son-in-law. And you would have done the right thing by her, wouldn't you?

Victoria: Really, Bill, I don't think you should talk about my mother like that.

William: If he's compromised her he ought to marry her.

Victoria: He hasn't compromised her and he can't marry her.

William: I don't want to seem inquisitive, but if you didn't marry Victoria's mother, who did you marry?

Frederick: Damn you, I married Victoria.

CURTAIN

Act II

The drawing-room at **Victoria's** *house. It is very bizarre.* **Victoria** *has put the decoration into the hands of an artist in futurism, and the result is very modern, outrageous, fantastic, but not ugly. There is no fire in the grate and all the windows are open.* **Frederick** *is sitting in a greatcoat with a rug round his legs, reading the paper.* **Mrs Shuttleworth** *enters.*

Mrs Shuttleworth: I'm going now.

Frederick: Are you?

Mrs Shuttleworth: I'm taking my dear little grandchildren away with me.

Frederick: Are you?

Mrs Shuttleworth: You don't seem in a very good temper this morning.

Frederick: I'm not.

Mrs Shuttleworth: Victoria will be down presently.

Frederick: Will she?

Mrs Shuttleworth: I should have thought you'd ask how she was after that dreadful shock.

Frederick: Would you?

Mrs Shuttleworth: She's better, poor darling, but she's terribly shaken. I put her to bed at once with hot-water bottles.

Frederick: Did you?

Mrs Shuttleworth: Of course, she was totally unfit to discuss this terrible situation yesterday.

Frederick: Was she?

Mrs Shuttleworth: Surely you can see that for yourself. The only thing was to keep her perfectly quiet till she'd had time to recover a little.

Frederick: Was it?

Mrs Shuttleworth: But this morning I have no doubt you'll find her prepared to go into the matter.

Frederick: Shall I?

Mrs Shuttleworth: If you have nothing else you wish to say to me I think I'll go now.

Frederick: Will you?

> **Mrs Shuttleworth** *purses her lips very tightly and goes towards the door. At that moment* **Taylor** *comes in.*

Taylor: Mr Leicester Paton has called, madam. Mrs Lowndes says, will you see him a minute. She's just getting out of her bath.

Mrs Shuttleworth: Certainly. Show him in here.

Taylor: Very good, madam.

> *Exit.*

Frederick: I'll go.

Mrs Shuttleworth: I wonder what he wants.

Frederick: Perhaps he wants Victoria's permission to pay you his address.

> *He goes out. In a minute* **Taylor** *announces* **Leicester Paton** *and then goes out.*

Taylor: Mr Leicester Paton.

Paton: Your daughter rang me up this morning. I thought the best thing I could do was to come along at once.

Mrs Shuttleworth: That's too good of you. I'm sure if anything can be done you are the man to do it.

Paton: It's an extraordinary situation.

Mrs Shuttleworth: Of course, I think it was very inconsiderate of Bill to turn up like that.

Paton: Poor thing, she must be quite upset.

Mrs Shuttleworth: Well, I can only tell you that the

shock entirely took the wave out of her hair. She only had it done yesterday, and it was as straight as a telegraph pole this morning.

Paton: You don't say so.

Mrs Shuttleworth: Here she is.

> **Victoria** *comes in. She has her dressing-gown on and bedroom slippers. Her hair is only partly done, but she manages to look perfectly ravishing.*

Victoria: I didn't want to keep you waiting. I came down just as I was. You mustn't look at me.

Paton: I can't help it.

Victoria: What nonsense. I know I look a perfect fright, but fortunately I have no personal vanity.

Paton (*holding her hand*): What a catastrophe! You must be beside yourself.

Victoria (*with a charming smile*): I knew I could rely on your sympathy.

Paton: What in heaven's name are you going to do?

Victoria: It's because I haven't an idea that I telephoned to you. You see, you've taught me to bring all my difficulties to you.

Paton: To whom else should you bring them? We must think. We must discuss the matter.

Victoria: The position is impossible.

Paton: It's wonderful that you bear it so bravely. I was expecting to find you in a state of collapse.

Victoria (*with a flash of the eyes*): With you to lean on?

Paton: I suppose you've been having the most terrible scenes.

Victoria: Heartrending. You see, they both adore me.

Paton: And you?

Victoria: I? I only want to do – my duty.

Paton: How like you! How exactly like you.

Mrs Shuttleworth: If there's nothing more I can do for you, darling, I think I'll go now.

201

Victoria: Do, darling.

Mrs Shuttleworth (*shaking hands with* **Leicester Paton**): Be very kind to her.

Paton: I'll try.

    Mrs Shuttleworth *goes out.*

Victoria (*almost tenderly*): It was very sweet of you to come and see me at once. I was afraid you wouldn't have time.

Paton: Do you imagine I should allow anything to stand in the way when you sent for me?

Victoria: Oh, but you know I shouldn't like to think that you were putting yourself out on my account.

Paton: I wish I could pretend I were. As a matter of fact, I was only going down to see a place I've just bought in the country, and as I wanted to try my new Rolls I thought I'd kill two birds with one stone.

Victoria: I didn't know you were buying a place.

Paton: Oh, it's a very modest little affair. The park is not more than three hundred acres, and there are only twenty-eight bedrooms. But you see, I'm a bachelor. I want so little.

Victoria: Where is it?

Paton: It's near Newmarket.

Victoria: A very nice neighbourhood.

Paton: A man in my position is bound to do something for the good of the country, and it seems to me that to patronize a good old English sport, which gives employment to numbers of respectable men, is an occupation which is truly patriotic. I'm going to take up racing.

Victoria: I think it's splendid of you. So many men waste their money on their own selfish pleasures. It's such a relief to come across anyone who is determined to make a thoroughly good use of it. I've often wondered that you didn't go into Parliament.

Paton: For the last four years I've been too busy winning the war to bother about governing the nation.

Victoria: Yes, but now. They want strong men of keen intelligence and dominating personality.

Paton: It's not impossible that very soon I shall have the opportunity to show of what mettle I am made. But not in the House of Commons.

Victoria (*all to pieces*): In the House of Lords?

Paton (*roguishly*): Ah, you mustn't ask me to betray the confidence of the Prime Minister.

Victoria: You'll look sweet in scarlet and ermine.

Paton (*gallantly*): But it's too bad of me to talk about my concerns when yours are so much more important.

Victoria: Oh, you can't think how I love to hear you talk about yourself. One feels a brain behind every word you say.

Paton: It's easy to be brilliant when one has a sympathetic listener.

Victoria: Of course, Bill and Freddie are dear good fellows, but their conversation is a little limited. During the war it was rather smart to talk about guns, and flying machines, and flea-bags, but now . . .

Paton: I understand you so well, dear lady.

Victoria: Why do you call me that?

Paton: Out of pure embarrassment. I don't know whether to call you Mrs Cardew or Mrs Lowndes.

Victoria: Why don't you split the difference and call me Victoria?

Paton: May I?

Victoria (*giving him her hand*): It will make me feel that you are not an entire stranger to me.

Paton (*with surprise*): Your wedding rings? You always used to wear two.

Victoria: As long as I thought that poor Bill was dead I didn't want to forget him.

Paton: But why have you removed them both?

Victoria: I'm all at sea. I'm married to two men, and I feel as if I were married to neither.

Paton: I wish you weren't. I wish will all my heart you weren't.

Victoria: How emphatic you are. Why?

Paton: Can't you guess?

Victoria (*looking down*): I must be very stupid.

Paton: Don't you know that I dote upon you? I curse my unhappy fate that I didn't meet you before you were married.

Victoria: Would you have asked me to marry you?

Paton: Morning, noon and night until you consented.

Victoria: I never want a Paris model so much as when I know it's just been sold to somebody else. I wonder if you'd want to marry me if I were free?

Paton: Yes. With all my heart.

Victoria: But I'm not free.

Paton: And you – if you were, would you marry me?

Victoria: Tell me, why do you wear spats?

Paton: I think they're so neat.

Victoria: Oh, not because you suffer from cold feet?

Paton: Oh no, my circulation is excellent.

Victoria: I don't believe you're the sort of man who'd ever take no for an answer.

Paton: You're perfectly adorable.

Victoria (*with a smile, shyly*): I wonder if you'd take me out to luncheon?

Paton: Give me the chance.

Victoria: I'll just dress myself. Come back in half an hour, and you'll find me ready.

Paton: Very well.

Victoria: Goodbye for the present.

> *They go out together.* **Williams's** *voice is heard outside.*

William: Victoria. (*He comes in, but sees nobody in the room.*) Hulloa! (*Shouting*) Freddie.

Frederick (*outside*): Hulloa.
William: Freddie.

  Frederick *comes in with his rug and his paper.*

William: I say, I can't find my boots.
Frederick: Your boots? What do you want your boots for?
William: To put them on. What else d'you think I want them for?
Frederick: I saw them lying about. I thought I'd better put them away in case of accidents.
William: Silly ass. Where did you put them?
Frederick: I was just trying to think.
William: You don't mean to say you don't know where they are.
Frederick: Of course I know where they are because I put them there, but I don't happen to remember just at the moment.
William: Well, you hurry up and remember.
Frederick: Don't fuss me. I can't possibly remember if you fuss me.
William: Try and think where you put them.
Frederick (*looking doubtfully at a vase*): I know I didn't put them in one of the flower vases.
William: So I should hope.
Frederick: They might be in the coal-scuttle.
William: If they are I'll black your face with them.
Frederick (*looking in the scuttle, with triumph*): I said they weren't in the coal scuttle.
William: Fathead. I don't want to know where they're not. I want to know where they are.
Frederick: If I knew that I shouldn't be hunting for them.
William: If you don't find them in two and a half seconds I'll break every bone in your body.
Frederick: It's no good losing your hair about it. If we can't find your boots we can't.

William (*irritably*): I say, what the devil have you got all the windows open for?

Frederick: I was trying to warm the room a bit. Besides, they say it's healthy.

William: A short life and a merry one for me. I like a fug.

He shuts the windows.

Frederick: That's won't make it any warmer. I've tried that.

William: You silly ass, why don't you light the fire?

Frederick: Don't be so damned unpatriotic. Victoria must have a fire in her bedroom, and we must have one in the nursery.

William: Why?

Frederick: For the children's bath.

William (*astonished*): What, every day?

Frederick: Yes, they wash children a lot nowadays.

William: Poor little beggars.

Frederick (*jumping up and going towards him*): Where the devil did you get that suit?

William: Rather saucy, I flatter myself. Victoria sent it in to me.

Frederick: She needn't have sent you the only new suit I've had since the war. Upon my soul, I think it's a bit thick.

William: Well, you didn't like the suit I wore yesterday. You can't expect me to go about in fig-leaves unless you have the house properly warmed.

Frederick: If you'd had the decency to ask *me* you might have had this suit I've got on.

William: Thanks, but I don't altogether like that one. It's a bit baggy at the knees for me.

Frederick: You're very much mistaken if you think you're going to wear all the new clothes and I'm going to wear all the old ones.

William: If you're going to be shirty about it, where the devil did you get that pin?

Frederick: Oh, Victoria gave it me on my birthday.

William: Well, it's mine. She gave it me on my
birthday first. And where did you get those links?

Frederick: Victoria gave them to me as a Christmas
present.

William: Oh, did she? She gave them to me as a
Christmas present before she gave them to you.
You jolly well take them off.

Frederick: I'll see you blowed first. At your death you
left everything to her in your will. If she chose to
give them to me it's no business of yours.

William: Well, I'm not going to argue about it, but I
think it's dashed bad form to swank about in a
dead man's jewellery.

Frederick: By the way, did you ever have a hammered
gold cigarette-case?

William: Rather. That was Victoria's wedding present
to me. Did you get it too?

Frederick: Thrifty woman, Victoria.

William: I say, unless I have a fire I shall turn into
the Albert Memorial.

Frederick: Apply a match and see what happens.

William: Thanks – I will.

*He strikes a match and lights the fire. The
flames leap up.*

Frederick: Now I'll take my coat off. Victoria will be
furious.

William: That's your look out. You'll have to take
the responsibility.

Frederick: It's got nothing to do with me. You're the
master of this house.

William: Not at all. I am but an honoured guest.

Frederick: Oh no, the moment you appeared I sank
into insignificance.

William: My dear fellow, where did I sleep last night?
In the spare bedroom. That proves conclusively
that I am a guest and nothing more.

Frederick: And where the devil do you think I slept? Here.

William: Why did you do that? You were perfectly sober when I went to bed.

Frederick: Victoria said I couldn't sleep in the next room to hers now you were back.

William: Oh, well, I dare say you made yourself very comfortable on the sofa.

Frederick: Look at the damned thing.

William: By the way, what's the matter with the furniture?

Frederick: When you were killed Victoria was naturally very much upset, so she had the drawing-room redecorated.

William: I dare say I'm not very bright so early in the morning, but I don't quite see the connection.

Frederick: You see, the old room had too many painful associations. She wanted to distract her mind.

William: Oh, I was under the impression that you'd undertaken that.

Frederick (*with dignity*): I was sympathetic. That is surely what you would have liked me to be.

William: Of course. I'm not blaming you.

Frederick: If you'd seen Victoria in tears you couldn't expect a man not to try and console her.

William: She's the only woman I ever knew who looks as pretty when she cries as when she smiles. It's a great power.

Frederick: I knew you'd take it like a sensible man.

William: Quite so.

Frederick: When would you like me to clear out?

William: My dear fellow, why should you wish to do that? Surely you don't for a moment imagine that I shall be in the way. I propose to make my visit quite a brief one.

Frederick: I'm sorry to hear that. Victoria will be disappointed. But of course that's no concern of mine. You and your wife must arrange that between you.

William: My dear old thing, you entirely misunderstand me. I am not the man to come between husband and wife.

Frederick: What the devil to you mean?

William: Well, if it comes to that, what the devil do you mean?

> **Victoria** *comes in. She now wears a most becoming morning dress. She carries a box of chocolates.*

Victoria: Good morning.

> *She goes to* **William** *and gives him her cheek to kiss.*

William: Good-morning.

Victoria: Good-morning.

> *She goes to* **Frederick** *and gives him the other cheek to kiss.*

Frederick: Good-morning.

Victoria (*with a nod of the head towards* **William**): I went to him first because he's been away so long.

Frederick: Naturally. And he was your husband long before I was.

Victoria: I don't want either of you to be jealous of the other. I adore you both and I'm not going to show any favouritism.

Frederick: I don't see why he should have the spare bedroom, while I have to double up on the drawing-room sofa.

William: I like that. What about the fatted calf?

Frederick: Not unless you've brought your coupons with you.

Victoria (*catching sight of the fire*): Who lit that fire?

Frederick: He did.

William: It was your match.

> **Victoria** *draws up a chair and sits down in*

front of the fire in such a way as to prevent any warmth from getting into the room.

Victoria (*eating a chocolate*): Of course you don't care if we run so short of coal that my wretched babies die of double pneumonia. It's simply criminal to have a fire here.

William: I'm tortured by the pangs of remorse. But, need you monopolize it?

Victoria: If there is a fire I may as well get some benefit out of it.

Frederick: Are those chocolates you're eating, Victoria?

Victoria: Yes, Bobbie Curtis sent them to me. They're delicious

Frederick: Are they?

Victoria: It's so hard to get good chocolates just now.

Frederick: I know it is. I haven't tasted one for months.

Victoria (*biting a chocolate*): Oh, this one's soft inside. How hateful. Would either of you like it?

William (*ironically*): It seems a pity to waste it, Victoria.

Victoria (*eating it*): I dare say you're right. One oughtn't to be too particular in war-time.

William: Ah, I suppose that's what you thought when you married Freddie.

Victoria: I did that for your sake, darling. He was such a pal of yours.

Frederick: She was simply inconsolable when you were killed.

William: It's lucky you were there to console her.

Victoria: It was Freddie who broke the news to me. He thought of the memorial service. He came to see me twice a day.

William: And with your practical mind I suppose you thought it hardly worth his while to wear out shoe-

leather when a trifling ceremony might save him
the journey.

Victoria: Of course we waited a year. I told him he
mustn't think of it till the year was up.

William: With leather so expensive? But you always
had nice feelings, Victoria.

Victoria: You know how helpless I am without a man.
I knew you wouldn't wish me to remain a widow.

Frederick: I felt I was the proper person to look after
her.

William: The way you've both of you sacrificed
yourselves for my sake is almost more than I can
bear. I can only hope that you didn't have to force
your inclinations too much?

Frederick: What do you mean by that?

William: Well, since it appears you married entirely
for my sake, I presume there was nothing between
you but – shall we say esteem?

Victoria: Oh, but, Bill darling, didn't I tell you that I
adored Freddie? It was his wonderful friendship for
you that won my heart.

Frederick: She was so devoted to you, Bill, I should
have been a brute not to care for her.

William: One would almost think you fell in love
with one another.

Victoria: Only over your dead body, darling.

Frederick: I should have thought you'd be rather
touched by it.

William: It gives me quite a lump in my throat.

Frederick: And Victoria never forgot you, old man.
Did you, Victoria.

Victoria: Never.

Frederick: I know quite well that I only came second
in her heart. So long as you were round and about
she would never have thought of me.

William: Oh, I don't know about that. Even the most
constant woman likes a change now and then.

Frederick: No, no. I know Victoria's faithful heart.

She can never really love any man but you.
Victoria, you know how I adore you. You are the
only woman in the world for me. But I realize that
there is only one thing for me to do. Bill has come
back. There is only one course open to me as a
gentleman and a man of honour. It is a bitter, bitter
sacrifice, but I am equal to it. I renounce all rights
in you. I will go away, a wiser and a sadder man,
and leave you to Bill. Goodbye, Victoria. Wipe
your mouth and give me one more kiss before we
part for ever.

Victoria: Oh, how beautiful you are, Freddie. What a
soul you've got.

Frederick: Goodbye, Victoria. Forget me and live
happily with a better man than I.

Victoria: I shall never forget you, Freddie. Goodbye.
Go quickly or I shall break down.

> **William** *has planted himself firmly in front of
> the door.* **Frederick** *goes up to him with
> outstretched hand.*

Frederick: Goodbye, Bill. Be kind to her. I couldn't do
this for anyone but you.

William (*deliberately*): Nothing doing.

Frederick: I am going out of your life for ever.

William: Not in those boots.

Frederick: Damn it all, what's the matter with them?
They're not yours.

William: A figure of speech, my lad.

Frederick: I don't think this is exactly the moment
for flippancy. You get away from that door.

William: You shall only pass over my dead body.

Frederick: What's the good of that? I shouldn't get the
chance then.

Victoria: Bill, why prolong a painful scene?

William: My dear Victoria, I am not the man to accept
a sacrifice like that. No. The War Office has
decided that I'm dead. You've had a memorial

service. You've redecorated the drawing-room.
You are happy. It would be monstrously selfish if I
disturbed a state of things which is eminently
satisfactory to you both. I will not come between
you.

Victoria: Oh, Bill, how noble.

William: Victoria, I am a gentleman and a soldier.
This being that you see before you,
notwithstanding the tolerable suit he wears, is a
disembodied wraith. To all intents and purposes I
am as dead as mutton. I will remain so.

Frederick: Victoria will never be happy with me now
that you've come back.

William: Not another word. She is yours.

Frederick: My dear Bill, you know me very little. I
am lazy, selfish, bad-tempered, mean, gouty, and
predisposed to cancer, tuberculosis and diabetes.

William: This is terrible, my poor Freddie. You must
take the greatest care of your health, and dear
Victoria will do her best to correct your defects of
character.

Frederick: If you really loved her you wouldn't expose
her to the certain misery that it must be to live
with a man like me.

William: Freddie, old man, I can no longer conceal
from you that with a constitution ruined by
dissipation in my youth and broken by the ravages
of war I have not much longer to live. Besides,
Victoria knows only too well that I am vindictive
and overbearing, extravagant, violent and
mendacious.

Victoria: I understand it all. You're both so noble.
You're both so heroic. You're both so unselfish.

   Taylor *comes in.*

Taylor: If you please, ma'am, someone to see you
from the Alexandra Employment Agency.

   She hands her a slip of paper.

Victoria: Oh, send her in at once.
Taylor: Very good, madam.

Exit.

Victoria: A cook. A cook. A cook.
Frederick: Good business. Is she plain or good?
Victoria: Plain and good.
William: How like a woman.

> **Taylor** *shows in* **Mrs Pogson** *and closes the door behind her.* **Mrs Pogson** *is large and heavy and authoritative. She is dressed like the widow of an undertaker.*

Mrs Pogson: Good-morning.
Victoria: Good-morning.

> **Mrs Pogson** *looks round her, and seeing a handy chair sits down on it.*

Mrs. Pogson: I 'ave your name on the list the Alexandra gave me as requiring a cook. I don't know as I very much like this neighbourhood, but I thought I'd just pop in and see if the position looked like suiting me.
Victoria (*ingratiatingly*): I'm sure you'd find it a very nice one.
Mrs Pogson: I couldn't stand them air-raids and I made up my mind I wouldn't come back to London not so long as the war lasted. And the streets all dark and I don't know what all. But of course I prefer London.
Victoria: Naturally.
Mrs Pogson: And now that the war's over if I can find anything that suits me I don't mind coming back. Why did the last cook leave you?
Victoria: She was going to be married.
Mrs Pogson: Ah, that's what all you ladies say. Of course, it may be so, and on the other 'and it may not.

Victoria: She told me she hadn't had a nicer place for the last three months.

Mrs Pogson: Now before we go any further I'd just like to know one thing. Have you got a garage?

Victoria: Well, we have, but there are no cars in it. We sold our car.

Mrs Pogson: Oh, well, that would be very convenient. I always bring my Ford with me.

Victoria: Yes, of course.

Mrs Pogson: Do you keep men-servants?

Victoria: No, I'm afraid not.

Mrs Pogson (*severely*): I've always been used to men-servants.

Victoria: You see, since the war . . .

Mrs Pogson: Oh, you don't 'ave to tell me. I know it's very difficult. And I suppose you 'aven't got a kitchen-maid either?

Victoria: One can't get one for love or money.

Mrs Pogson: That's a thing I shall never forgive the Government for. Taking all them girls and putting them in munitions. Still, that's not your fault, I will say that. There's many cooks I know as say they *will not* go without a kitchen-maid, but I say, it's war-time and everyone ought to do his bit. If I must do without a kitchen-maid, well, I will do without a kitchen-maid

Victoria: I think it's very patriotic of you.

Mrs Pogson: Of course, I leave you to make any arrangements you like about lighting the kitchen fire. All I ask is that it should be alight when I come down in the morning.

Victoria: Oh! Naturally, I see your point. But I don't quite know how I should manage about that.

Mrs Pogson: In my last position the gentleman of the house lit the fire every morning.

Victoria: Oh, I hadn't thought of that.

William: I wouldn't if I were you, Victoria.

Mrs Pogson: A very nice gentleman he was too.

Brought me up a cup of tea and a slice of thin bread
and butter every day before I got up.

Victoria: I'm sure we'd do everything we could to
make you comfortable.

Mrs Pogson: What cooking would you require?

Victoria: I'm sure you'd satisfy us there. I can see at
once that you're a first-rate cook.

Mrs Pogson: I don't 'old with a lot of fancy things
meself, not in war-time. I say, be thankful you get
anything to eat at all.

Victoria: Of course, I know it's very difficult to have
a great variety now. I'm sure you'll do the best
you can. We're out for luncheons a good deal and
we dine at eight.

Mrs Pogson: Of course, you can please yourselves
there, but I never do any cooking after mid-day.

Victoria: That's rather awkward.

Mrs Pogson: If you don't think I'll suit you needn't
waste any more of my time. I've got ten to a dozen
ladies that I must interview this morning.

Victoria: Oh, I wouldn't make a point of that. I dare
say we can arrange our hours to suit you.

Mrs Pogson: Well, I always serve up my dinner at one
o'clock. A nice little bit of meat and a milk-
pudding. And should you want anything after that
you can always 'ave the cold meat for your supper
and any little sweet I 'appen to 'ave in the kitchen.

Victoria: I see. And what – what wages are you
asking?

Mrs Pogson: I don't know as I'm asking any wages.
I'm prepared to accept a salary of two pound a week.

Victoria: That's rather more than I've been in the
habit of paying.

Mrs Pogson: If you aren't prepared to pay that there
are plenty as are.

Victoria: We won't quarrel about that. I'm sure you're
worth the money.

Mrs Pogson: I don't think there are any more
questions I need to ask you.

Victoria: No, I think that's everything. When would
you be able to come in?

Mrs Pogson: I'll just go and see these other ladies and
see what they 'ave to offer me, and then if I come
to the conclusion that you'll suit me I'll just drop
you a line.

Victoria: I do hope you'll come here. I'm sure you'd
be happy.

Mrs Pogson: That's what I always say, the great thing
is to be 'appy. And I like your face. I don't mind
telling you that I've taken quite a fancy to you.

Victoria: I'm very glad to hear it.

Mrs Pogson: There, I was just going away and I knew
I 'ad one more question to ask you. My 'ead's like a
perfect sieve this morning. How many are you in
the family?

Victoria: Well, I have two children, but they give no
trouble at all, and just at present they're not
staying here.

Mrs Pogson: Oh, I don't mind children. I've had too
many meself to do that.

Victoria: And then there's just me and these two
gentlemen.

Mrs Pogson: I suppose you are married to one of them.

Victoria: I don't know what you mean by that, I'm
married to both.

Mrs Pogson: Both? Legally?

Victoria: Of course.

Mrs Pogson: Well, I do call that going it. (*With
growing indignation*) If it 'ad been just a
gentleman friend I'd 'ave 'ad nothing to say. I've
lived in the very best families and I'm quite used
to that. It keeps the lady quiet and good-tempered
and she ain't always fussing about one thing and
another. And if he lives in the 'ouse she ain't likely
to keep dinner waiting for 'alf an hour every other

217

day. But if you're married to 'im that's quite
another thing. It's not justice. If you ladies think
you're going to 'ave two 'usbands while many a
working woman can't even get one – well, all I
say is, it's not justice. I've bin a Conservative all
my life, but thank God I've got a vote now, and I
tell you straight what I'm going to do, I'm going to
vote Labour.

> *She flaunts out of the room and slams the door
> behind her.*

William: Bang!

Victoria (*furiously*): The position is intolerable. I
must have one husband. There are all sorts of ways
in which a husband is indispensable. But only one,
I cannot and will not have two.

Frederick: I have an idea.

William: It's sure to be a rotten one.

Frederick: Let's draw lots.

William: I knew it was a rotten one.

Victoria: How d'you mean, Freddie?

Frederick: Well, we'll take two pieces of paper and
make a cross on one of them. Then we'll fold them
up and put them in a hat. We'll draw, and the one
who draws the cross gets Victoria.

Victoria (*mollified*): That'll be rather thrilling.

William: I'd sooner toss for it. I'm lucky at tossing.

Frederick: Do you mean to say you funk it?

William: I didn't exactly funk it. It's an awful risk to
take.

Victoria: It'll be so romantic. Get some paper, Freddie.

Frederick: All right.

William (*worried*): I don't like it. This isn't my lucky
day. I saw the new moon through glass. I knew
something was going wrong the moment I opened
my egg this morning.

> **Frederick** *goes to a desk and takes out a sheet*

of paper which he tears in two. Then with his back turned he draws a cross.

Frederick: Whoever draws the blank paper renounces all claim to Victoria. He vanishes from the scene like a puff of smoke. He will never be heard of again.

William: I don't like it. I repeat that I only do it under protest.

Victoria: Now, Bill, don't be disagreeable the moment you come back.

Frederick: You'll have plenty of time for that during the next forty years.

Victoria: You seem rather above yourself, Freddie. Supposing *you* draw the blank?

Frederick: I saw a dappled horse this morning. What shall we put them in?

Victoria: The wastepaper basket is the best thing.

Frederick: I'll get it. Now you quite understand. One of these papers has a cross on it. I will put the two papers in the basket, and Victoria shall hold it. It is agreed that whoever draws a blank shall leave the house at once.

William (*faintly*): Yes.

Frederick (*handing her the basket*): Here you are, Victoria.

William (*with agitation*): Shake 'em well.

Victoria: All right. I say, isn't this thrilling?

Frederick: You draw first, Bill.

William (*shaking like a leaf*): No, I can't. I really can't.

Frederick: It's your right. You are Victoria's first husband.

Victoria: He's right there, Bill. You must have the first dip in the lucky bag.

William: This is awful. I'm sweating like a pig.

Victoria: It's too exciting. My heart is simply going pit-a-pat. I wonder which of you will get me.

William (*hesitating*): Going over the top is nothing to it.

Frederick: Courage, old man, courage.

William: It's no good, I can't. You must remember that my nerves are all to pieces after three years in a German prison.

Victoria: I see how much you love me, Bill.

Frederick: Shut your eyes, man, and make a plunge for the basket.

William: The only thing is to get it over. I wish I'd been a better man.

He draws out one of the pieces of paper and **Frederick** *takes the other. For a moment he looks at it nervously, unable to bring himself to unfold it.* **Frederick** *opens his, gives a sudden cry, and starts back.*

Frederick (*dramatically*): Blank. Blank. Blank.

William *gives a start, and quickly unravels the paper in his hand. He stares at it in horror.*

William: My God!

Victoria: Oh, my poor Freddie!

Frederick (*with enormous feeling*): Don't pity me, Victoria. I want all my courage now. I've lost you and I must bid you goodbye for ever.

Victoria: Oh, Freddie, this is too dreadful! You must come and see me from time to time.

Frederick: I couldn't. That is more than I could bear. I shall never forget you. You are the only woman I have ever loved.

At these words **William** *looks up and observes him curiously.*

Victoria: You'll never love another, will you? I shouldn't like that.

Frederick: How could I love anyone after you? Why, you might as well ask a man to see when the sun has gone down.

William: He can turn on the electric light, you know.

Frederick: Ah, you can jest. I am a broken-hearted and a ruined man.

William: I was only suggesting the possibility of consolation.

Victoria: I don't think that's very nice of you, Bill. I thought what he said extremely poetic. Besides, I don't want him to be consoled.

Frederick: Give me one last kiss, Victoria.

Victoria: Darling!

He seizes her in his arms and kisses her.

Frederick (*the hero of romance*): Goodbye. I go into the night.

William: Oh, aren't you going at once?

Frederick: I am.

William: Well, it happens to be the middle of the day.

Frederick (*with dignity*): I was speaking in metaphor.

William: Before you go you might just let me have a look at that other bit of paper, the one with the blank on it.

Frederick (*walking towards the door*): Oh, don't delay me with foolish trifling.

William (*intercepting him*): I'm sorry to detain you.

Frederick (*trying to dodge round him*): Why d'you want to see it?

William (*preventing him*): Mere curiosity.

Frederick (*trying the other side*): Really, Bill, I don't know how you can be so heartless as to give way to curiosity when my heart is one great aching wound.

William: I should like to have the two pieces framed, an interesting souvenir of an important occasion.

Frederick: Any other piece will do just as well. I threw that one in the fire.

William: Oh no, you didn't. You put it in your pocket.

Frederick: I've had enough of this. Can't you see that I'm a desperate man?

William: Not half so desperate as I am. If you don't give me that bit of paper quietly I'll take it from you.

Frederick: Go to blazes!

William: Give it up.

He makes a dash for **Frederick**, *who dodges; he pursues him round the room.*

Victoria: What's the matter? Have you both gone mad?

William: You'll have to sooner or later.

Frederick: I'll see you damned first.

Victoria: Why don't you give it him?

Frederick: Not if I know it.

Victoria: Why not?

Frederick: I won't have my feelings hurt like this.

William: I'll hurt a lot more than your feelings in a minute.

Frederick *makes a sudden bolt for the door, but* **William** *catches him.*

William: Gotcher. Now will you give it up?

Frederick: Not on your life.

William: I'll break your bally arm if you don't.

Frederick (*writhing*): Oh, you devil! Stop it. You're hurting me.

William: I'm trying to.

Frederick: Hit him on the head with the poker, Victoria.

William: Don't be unladylike, Victoria.

Frederick: You filthy Boche. All right, here it is.

William *lets him go and* **Frederick** *takes the paper out of his pocket. Just as* **William** *thinks he is going to give it him, he puts it in his mouth.*

William (*seizing him by the throat*): Take it out of your mouth.

Frederick *takes it out and throws it on the floor.*

Frederick: I don't know if you call yourself a gentleman.

    William *takes up the paper and unfolds it.*

William: You dirty dog.
Victoria: What's the matter?

    He walks over and hands it to her.

William: Look.
Victoria: Why, it's got a cross on it.
William (*indignantly*): They both had crosses on them.
Victoria: I don't understand.
William: Don't you? He was making quite sure that *I* shouldn't draw a blank.

    Victoria *looks at him in astonishment. There is a moment's pause.*

Frederick (*magnanimously*): I did it for your sake, Victoria. I knew that your heart was set on Bill, only you couldn't bear to hurt my feelings, so I thought I'd make it easier for you.
Victoria: That was just like you, Freddie. You have a charming nature.
William (*acidly*): It almost brings tears to my eyes.
Frederick: I'm made that way. I can't help sacrificing myself for others.

    Taylor *comes in.*

Taylor: May I speak to you for a minute, madam.
Victoria: Not now, I'm busy.
Taylor: I'm afraid it's very urgent, madam.
Victoria: Oh, very well, I'll come. Don't say anything important till I come back.

    Taylor *holds the door open for her, and she goes out.*

Frederick: How did you guess?

223

William: You were so devilish calm about it.

Frederick: That was the calm of despair.

> **William** *is sitting on the sofa. He happens to put his hand behind him and feels something hard. With a puzzled expression he puts down his hand between the seat and the back of the sofa and draws out first one boot and then another.*

William: My boots!

Frederick: I knew I'd put them somewhere.

William: You didn't put them anywhere. You hid them, you dirty dog.

Frederick: It's a lie. Why the dickens should I hide your rotten old boots?

William: You were afraid I'd do a bunk.

Frederick: You needn't get ratty about it. I only ascribed to you the disinterested motives that I – that I have myself. I may be wrong, but, after all, it's a noble error.

William: One might almost think you didn't want Victoria.

> **Frederick** *looks at him for a moment thoughtfully, then he makes up his mind to make a clean breast of it.*

Frederick: Bill, old chap, you know I'm not the sort of man to say a word against my wife.

William: Nor am I the sort of man to listen to a word against mine.

Frederick: But, hang it all, if a fellow can't discuss his wife dispassionately with her first husband, who can he discuss her with?

William: I can't imagine unless it's with her second.

Frederick: Tell me what you really think of Victoria.

William: She's the sweetest little woman in the world.

Frederick: No man could want a better wife.

William: She's pretty.

Frederick: Charming.

William: Delightful.

Frederick: I confess that sometimes I've thought it hard that when I wanted a thing it was selfishness, and when she wanted it, it was only her due.

William: I don't mind admitting that sometimes I used to wonder why it was only natural for me to sacrifice my inclinations, but in her the proof of a beautiful nature.

Frederick: It has tried me now and then that in every difference of opinion I should always be wrong and she should always be right.

William: Sometimes I couldn't quite understand why my engagements were made to be broken, while nothing in the world must interfere with hers.

Frederick: I have asked myself occasionally why my time was of no importance while hers was so precious.

William: I did sometimes wish I could call my soul my own.

Frederick: The fact is, I'm not worthy of her, Bill. As you so justly say, no man could want a better wife . . .

William (*interrupting*): No, you said that.

Frederick: But I'm fed up. If you'd been dead I'd have seen it through like a gentleman, but you've turned up like a bad shilling. Now you take up the white man's burden.

William: I'll see you damned first.

Frederick: She must have one husband.

William: Look here, there's only one thing to do. She must choose between us.

Frederick: That's not giving me a chance.

William: I don't know what you mean by that. I think it's extraordinarily magnanimous on my part.

Frederick: Magnanimous be hanged. I've got a charming nature and I'm extremely handsome. Victoria will naturally choose me.

William: Heaven knows I'm not vain, but I've always been given to understand that I'm an almost perfect specimen of manly beauty. My conversation is not only amusing, but instructive.

Frederick: I'd rather toss for it.

William: I'm not going to risk anything like that. I've had enough of your hanky-panky.

Frederick: I thought I was dealing with a gentleman.

William: Here she comes.

Victoria *comes in. She is in a temper.*

Victoria: All the servants have given notice now.

Frederick: They haven't!

Victoria: I've done everything in the world for them. I've given them double wages. I've fed them on the fat of the land. I've given them my own butter and my own sugar to eat.

Frederick: Only because they were bad for your figure, Victoria.

Victoria: They didn't know that. I've given them all the evenings out that I really didn't want them. I've let them bring the whole British army to tea here. And now they give me notice.

William: It's a bit thick, I must say.

Victoria: I argued with them, I appealed to them, I practically went down on my knees to them. They wouldn't listen. They're going to walk out of the house this afternoon.

William: Oh, well, Freddie and I will do the housework until you get some more.

Victoria: Do you know that it's harder to get a parlour-maid than a peerage? Why, every day at Paddington Registry Office you'll see a queue of old bachelors taking out licences to marry their cooks. It's the only way to keep them.

William: Well, Victoria, we've decided that there's only one thing to be done. You must choose between us.

Victoria: How can I? I adore you both. Besides, there's so little to choose between you.

William: Oh, I don't know about that. Freddie has a charming nature and he's extremely handsome.

Frederick: I wish you wouldn't say that, Bill. Heaven knows you're not vain, but I must tell you to your face that you're an almost perfect specimen of manly beauty, and your conversation is not only amusing but instructive.

Victoria: I don't want to hurt anybody's feelings.

Frederick: Before you decide, I feel it only fair to make a confession to you. I could not bear it if our future life were founded on a lie. Victoria, in my department there is a stenographer. She is of the feminine gender. She has blue eyes and little yellow curls at the nape of her neck. The rest I leave to your imagination.

Victoria: How abominable. And I always thought you had such a nice mind.

Frederick: I am unworthy of you. I know it only too, too well. You can never forgive me.

William: Dirty dog.

Victoria: That certainly simplifies matters. I don't quite see myself as the third lady in the back row of a harem.

William: You would run no risk of being that in Canada. Women are scarce in Manitoba.

Victoria: What *are* you talking about?

William: I have come to the conclusion that England offers me no future now the war is over. I shall resign my commission. The empire need workers, and I am ready to take my part in reconstruction. Make me the happiest of men, Victoria, and we'll emigrate together.

Victoria: To Canada?

Frederick: Where the sables come from.

Victoria: Not the best ones.

William: I shall buy a farm. I think it would be a very

good plan if you employed your leisure in learning how to cook the simple fare on which we shall live. I believe you can wash?

Victoria (*with asperity*): Lace.

William: But I think you should also learn how to milk cows.

Victoria: I don't like cows.

William: I see the idea appeals to you. It will be a wonderful life, Victoria. You'll light the fire and scrub the floors, and you'll cook the dinner and wash the clothes. You'll vote.

Victoria: And what shall I do in my spare moments?

William: We will cultivate your mind by reading the *Encyclopaedia Britannica* together. Take a good look at us, Victoria, and say which of us it's to be.

Victoria: To tell you the truth, I don't see why it should be either.

Frederick: Hang it all, it must be one or the other.

Victoria: I think no one can deny that since the day I married you I've sacrificed myself in every mortal way. I've worked myself to the bone to make you comfortable. Very few men have ever had such a wife as I've been to both of you! But one must think of oneself sometimes.

William: How true.

Victoria: The war is over now, and I think I've done my bit. I've married two D.S.O.s. Now I want to marry a Rolls-Royce.

Frederick (*astonishment*): But I thought you adored us.

Victoria: Well, you see, I adore both of you. It's six of one and half a dozen of the other, and the result is . . .

William: A wash-out.

Frederick: Hang it all, I think it's a bit thick. Do you mean to say that you've fixed up to marry somebody else behind our back?

Victoria: You know I wouldn't do a thing like that, Freddie.

Frederick: Well, I don't tumble.

Victoria: My dear Freddie, have you ever studied the domestic habits of the unicorn?

Frederick: I am afraid my education was very much neglected.

Victoria: The unicorn is a shy and somewhat timid animal, and it is impossible to catch him with the snares of the hunter. But he is strangely impressionable to the charms of the fair sex. When he hears the frou-frou of a silk petticoat he forgets his native caution. In short, a pretty woman can lead him by the nose.

Taylor comes in.

Taylor: Mr Leicester Paton is downstairs in his car, madam.

Victoria: Is it the Rolls-Royce?

Taylor: I think it is, madam.

Victoria (*with a smile of triumph*): Say I'll come down at once.

Taylor: Very good, madam.

Exit.

Victoria: The unicorn's going to take me out to luncheon.

She makes a long nose at them and goes out.

CURTAIN

Act III

The kitchen. At one end is a range, with a gas-stove; at the other end a dresser on which are plates and dishes. At the back a door leads out to the area and near it is a window, with iron bars, through which

229

can be seen the area steps and persons ascending and descending them. In the middle of the room is a kitchen table, and here and there kitchen chairs. There is a linoleum on the floor. The place is clean, sanitary, and cheerful.

William *is sitting on one of the chairs with his feet on another, reading a thin, paper-bound novel of the sort that is published at threepence and sold by the newsagent round the corner.* **Frederick** *comes in with a scuttle full of coals.*

Frederick (*putting down the scuttle*): I say, these coals weigh about a ton. You might carry them upstairs.

William (*cheerfully*): I might, but I'm not going to.

Frederick: I wouldn't ask you, only since I was wounded in the arm serving my country I haven't the strength I had once.

William (*suspiciously*): Which arm were you wounded in?

Frederick (*promptly*): Both arms.

William: Carry the coals on your head then. I believe that's the best way really. And they say it improves the figure.

Frederick: You heartless devil.

William: I'd do it like a shot, old man, only the doctor said it was very bad for my heart to carry heavy weights.

Frederick: What's the matter with your heart? You said you were wounded in the head.

William: Besides, it isn't my work. I'm doing the cooking. You really can't expect me to do housework as well.

Frederick: *Are* you doing the cooking? It looks to me as though you were just sitting about doing nothing. I don't see why I should have to sweat my life out.

William: You see, you have no organization.

Housework's perfectly simple, only you must have organization. I have organization. That's my secret.

Frederick: I was a mug to say I'd do the housework. I might have known you'd freeze on to a soft job if there was one.

William: I naturally undertook to do what I could do best. That is one of the secrets of organization. Cooking is an art. Any fool can do housework.

Frederick: I'll give you a thick ear in a minute. You just try and get a shine on a pair of boots and see if it's easy.

William: I don't believe you know how to shine a pair of boots. Do you spit on them?

Frederick: No, only on the silver.

William: You just look nippy and get the table laid while I finish my book.

Frederick (*gloomily*): Is it luncheon or dinner?

William: I don't know yet, but we're going to have it down here because it's easier for dishing up. Organization again.

Frederick: What does Victoria say to that?

William: I haven't told her yet.

Frederick: She's in an awful temper this morning.

William: Why?

Frederick: Because the water in the bathroom wasn't hot.

William: Wasn't it?

Frederick: You know very well it wasn't.

William: I think cold baths are much better for people. There'd be a damned sight less illness about if cold baths were compulsory.

Frederick: Tell that to the horse-marines. You were too lazy to get up in time. That's all there is to it.

William: I wish you'd get on with your work instead of interrupting me all the time.

Frederick: You don't look as if you were so busy as all that.

William: I want to find out if the nursery governess

married the duke after all. You should read this after I've finished it.

Frederick: I don't have time for reading. When I take on a job I like to do it properly.

William: I wish you wouldn't mumble.

Frederick: What is there for lunch? (*He goes over to the stove and takes a cover off a saucepan.*) What's this mess?

William: Those are potatoes. You might give one of them a jab with a fork to see how they're getting on.

Frederick: It seems rather unfriendly, doesn't it?

William: Oh no, they're used to it.

> **Frederick** *takes a fork and tries to transfix a potato.*

Frederick: Damn it all, they won't stop still. They're wriggling all over the place. Wriggle, wriggle, little tater. How I wonder who's your mater. Poetry! Come here, you little devil. Woa there.

William: I say, don't make such a row. This is awfully exciting. He's plunged both his hands into her hair.

Frederick: Dirty trick, I call it.

William: Why? She'd washed it.

Frederick (*bringing out a potato*): Damn it all, they're not skinned.

William: I suppose you mean peeled.

Frederick: If there's anything I dislike it's potatoes in their skins.

William: It's simply waste to peel potatoes. I never peel potatoes.

Frederick: Is that organization?

William: Well, if you ask me, that's just what it is.

Frederick: Ever since I've been at the War Office I've heard fellows talk of organization, but I never could find anyone to tell me just what it was. It's beginning to dawn on me now.

William (*still reading*): Well, what is it?

Frederick: I'm not going to tell you unless you listen.

William (*looking up*): He's just glued his lips to hers. Well?

Frederick: Organization means getting someone else to do your job for you if you can, and if you can't, letting it rip.

William: I suppose you think you're funny.

Frederick (*putting the potato back in the saucepan*): The steak smells as though it was almost done.

William: Done? It's only been on about a quarter of an hour.

Frederick: But in a grill-room they do you steak in ten minutes.

William: I don't care about that. You cook meat a quarter of an hour for every pound. I should have thought any fool knew that.

Frederick: What's that got to do with it?

William: I bought three pounds of steak, so I'm going to cook it for three-quarters of an hour.

Frederick: Well, it looks to me as if it wanted eating now.

William: That's only its cunning. It won't be ready for ages yet. I wish you'd let me get on with my story.

Frederick (*puzzled*): But look here, if there were three steaks of a pound each you'd cook them a quarter of an hour each.

William: Exactly. That's what I say. That comes to three-quarters of an hour.

Frederick: But, hang it all, it's the same quarter of an hour.

William: You make me tired. You might just as well say that because three men can walk four miles an hour each man can walk twelve miles an hour.

Frederick: But that's just what I do say.

William: Well, it's damned idiotic, that's all.

Frederick: No, but I mean exactly the opposite. That's

what *you* say. You've got me confused now. We'll have to start all over again.

William: I shall never finish this story if you go on like this.

Frederick: It's a very important matter. Let's get a pencil and a piece of paper and work it out. We must get it right.

William: For goodness' sake go and clean knives or something, and don't bother your head about things that are no concern of yours.

Frederick: Who's going to eat the steak?

William: You won't if you're not careful.

Frederick: If I'm careful I don't think I will.

William (*beginning to get peevish*): Cooking has its rules like everything else, and it's just as little use arguing about them as arguing about women.

Frederick: Now look here, if you cut that steak into three, would there be three pounds of steak or not?

William: Certainly not. There'd be three steaks of one pound, and that's quite another matter.

Frederick: But it would be the same steak.

William (*emphatically*): It wouldn't be the same steak. It would be an entirely different steak.

Frederick: Do you mean to tell me that if you had a steak of a hundred pounds you'd cook it for twenty-five hours?

William: Yes, and if I had a steak of a thousand pounds I'd cook it for ten days.

Frederick: It seems an awful waste of gas.

William: I don't care about that, it's logic.

Enter **Victoria.**

Victoria: I really think it's too bad of you. I've been ringing the bell for the last quarter of an hour. There are two men in the house, and you neither of you pay the least attention.

William: We were having an argument.

Frederick: Let me put it before you, Victoria.

William: It has nothing to do with Victoria. I'm the cook, and I won't have anyone come interfering in my kitchen.

Frederick: You must do something, Victoria. The steak will be absolutely uneatable.

Victoria: I don't care. I never eat steak.

William: It's all you'll get for luncheon.

Victoria: I shan't be here for luncheon.

William: Why not?

Victoria: Because – because Mr Leicester Paton has made me an offer of marriage and I have accepted it.

Frederick: But you've got two husbands already, Victoria.

Victoria: I imagine you'll both be gentleman enough to put no obstacle in the way of my getting my freedom.

A ring is heard.

Frederick: Hulloa, who's that?

Victoria: That is my solicitor.

Frederick: Your what?

Victoria: I told him to come at once. Go and open the door, Freddie, will you?

Frederick: What the dickens does he want?

Victoria: He's going to fix up my divorce.

Frederick: You're not letting the grass grow under your feet.

He goes out.

William: This is a desperate step you're taking, Victoria.

Victoria: I had to do something. You must see that it's quite impossible for a woman to live without servants. I had no one to do me up this morning.

William: How an earth did you manage?

Victoria: I had to put on something that didn't need doing up.

William: That seems an adequate way out of the difficulty.

Victoria: It so happens that the one frock that didn't need doing up was the one frock I didn't want to wear.

William: You look ravishing in it all the same.

Victoria (*rather stiffly*): I'd sooner you didn't pay me compliments, Bill.

William: Why not?

Victoria: Well, now that I'm engaged to Leicester Paton I don't think it's very good form.

William: Have you quite made up your mind to divorce me?

Victoria: Quite.

William: In that case, I can almost look upon you as another man's wife.

Victoria: What do you mean by that?

William: Only that I can make love to you without feeling a thundering ass.

Victoria (*smiling*): I'm not going to let you make love to me.

William: You can't prevent me from telling you that you're the loveliest thing that ever turned a poor man's head.

Victoria: I can close my ears.

William (*taking her hands*): Impossible, for I shall hold your hands.

Victoria: I shall scream.

William: You can't because I shall kiss your lips.

He does so.

Victoria: Oh, Bill, what a pity it is you were ever my husband. I'm sure you'd make a charming lover.

William: I have often thought that is the better part.

Victoria: Take care. They're just coming. It would never do for my solicitor to find me in my husband's arms.

William: It would be outrageous.

Frederick ushers in the visitor. **Mr. A. B.
Raham** *is a solicitor. There is nothing more
to be said about him.*

Victoria: How do you do, Mr Raham? Do you know
my husbands?

Mr Raham: I'm pleased to meet you, gentlemen. I
dare say it would facilitate matters if I am told which
of you is which, and which is the other.

Victoria: This is Major Cardew, my first husband, and
this is my second husband, Major Lowndes.

Mr Raham: Ah, that makes it quite clear. Both majors.
Interesting coincidence.

William: I suppose that Mrs Lowndes has put you in
possession of the facts, Mr Raham?

Mr Raham: I think so. We had a long talk at my office
yesterday.

Frederick: You can quite understand that it's a
position of some delicacy for Mrs Cardew.

Mr Raham (*puzzled*): Mrs Cardew? Where does Mrs
Cardew come in?

Frederick: This is Mrs Cardew.

Mr Raham: Oh, I see what you mean. That, in short,
is the difficulty. Is this lady Mrs Cardew or Mrs
Lowndes? Well, the fact is, she has decided to be
neither.

Victoria: I've just broken it to them.

William: You find us still staggering from the shock.

Frederick: Staggering.

Mr Raham: She has determined to divorce you both.
I have told her that this is not necessary, since she
is obviously the wife of only one of you.

Victoria (*argumentatively*): In that case, what am I to
the other?

Mr Raham: Well, Mrs Cardew, or shall we say
Lowndes? I hardly like to mention it to a lady, but
if you'll excuse me saying so, you're his concubine.

William: I rather like that, it sounds so damned Oriental.

Victoria (*indignantly*): I never heard of such a thing.

William: Oh, Fatima, your face is like the full moon, and your eyes are like the eyes of a young gazelle. Come, dance to me to the sound of the lute.

Victoria: Well, that settles it. I shall divorce them both just to prove to everyone that they're both my husbands.

Frederick: I think it's just as well to take no risks.

Mr Raham: Do I understand that you two gentlemen are agreeable?

William: Speaking for myself, I am prepared to sacrifice my feelings, deep as they are, to the happiness of Victoria.

Mr Raham: Very nicely and feelingly put.

Victoria: He always was a gentleman.

Mr Raham (*to Frederick*): Now you, Major Cardew.

Frederick: My name is Lowndes.

Mr Raham: My mistake. Of course you're Major Lowndes. I made a mental note of it when we were introduced. Cardew – camel-face. Lowndes – litigation. Pelmanism, you know.

Frederick: I see. It doesn't seem very effective, though.

Mr Raham: Anyhow, that is neither here nor there. Will you give this lady the freedom she desires?

Frederick: I will. (*With a puzzled look*) When did I last say those words? (*Remembering*) Of course, the marriage service.

Mr Raham: Well, so far so good. I am under the impression that when it comes to the point we shall not need to take both you gentlemen to court, but I quite agree with Mrs Lowndes-Cardew that it will save time and trouble if we get up the case against both of you in the same way. Since you will neither of you defend the case, there is no need for you to go the expense of legal advice, so I propose to go into the whole matter with you now.

Victoria: You can feel quite easy taking to Mr Raham's advice. He has arranged more divorce cases than any man in England.

Mr Raham: I venture to say that there are few of the best families in this country that haven't made use of my services in one way or another. Outraged husband, deceived wife, co-respondent or intervener; it's hardly likely that anyone who is anyone won't figure sooner or later in one or other of these capacities. And although it's I as says it, if he's wise he comes to me. My maxim has always been: Do it quickly; don't let's have a lot of fuss and bother. And, just to show you how my system works, there are ladies for whom I've got a divorce from three or four successive husbands, and never a word of scandal has sullied the purity of their fair name.

William: You must be a very busy man.

Mr Raham: I assure you, major, I'm one of the busiest men in London.

William: Fortunately, some marriages are happy.

Mr Raham: Don't you believe it, Major Cardew. There are no happy marriages. But there are some that are tolerable.

Victoria: You are a pessimist, Mr Raham. I have made both my husbands ideally happy.

Mr Raham: But I will come to the point. Though, perhaps, it is hardly necessary, I will point out to you gentlemen what the law of the country needs in order to free a couple who, for reasons which merely concern themselves, have decided that they prefer to part company. If a husband wishes to divorce his wife he need prove nothing but adultery, but the English law recognizes the natural polygamy of man, and when a wife desires to divorce her husband she must prove besides cruelty or desertion. Let us take these first. Do you wish the cause of offence to be cruelty *or* desertion?

Victoria: Personally, I should prefer desertion.

William: Certainly. I should very much dislike to be cruel to you, Victoria.

Frederick: And you know I could never hurt a fly.

Mr Raham: Then we will settle on desertion. I think myself it is the more gentlemanly way, and besides, it is more easily proved. The procedure is excessively simple. Mrs Cardew-Lowndes will write you a letter, which I shall dictate, asking you to return to her – the usual phrase is 'to make a home for her' – and you will refuse. I propose that you should both give me your refusals now.

William (*surprised*): Before we've had the letter?

Mr Raham: Precisely. The letter which she will write, and which is read out in court, is so touching that on one occasion the husband, about to be divorced, was so moved that he immediately returned to his wife. She was very angry indeed, and so now I invariably get the refusal first.

William: It's so difficult to write an answer to a letter that hasn't been written.

Mr Raham: To meet that difficulty I have also prepared the replies. Have you a fountain-pen?

William: Yes.

Mr Raham (*taking a piece of paper from his pocket-book and two sheets of paper*): If you will kindly write to my dictation, we will settle the matter at once. Here is a sheet of paper.

William (*taking it*): The address is – Hotel Majestic.

Mr Raham: You will see the point later. Here is a piece for you, major.

He gives it to **Frederick.**

Frederick: Do we both write the same letter?

Mr Raham: Certainly not. I have two letters that I generally make use of, and I propose that you

should each of you write one of them. The note of
one is sorrow rather than anger. The other is
somewhat vituperative. You can decide among
yourselves which of you had better write which.

Victoria: They both habitually swore at me, but I
think Bill's language was more varied.

Mr Raham: That settles it. Are you ready, Major
Lowndes?

Frederick (*getting ready to write*): Fire away.

Mr Raham (*dictating*): My dear Victoria, I have given
your letter anxious consideration. If I thought
there was any hope of our making a greater success
of married life in the future than we have in the
past I should be the first to suggest that we should
make one more attempt.

William: Very touching.

Mr Raham (*continuing*): But I have regretfully come
to the conclusion that to return to you would only
be to cause a recurrence of the unhappy life from
which I know that you have suffered no less than
I. I am bound therefore definitely to refuse your
request. I do not propose under any circumstances
to return to you. Yours sincerely. – Now sign your
full name.

Victoria: A very nice letter, Freddie. I shall always
think pleasantly of you.

Frederick: I have my points.

Mr Raham: Now, Major Cardew, are you ready?

William: Quite.

Mr Raham: My dear Victoria, I am in receipt of your
letter asking me to return to you. Our life together
has been a hell upon earth, and I have long realized
that our marriage was a tragic mistake. You have
sickened me with scenes and tortured me with
jealousy. If you have tried to make me happy you
have succeeded singularly ill. I trust that I shall
never see you again, and nothing in the world will

induce me ever to resume a life which I can only
describe as a miserable degradation.

William: Thick, eh?

Mr Raham: Now the crowning touch. Mark the irony
of the polite ending: I beg to remain yours most
sincerely. – Now sign your name.

William: I've signed it.

Mr Raham: Then that is settled. Now we only have
to go into court, apply for a decree for restitution
of conjugal rights, and six months later bring an
action for divorce.

Victoria: Six months later! But when shall I be free,
then?

Mr Raham: In about a year.

Victoria: Oh, but that won't do at all. I must have
my freedom by – well, before the season ends, at all
events.

Mr Raham: As soon as that?

Victoria: The Derby, if possible. Certainly by the Two
Thousand Guineas.

Mr Raham (*shrugging his shoulders*): In that case the
only thing is cruelty.

Victoria: It can't be helped. They'll have to be cruel.

Frederick: I don't like the idea, Victoria.

Victoria: Try and be a little unselfish for once, darling.

William: I could never strike a woman.

Victoria: If I don't mind I don't see why you should.

Mr Raham: Cruelty has its advantages. If it's properly
witnessed it has a convincing air which desertion
never has.

Victoria: My mother will swear to anything.

Mr Raham: Servants are better. The judges are often
unduly suspicious of the mother-in-law's testimony.
Of course, one has to be careful. Once, I remember,
on my instructions the guilty husband hit the lady
I was acting for in the jaw, which unfortunately
knocked out her false teeth. The gentleman she
had arranged to marry happened to be present and

he was so startled that he took the night train for the Continent and has never been heard of since.

William: I'm happy to say that Victoria's teeth are all her own.

Mr Raham: On another occasion I recommended a gentleman to take a stick and give his wife a few strokes with it. I don't know if he got excited or what, but he gave her a regular hiding.

Victoria: How awful!

Mr Raham: It was indeed, for she threw her arms round his neck, and, saying she adored him, refused to have anything more to do with the divorce. She was going to marry a colonel in the army, and he was most offensive to me about it. I had to tell him that if he didn't leave my office I would send for the police.

Victoria: You're dreadfully discouraging.

Mr Raham: Oh, I merely tell you that to show you what may happen. But I have devised my own system and have never known it fail. I always arrange for three definite acts of cruelty. First the dinner-table. Now, please listen to me carefully, gentlemen, and follow my instructions to the letter. When you have tasted your soup you throw down the spoon with a clatter and say: Good Lord, this soup is uneatable. Can't you get a decent cook? You madam, will answer: I do my best, darling. Upon which you, crying with a loud voice: Take that, you damned fool, throw the plate straight at her. With a little ingenuity the lady can dodge the plate, and the only damage is done to the tablecloth.

Victoria: I like that.

Mr Raham: The second act is a little more violent. I suppose you have a revolver.

William: At all events, I can get one.

Mr Raham: Having carefully removed the cartridges, you ring the bell for the servant, and just as she opens the door, you point it at the lady and say: You lying devil, I'll kill you. Then you, madam, give a loud shriek, and cry to the maid: Oh, save me, save me.

Victoria: I shall love doing that. So dramatic.

Mr Raham: I think it's effective. When the servant tells her story in court it is very seldom that an audible thrill does not pass over the audience. They describe it in the papers as: Sensation.

Victoria (*practising*): Oh, save me. Save me.

Mr Raham: Now we come to physical as opposed to moral cruelty. It's as well to have two witnesses to this. The gentleman takes the lady by the throat, at the same time hissing malevolently: I'll throttle you if I swing for it, by God. It's very important to leave a bruise so that the doctor, who should be sent for immediately, can swear to it.

Victoria: I don't like that part so much.

Mr Raham: Believe me, it's no more unpleasant than having a tooth stopped. Now if one of your gentlemen would just go up to the lady we'll practise that. I set great store on this particular point, and it's important that there should be no mistake. Major Cardew, would you mind obliging?

William: Not at all.

Victoria: Be careful, Bill.

William: Do I take her with both hands or only one?

Mr Raham: Only one.

William *seizes* Victoria *by the throat.*

Mr Raham: That's right. If he doesn't press hard enough kick him on the shins.

William: If you do, Victoria, I swear I'll kick you back.

Mr Raham: That's the spirit. You can't make a bruise without a little violence. Now hiss.

Victoria: I'm choking.

Mr Raham: Hiss, hiss.

William: I'll throttle you if I swing for it, by God.

Mr Raham: Splendid! A real artist. You're as good as divorced already.

Victoria: He did say it well, didn't he? It really made my blood turn cold.

Frederick: Do you want me to do it too?

Mr Raham: Now you've seen the idea I think it'll do if you just practice it once or twice with Major Cardew.

Frederick: Oh, all right.

Mr Raham: Now we come to a point trivial enough in itself, but essential in order to satisfy the requirements of our English law. Adultery.

William: That I think you can safely leave to us.

Mr Raham: By no means. I think that would be most dangerous.

William: Hang it all, man, human nature can surely be trusted there.

Mr Raham: We are not dealing with human nature, we are dealing with law.

William: Law be blowed. With the price of a supper in my pocket and an engaging manner I am prepared to supply you with all the evidence you want.

Mr Raham: I am shocked and horrified by your suggestion. Do you expect a man in my position to connive at immorality.

William: Immorality. Well, there must be – shall we say a *soupçon* of it – under the painful circumstances.

Mr Raham: Not at all. I always arrange this part of the proceedings with the most scrupulous regard to propriety. And before we go any further I should like to inform you that unless you are prepared to put out of your mind anything that is suggestive of indecent behaviour I shall decline to have anything more to do with the case.

Victoria: I think you must have a nasty mind, Bill.

William: But, my dear Victoria, I only wanted to make

things easy for you. I apologize. I put myself in your hands, Mr Raham.

Mr Raham: Then please listen to me. I will engage a suite of rooms for you at the Hotel Majestic. You will remember it was from there you wrote the letter in which you declined to return to your wife. The judge never fails to remark on the coincidence. On a date to be settled hereafter you will come to my office, where you will meet a lady.

William: Do you mean to say you provide her too?

Mr Raham: Certainly.

Frederick: What's she like?

Mr Raham: A most respectable person. I have employed her in these cases for many years.

William: It sounds as though she made a business of it.

Mr Raham: She does.

Frederick: What!

Mr Raham: Yes, she had the idea – a most ingenious one to my mind – that in these days of specialized professions there was great need for someone to undertake the duties of intervener. That is the name by which the lady is known adultery with whom is the motive for divorce. She has been employed by the best legal firms in London, and she has figured in practically all the fashionable divorces of the last fifteen years.

William: You amaze me.

Mr Raham: I have felt it my duty to give her all the work I can on account of a paralysed father, whom she supports entirely by her exertions.

Victoria: Not an unpleasant existence, I should imagine.

Mr Raham: If you knew her you would realize that no thought of that has ever entered her mind. A most unselfish, noble-minded woman.

William: Does she make money by it?

Mr Raham: Sufficient for her simple needs. She only charges twenty guineas for her services.

William: I'm sure I could get it done for less.

Mr Raham: Not by a woman of any refinement.

William: Well, well, with most of us it's only once in a lifetime.

Mr Raham: I will proceed. You will fetch this lady at my office, and you will drive with her to the Hotel Majestic, where you will register as Major and Mrs Cardew. You will be shown into the suite of rooms which I shall engage for you, and supper will be served in the sitting-room. You will partake of this, and you will drink champagne.

William: I should like to choose the brand myself.

Mr Raham (*magnanimously*): I have no objection to that.

William: Thanks.

Mr Raham: Then you will play cards. Miss Montmorency is a wonderful card-player. She not only has an unparalleled knowledge of all games for two, but she can do a great number of tricks. In this way you will find the night passes without tediousness, and in the morning you will ring for breakfast.

Frederick: I'm not sure if I should have much appetite for it.

Mr Raham: I never mind my clients having brandy and soda instead. It looks well in the waiter's evidence. And after having paid your bill, you will take Miss Montmorency in a taxi-cab and deposit her at my office.

William: It sounds a devil of a beano.

Frederick: I should like to see her first.

Mr Raham: That is perfectly easy. I know that ladies in these cases often like to see the intervener themselves. Ladies are sometimes very suspicious, and even though they're getting rid of their husbands, they don't want them to – well, run any risks; and so I took the liberty of bringing Miss Montmorency with me. She is waiting in the taxi at the door, and if you like I will go and fetch her.

Frederick: A1. I'll go along and bring her down.

Victoria: Is she the sort of person I should like to meet, Mr Raham?

Mr Raham: Oh, a perfect lady. She comes from one of the best families in Shropshire.

Victoria: Do fetch her, Freddie. Now I come to think of it, I should like to see her. Men are so weak, and I shall be easier in my mind if I can be sure that these poor boys won't be led astray.

     Frederick *goes out.*

William: Do you mean to say that with this evidence you will be able to get a divorce?

Mr Raham: Not a doubt of it. I've got hundreds.

William: I am only a soldier, and I dare say you will not be surprised if I am mentally deficient.

Mr Raham: Not at all. Not at all.

William: Why on earth does such a state of things exist?

Mr Raham: Ah, that is a question which at one time I often ask myself. I confess it seemed to me that when two married persons agreed to separate it was nobody's business but their own. I think if they announced their determination before a justice of the peace, and were given six months to think the matter over, so that they might be certain they knew their minds, the marriage might then be dissolved without further trouble. Many lies would never be told, much dirty linen would never be washed in public, and the sanctity of the marriage tie would be strengthened rather than lessened if the world were spared the spectacle of the sordid aspect the state which is called blessed too often wears. There would be a notable saving of time, money and decency. But at last I hit upon the explanation.

William: What is it, then?

Mr Raham: If the law were always wise and reasonable it would be obeyed so easily that to obey the law would become an instinct. Now, it is not for the good of the community that the people should be too law-abiding. So our ancestors in the wisdom of their hearts devised certain laws which were vexatious or absurd, so that men should break them and therefore be led insensibly to break others.

William: But why is it not for the good of the community that the people should be too law-abiding.

Mr Raham: My dear sir, how else would the lawyers earn their living?

William: I had forgotten. I see your point.

Mr Raham: I hope I have convinced you.

William: Completely.

At this moment **Frederick** *comes in. He is pale and dishevelled. He staggers into the room like a man who has been exposed to a tremendous shock.*

Frederick (*gasping*): Brandy! Brandy!

William: What's the matter?

Frederick: Brandy!

He fills half a glass of brandy and tosses it off. A voice is heard outside the door.

Miss Montmorency: Is this the way?

Mr Raham: Come straight in, Miss Montmorency.

She enters. She is a spinster of uncertain age. She might be fifty-five. She looks rather like a hard-boiled egg, but there is in her gestures a languid grace. She speaks with a slight drawl, pronouncing her words with

*refinement, and her manner is a mixture of
affability and condescension. She might be a
governess of a very good family in the
suburbs. Her respectability is portentous.*

Miss Montmorency: But this is the kitchen.

> **William** *takes a long look at her, then gets up
> and goes to the brandy. His hands shakes so
> violently that the neck of the bottle rattles
> against the glass. He takes a long drink.*

Victoria: I'm afraid it's the only room in the house
that's habitable at the moment.

Miss Montmorency: To the practised observer the
signs of domestic infelicity jump to the eye, as the
French say.

Mr Raham: Miss Montmorency – Mrs Frederick
Lowndes.

Miss Montmorency (*graciously*): I'm charmed to
make your acquaintance. The injured wife, I
presume?

Victoria: Er – yes.

Miss Montmorency: So sad. So sad. I'm afraid the war
is responsible for the rupture of many happy
marriages. I'm booked up for weeks ahead. So sad.
so sad.

Victoria: Do sit down, won't you.

Miss Montmorency: Thank you. Do you mind if I get
out my note-book? I like to get everything perfectly
clear, and my memory isn't what it was.

Victoria: Of course.

Miss Montmorency: And now, which of these
gentlemen is the erring husband?

Victoria: Well, they both are.

Miss Montmorency: Oh, really. And which are you
going to marry after you've got your divorce.

Victoria: Neither.

Miss Montmorency: This is a very peculiar case, Mr
Raham. When I saw these two gentlemen I

naturally concluded that one of them was the
husband Mrs Frederick Lowndes was discarding
and the other the husband she was acquiring. The
eternal triangle, you know.

William: In this case the triangle is four-sided.

Miss Montmorency: Oh, how very peculiar.

Mr Raham: We see a lot of strange things in our
business, Miss Montmorency.

Miss Montmorency: To whom do you say it, as the
French say.

Victoria: I don't want you to think that I've been at
all light or careless, but the fact is, through no
fault of my own, they're both my husbands.

Miss Montmorency (*taking it as a matter of course*):
Oh, really. How very interesting. And which are
you divorcing?

Victoria: I'm divorcing them both.

Miss Montmorency: Oh, I see. Very sad. Very sad.

William: We're taking as cheerful a view of it as we
can.

Miss Montmorency: Ah, yes, that's what I say to my
clients. Courage. Courage.

Frederick (*with a start*): When?

Victoria: Be quiet, Freddie.

Miss Montmorency: I think I ought to tell you at
once that I shouldn't like to misconduct myself – I
use the technical expression – with both these
gentlemen.

Mr Raham: Oh, Miss Montmorency, a woman of your
experience isn't going to strain at a gnat.

Miss Montmorency: No, but I shouldn't like to
swallow a camel.

Mr Raham: We shall be generous, Miss
Montmorency.

Miss Montmorency: I have to think of my self-
respect. One gentleman is business, but two would
be debauchery.

Mr Raham: Mrs Lowndes is anxious to put this matter through as quickly as possible.

Miss Montmorency: I dare say my friend Mrs Onslow Jervis would oblige if I asked her as a personal favour.

Victoria: Are you sure she can be trusted?

Miss Montmorency: Oh, she's a perfect lady and most respectable. She's the widow of a clergyman and she has two sons in the army. They've done so well in the war.

Mr Raham: Unless we can get Miss Montmorency to reconsider her decision I'm afraid we shall have to put up with Mrs Onslow Jervis.

Miss Montmorency: I am adamant, Mr Raham. Adamant.

Frederick: I'm all for Mrs Onslow Jervis personally.

Miss Montmorency: Then you fall on me, major . . . I didn't catch your name.

William: Cardew.

Miss Montmorency: I hope you play cards.

William: Sometimes.

Miss Montmorency: I'm a great card-player. Piquet, écarté, cribbage, double dummy, baccarat, bezique, I don't mind what I play. It's such a relief to find a gentleman who's fond of cards.

William: Otherwise I daresay the night seems rather long.

Miss Montmorency: Oh, not to me, you know. I'm such a student of human nature. But my gentlemen begin to grow a little restless when I've talked to them for six or seven hours.

William: I can hardly believe it.

Miss Montmorency: One gentleman actually said he wanted to go to bed, but, of course, I told him that would never do.

Victoria: Forgive my asking – you know what men are – do they never attempt to take any liberties with you?

Miss Montmorency: Oh no. If you're a lady you can

always keep a man in his place. And Mr Raham only takes the very best sort of divorces. The only unpleasantness I've ever had was with a gentleman sent to me by a firm of solicitors in a cathedral city. I took a dislike to him the first moment I saw him, and when he refused to drink anything at supper but ginger-beer I was on my guard. A cold sensualist, I said to myself.

Victoria: Oh, I know so well what you mean.

Miss Montmorency: He had no sooner finished his second bottle of ginger-beer then, without any warning at all, he said: 'I am going to kiss you.' You could have heard a pin drop. I pretended to think he was joking, so I said: 'We have met for business rather than pleasure.' And what d'you think he answered? He said: 'This is one of the rare occasions on which one can combine the two.' I didn't lose my presence of mind. I expostulated with him. I told him I was a woman and defenceless, and he said: 'That's just it.' Not a gentleman, if course, not in the best sense of the word. I appealed to his better nature. But all in vain. I didn't know what to do, when suddenly I had an inspiration. I rushed to the door and called in the detective who was watching us. He protected me.

Mr Raham: It was risky, Miss Montmorency. The judge might have said there was collusion.

Miss Montmorency: Necessity knows no law, Mr Raham, as those dreadful Germans say, and I was terribly frightened.

William: I assure you, Miss Montmorency, that you need not fear that I shall take advantage of your delicate position.

Miss Montmorency: Of course, you will divest yourself of none of your raiment.

William: On the contrary, I propose to put on an extra suit of clothes.

Miss Montmorency: Oh, Mr Raham, please don't

forget that I only drink Pommery. In the Twickenham divorce they sent up Pol Roger, and Pol Roger always gives me indigestion.

Fortunately the dear marquis, who suffers from dyspepsia, had some pepsin tabloids with him or I don't know what I should have done.

Mr Raham: I'll make a note of it at once.

Miss Montmorency: 1906. (*To* **William**) I'm sure we shall have a delightful night. I can see that we have much in common.

William: It's too good of you to say so.

Miss Montmorency (*to* **Frederick**): And I know you'll like Mrs Onslow Jervis. A perfect lady. She has such charm of manner. So much ease. You can see that she did a lot of entertaining when her husband was Vicar of Clacton. They have a nice class of people at Clacton.

Frederick: I shall be charmed to meet her.

Miss Montmorency: You will take care not to be at all risqué, as the French say, in your conversation, won't you? Of course, she's a woman of the world, but as the widow of the Vicar of Clacton she feels it only due to herself to be a little particular.

Frederick: I promise you I'll be very careful.

Miss Montmorency: I don't know what Mr Raham would say to our sharing a suite. We could play bridge. She's a very fine bridge-player, and we only play threepence a hundred, because in her position she can hardly gamble, can she?

Mr Raham: I always like to oblige you, Miss Montmorency, but I hardly think that arrangement will do. You know how fussy the judges are. We might hit upon one of them who saw nothing in it.

Miss Montmorency: I know. They're tiresome, silly creatures.

Mr Raham: Why, the other day I came across one who wouldn't believe the worst had happened when a man and a woman, not related in any way, mind you, were proved to have been alone in a room together for three-quarters of an hour.

Miss Montmorency: Oh, well, let us take no risks. Business is business. It must be you and me alone then, Major Cardew. You will let me know in good time when you fix the fatal night. I'm very much booked up just now.

Mr Raham: Of course, we will do everything to suit your convenience, Miss Montmorency. And now, Mrs Lowndes, since we have settled everything. I think Miss Montmorency and I will go.

Victoria: I can't think of anything else.

Miss Montmorency: Excuse my taking the liberty, Mrs Frederick Lowndes, but after your great trouble is over should you be wanting any face massage, may I give you my card?

Victoria: Oh, do you do face massage?

Miss Montmorency: Only for ladies who are personally recommended to me. Here is my card.

Victoria (*looking at it*): Esmeralda.

Miss Montmorency: Yes, it's a pretty name, isn't it? I also make the Esmeralda cream. The Marchioness of Twickenham's face was simply ravaged when she was divorcing the Marquis, and, believe me, after a course of twelve treatments you wouldn't have known her.

Victoria: Of course, all this sort of thing is a great nervous shock.

Miss Montmorency: Oh, I know. And there's nothing like face massage for soothing the nerves.

Victoria: I'll certainly keep your card.

Miss Montmorency: Goodbye, then. (*To William*) I'm not going to say good-bye to you, but au revoir.

William: Believe me, I look forward to our next meeting.

Mr Raham: Good morning, Mrs Lowndes. Good

morning. (*Moving towards the door that leads into the area*) Shall we go out this way?

Miss Montmorency (*just a little taken aback*): The area steps? Oh, very well. It's so quaint and old-fashioned. I always think a lady if she is a lady can do anything.

> *She gives a gracious bow and goes out, followed by* **Mr Raham**.

William: This is a bit of all right that you've let us in for, Victoria.

Victoria: Well, darling, it's the only thing I've ever asked you to do for me in all my life, so you needn't complain.

William: I will bear it like a martyr.

Victoria: Now, the only thing left is for me to bid you goodbye.

Frederick: Already?

Victoria: You must understand that under the circumstances it wouldn't be nice for me to stay here. Besides, without servants, it's beastly uncomfortable.

William: Won't you even stay to luncheon?

Victoria: I don't think I will, thanks. I think I shall get a better one at my mother's.

Frederick: Oh, are you going there?

Victoria: Where else do you expect a woman to go in a crisis like this?

William: I should think the steak was about done, Freddie.

Frederick: Oh, I'd give it another hour or two to make sure.

Victoria: Of course, I realize that it's a painful moment for both of you, but as you say, we shan't make it any easier by dragging it out.

William: True.

Victoria: Goodbye, Bill. I forgive you everything, and I hope we shall always be good friends.

William: Goodbye, Victoria. I hope this will not be by any means your last marriage.

Victoria: When everything is settled you must come and dine with us. I'm sure you'll find that Leicester has the best wines and cigars that money can buy.

She turns to him an indifferent cheek.

William (*kissing it*): Goodbye.

Victoria: And now, Freddie, it's your turn. Now that there's nothing more between us you might give me back that pin I gave you.

Frederick (*taking it out of his tie*): Here you are.

Victoria: And there was a cigarette-case.

Frederick (*giving it her*): Take it.

Victoria: They say jewellery has gone up tremendously in value since the war. I shall give Leicester a cigarette-case as a wedding present.

William: You always do, Victoria.

Victoria: Men like it. Goodbye, Freddie dear. I shall always have a pleasant recollection of you.

She turns the other cheek to him.

Frederick: Goodbye, Victoria.

William: Would you like a taxi?

Victoria: No thanks, I think the exercise will do me good.

She goes out, and is seen tripping up the area steps.

Frederick: A wonderful woman.

William: I shall never regret having married her. Now let's have lunch.

Frederick: I wish I looked forward to it as much as you do.

William: Dear old man, has this affecting scene taken away your appetite?

Frederick: It's not the appetite I'm doubtful about. It's the steak.

William: Oh, don't you worry yourself about that. I'll just dish up. (*He goes over to the stove and tries to get the steak out of the frying-pan.*) Come out, you great fat devil. It won't come out.

Frederick: That's your trouble.

William (*bringing the frying-pan to the table*): Oh, well, we can eat it just as well out of the frying-pan. Shall I carve it?

Frederick (*sitting down*): Please.

> **William** takes a knife and starts to cut the steak. It won't cut. He applies force. The steak resists stealthily. A little surprised, **William** puts somewhat more strength into it. He makes no impression. He begins to grow vexed. He starts to struggle. He sets his teeth. It is all in vain. The sweat pours from his brow. **Frederick** watches him in gloomy silence. At last in a passion **William** throws down the knife.

William (*furiously*): Why don't you say something, you fool?

Frederick (*gently*): Shall I go and fetch my little hatchet?

William (*attacking the steak again angrily with the knife*): I know my theory's right. If you cook a pound of meat a quarter of an hour you must cook three pounds of meat three quarters of an hour.

> A **Boy**, carrying a large, square, covered basket, is seen coming down the area steps. He knocks at the door.

Frederick: Hulloa, who's this. (*He goes to the door and opens.*) What can I do for you, my son?

Clarence: Does Mrs Frederick Lowndes live here?

Frederick: In a manner of speaking.

Clarence (*coming in*): From the Ritz Hotel.

Frederick: What's that? Walk right in, my boy. Put it on the table.

William (*looking at the label*): With Mr Leicester Paton's compliments.

Frederick: It's luncheon.

Clarence: I was told to give the basket to the lady personally.

Frederick: That's all right, my boy.

Clarence: If the lady's not here I'm to take it back again.

William (*promptly*): She's just coming downstairs. (*He goes to the door and calls*) Victoria, my darling, that kind Mr Leicester Paton has sent you a little light refreshment from the Ritz.

Frederick: There's half-a-crown for you, my lad. Now, you hop it quick.

Clarence: Thank you, sir.

> *He goes out.*

Frederick: Now you can eat the steak if you like. I'm going to eat Victoria's luncheon.

William: It's a damned unscrupulous thing to do. I'll join you.

> *They hurriedly begin to unpack the basket.*

Frederick (*taking off a cover*): What's here? Chicken *en casserole*?

William: That's all right. Here, give me that bottle and see me open it.

> *He takes out a bottle of champagne and proceeds to open it.*

Frederick: *Pâté de foie gras*. Good. Caviare? No. Smoked salmon. Stout fellow, Mr Leicester Paton.

William: Don't stand there staring at it. Get it out.

Frederick: This is a regular beano.

William: I'm beginning to think the wangler won the war after all.

Frederick: *Mousse au jambon*. He's got some idea of Victoria's appetite.

William: My dear fellow, love is always blind.

Frederick: Thank God for it, that's all I say. How's that cork going?

William: Half a mo. It's just coming.

Frederick: That is what I call a nice little snack. Dear Victoria, she was a good sort.

William: In her way.

Frederick: But give me *pâté de foie gras*.

William (*getting the bottle opened*): Pop. Hand over your glass.

Frederick: Here you are. I'm as hungry as a trooper.

William: Before we start, I want you to drink a toast.

Frederick: I'll drink anything.

William (*holding up his glass*): Victoria's third husband.

Frederick: God help him!

William: And for us – liberty.

   *As they drain their glasses the curtain falls
   quickly.*

   CURTAIN

Lady Frederick

A COMEDY IN THREE ACTS

Characters

Lady Frederick Berolles
Sir Gerald O'Mara
Mr Paradine Fouldes
Marchioness of Mereston
Marquess of Mereston
Admiral Carlisle
Captain Montgomerie
Rose
Lady Frederick's Dressmaker
Lady Frederick's Footman
Lady Frederick's Maid
Thompson
A Waiter

Time: 1890

Act I

Scene: *Drawing-room of the Hotel de Paris at Monte Carlo. A large, sumptuously furnished room, with doors right and left, and windows at the back leading on to a terrace. Through these is seen the starry southern night. On one side is a piano, on the other a table with papers neatly laid on it. There is a lighted fire.*

Lady Mereston, *in evening dress, rather magnificently attired, is reading the papers. She is a handsome woman of forty. She puts down the paper impatiently and rings the bell. A servant answers.*

Lady Mereston: Did Mr Paradine Fouldes come this evening?

Servant: Yes, miladi.

Lady Mereston: Is he in the hotel now?

Servant: Yes, miladi.

Lady Mereston: Will you send someone up to his room to say I'm waiting to see him?

Servant: Pardon, miladi, but the gentleman say 'e was on no account to be disturbed.

Lady Mereston: Nonsense. Mr Fouldes is my brother. You must go to him immediately.

Servant: Mr Fouldes his valet is in the 'all. Will your ladyship speak with him?

Lady Mereston: Mr Fouldes is more difficult to see than a cabinet minister. Send his servant to me.

Servant: Very good, miladi.

> *Exit* **Servant**, *and presently* **Thompson**, *Mr Fouldes' man, comes in.*

Thompson: Your ladyship wished to see me.

263

Lady Mereston: Good evening, Thompson. I hope you had a comfortable journey.

Thompson: Yes, my lady. Mr Fouldes always has a comfortable journey.

Lady Mereston: Was the sea calm when you crossed?

Thompson: Yes, my lady. Mr Fouldes would look upon it as a great liberty if the sea was not calm.

Lady Mereston: Will you tell Mr Fouldes that I should like to see him at once?

Thompson (*looking at his watch*): Excuse me, my lady, but Mr Fouldes said no one was to disturb him till ten o'clock. It's more than my place is worth to go to him at five minutes to.

Lady Mereston: But what on earth's he doing?

Thompson: I don't know at all, my lady.

Lady Mereston: How long have you been with Mr Fouldes?

Thompson: Twenty-five years, my lady.

Lady Mereston: I should have thought you knew how he spent every minute of his day.

> **Paradine** *comes in. He is a very well-dressed man of forty-odd. Self-possessed, worldly, urbane. He is never at a loss or put out of countenance. He overhears* **Lady Mereston's** *last words.*

Fouldes: When I engaged Thompson I told him the first thing he must learn was the very difficult feat of keeping his eyes open and shut at one and the same time.

Lady Mereston: My dear Paradine, I've been waiting to see you for the last two hours. How tiresome you are.

Fouldes: You may give me a kiss, Maud, but don't be rough.

Lady Mereston (*kissing his cheek*): You ridiculous creature. You really might have come to see me at once.

Fouldes: My dear, you cannot grudge me a little repose after a long and tedious journey. I had to repair the ravages to my person caused by twenty-seven hours in the train.

Lady Mereston: Don't be so absurd. I'm sure your person is never ravished.

Fouldes: Ravaged, my dear, ravaged. I should look upon it as an affectation at my age if I were not a little upset by the journey from London to Monte Carlo.

Lady Mereston: I'll be bound you ate a very hearty dinner.

Fouldes: Thompson, did I eat any dinner at all?

Thompson (*stolidly*): Soup, sir.

Fouldes: I remember looking at it.

Thompson: Fish, sir.

Fouldes: I trifled with a fried sole.

Thompson: Vol-au-vent Rossini, sir.

Fouldes: It has left absolutely no impression upon me.

Thompson: *Tournedos à la Splendide.*

Fouldes: They were distinctly tough, Thompson. You must lodge a complaint in the proper quarter.

Thompson: Roast pheasant, sir.

Fouldes: Yes, yes, now you mention it, I do remember the pheasant.

Thompson: *Pêches* Melba, sir.

Fouldes: They were too cold, Thompson. They were distinctly too cold.

Lady Mereston: My dear Paradine, I think you dined uncommonly well.

Fouldes: I have reached an age when love, ambition and wealth pale into insignificance beside a really well-grilled steak. That'll do, Thompson.

Thompson: Very well, sir.

He goes out.

Lady Mereston: It's too bad of you, Paradine, to

Lady Frederick

devour a substantial meal when I'm eating out my
very heart with anxiety.

Fouldes: It seems to agree with you very well. I've
not seen you look better for years.

Lady Mereston: For heaven's sake be serious and
listen to me.

Fouldes: I started immediately I got your telegram.
Pray tell me what I can do for you?

Lady Mereston: My dear Paradine, Charlie's head over
ears in love.

Fouldes: It's not altogether an unexpected condition
for a young man of twenty-two. If the lady's
respectable, marry him and resign yourself to being
a dowager. If she's not, give her five hundred
pounds and pack her off to Paris or London or
wherever else she habitually practices her arts and
graces.

Lady Mereston: I wish I could. But who d'you think
it is?

Fouldes: My dear, there's nothing I detest more than
riddles. I can imagine quite a number of fair ladies
who would look without disdain upon a young
marquess with fifty thousand a year.

Lady Mereston: Lady Frederick Berolles.

Fouldes: By Jupiter!

Lady Mereston: She's fifteen years older than he is.

Fouldes: Then she's not old enough to be his mother,
which is a distinct advantage.

Lady Mereston: She dyes her hair.

Fouldes: She dyes it uncommonly well.

Lady Mereston: She paints.

Fouldes: Much better than a Royal Academician.

Lady Mereston: And poor Charlie's simply infatuated.
He rides with her all the morning, motors with
her all the afternoon, and gambles with her half the
night. I never see him.

Fouldes: But why should you think Lady Frederick
cares two straws for him?

266

Lady Mereston: Don't be ridiculous, Paradine. Every one knows she hasn't a penny, and she's crippled with debts.

Fouldes: One has to keep up appearances in this world Life nowadays for the woman of fashion is a dilemma of which one horn is the Bankruptcy Court and the other – the President of the Divorce Court.

Lady Mereston: I wish I knew how she manages to dress so beautifully. It's one of the injustices of fate that clothes only hang on a woman really well when she's lost every shred of reputation.

Fouldes: My dear, you must console yourself with the thought that she'll probably frizzle for it hereafter.

Lady Mereston: I hope I'm not wicked, Paradine, but to wear draperies and wings in the next world offers me no compensation for looking dowdy in a Paquin gown in this.

Fouldes: I surmised she was on the verge of bankruptcy when I heard she'd bought a new brougham. And you seriously think Charlie wants to marry her?

Lady Mereston: I'm sure of it.

Fouldes: And what d'you want me to do?

Lady Mereston: Good heavens, I want you to prevent it. After all he has a magnificent position; he's got every chance of making a career for himself. There's no reason why he shouldn't be Prime Minister – it's not fair to the boy to let him marry a woman like that.

Fouldes: Of course you know Lady Frederick?

Lady Mereston: My dear Paradine, we're the greatest friends. You don't suppose I'm going to give her the advantage of quarrelling with me. I think I shall ask her to luncheon to meet you.

Fouldes: Women have such an advantage over men in affairs of this sort. They're troubled by no scruples, and like George Washington, never hesitate to lie.

Lady Mereston: I look upon her as an abandoned creature, and I tell you frankly I shall stop at nothing to save my son from her clutches.

Fouldes: Only a thoroughly good woman could so calmly announce her intention of using the crookedest ways to gain her ends.

Lady Mereston (*looking at him*): There must be some incident in her career which she wouldn't like raked up. If we could only get hold of that. . . .

Fouldes (*blandly*): How d'you imagine I can help you?

Lady Mereston: A reformed burglar is always the best detective.

Fouldes: My dear, I wish you could be frank without being sententious.

Lady Mereston: You've run through two fortunes, and if we all got our deserts you would be starving now instead of being richer than ever.

Fouldes: My second cousins have a knack of dying at the psychological moment.

Lady Mereston: You've been a horrid, dissipated wretch all your life, and heaven knows the disreputable people who've been your bosom friends.

Fouldes: With my knowledge of the world and your entire lack of scruple we should certainly be a match for one defenceless woman.

Lady Mereston: Common report says that at one time you were very much in love with her.

Fouldes: Common report is an ass whose long ears only catch its own braying.

Lady Mereston: I was wondering how far things went. If you could tell Charlie of the relations between you. . . .

Fouldes: My good Maud, there were no relations – unfortunately.

Lady Mereston: Poor George was very uneasy about you at the time.

Fouldes: Your deceased husband, being a strictly

religious man, made a point of believing the worst about his neighbours.

Lady Mereston: Don't, Paradine; I know you didn't like one another, but remember that I loved him with all my heart. I shall never get over his death.

Fouldes: My dear girl, you know I didn't mean to wound you.

Lady Mereston: After all, it was largely your fault. He was deeply religious, and as the president of the Broad Church Union he couldn't countenance your mode of life.

Fouldes (*with great unction*): Thank God in my day I've been a miserable sinner!

Lady Mereston (*laughing*): You're quite incurable, Paradine. But you will help me now. Since his father's death, the boy and I have lived a very retired life, and now we're quite helpless. It would break my heart if Charlie married that woman.

Fouldes: I'll do my best. I think I can promise you that nothing will come of it.

> *The door is flung open, and* **Lady Frederick**
> *enters, followed by* **Mereston,** *a young man*
> *of twenty-two; by her brother,* **Sir Gerald**
> **O'Mara,** *a handsome fellow of six-and-*
> *twenty; by* **Captain Montgomerie, Admiral**
> **Carlisle,** *and* **Rose,** *his daughter.* **Lady**
> **Frederick** *is a handsome Irish woman of thirty*
> *to thirty-five, beautifully dressed. She is very*
> *vivacious. She has all the Irish recklessness*
> *and unconcern for the morrow. Whenever she*
> *wants to get round anybody she falls into an*
> *Irish brogue, and then, as she knows very*
> *well, is quite irresistible.* **Captain**
> **Montgomerie** *is a polished, well-groomed*
> *man of thirty-five, with suave manners. The*
> **Admiral** *is bluff and downright.* **Rose** *is a*
> *pretty ingénue of nineteen.*

Lady Mereston: Here they are.

Lady Frederick (*enthusiastically going to him with open arms*): Paradine! Paradine! Paradine!

Mereston: Oh, my prophetic soul, mine uncle!

Fouldes (*shaking hands with* **Lady Frederick**): I heard you were at the Casino.

Lady Frederick: Charlie lost all his money, so I brought him away.

Lady Mereston: I wish you wouldn't gamble, Charlie dear.

Mereston: My dear mother, I've only lost ten thousand francs.

Lady Frederick (*to* **Paradine Fouldes**): I see you're in your usual robust health.

Fouldes: You needn't throw it in my face. I shall probably be very unwell to-morrow.

Lady Frederick: D'you know Admiral Carlisle? This is my brother Gerald.

Fouldes (*shaking hands*): How d'you do?

Lady Frederick (*introducing*): Captain Montgomerie.

Captain Montgomerie: I think we've met before.

Fouldes: I'm very pleased to hear it. How do'you do. (*To* **Mereston**) Are you having a good time in Monte Carlo, Charles?

Mereston: A1, thanks.

Fouldes: And what do you do with yourself?

Mereston: Oh, hang about generally, you know – and there's always the tables.

Fouldes: That's right, my boy; I'm glad to see that you prepare yourself properly for your duties as a hereditary legislator.

Mereston (*laughing*): Oh, shut it, Uncle Paradine.

Fouldes: I rejoice also to find that you have already a certain command of the vernacular.

Mereston: Well, if you can browbeat a London cabby and hold your own in repartee with a barmaid, it oughtn't to be difficult to get on all right in the House of Lords.

Fouldes: But let me give you a solemn warning. You
have a magnificent chance, dear boy, with all the
advantages of wealth and station. I beseech you not
to throw it away by any exhibition of talent. The
field is clear and the British people are waiting for
a leader. But remember that the British people like
their leaders dull. Capacity they mistrust,
versatility they cannot bear, and wit they utterly
abhor. Look at the fate of poor Lord Parnaby. His
urbanity gained him the premiership, but his
brilliancy overthrew him. How could the fortunes
of the nation be safe with a man whose speeches
were pointed and sparkling, whose mind was so
quick, so agile, that it reminded you of a fencer's
play? Every one is agreed that Lord Parnaby is
flippant and unsubstantial; we doubt his
principles and we have grave fears about his
morality. Take warning, my dear boy, take
warning. Let the sprightly epigram never lighten
the long periods of your speech nor the Attic salt
flavour the roast beef of your conversation. Be
careful that your metaphors show no imagination
and conceal your brains as you would a
discreditable secret. Above all, if you have a sense
of humour, crush it. Crush it.

Mereston: My dear uncle, you move me very much.
I will be as stupid as an owl.

Fouldes: There's a good, brave boy.

Mereston: I will be heavy and tedious.

Fouldes: I see already the riband of the Garter
adorning your shirt-front. Remember, there's no
damned merit about that.

Mereston: None shall listen to my speeches without
falling into a profound sleep.

Fouldes (*seizing his hand*): The premiership itself is
within your grasp.

Lady Mereston: Dear Paradine, let us take a stroll on
the terrace before we go to bed.

Fouldes: And you shall softly whisper all the latest scandal in my ear.

He puts on her cloak and they go out.

Lady Frederick: May I speak to you, admiral?

Admiral: Certainly, certainly. What can I do for you?

While **Lady Frederick** *and the* **Admiral** *talk, the others go slowly out. Through the conversation she uses her Irish brogue.*

Lady Frederick: Are you in a good temper?

Admiral: Fairly, fairly.

Lady Frederick: I'm glad of that because I want to make you a proposal of marriage.

Admiral: My dear Lady Frederick, you take me entirely by surprise.

Lady Frederick (*laughing*): Not on my own behalf, you know.

Admiral: Oh, I see.

Lady Frederick: The fact is, my brother Gerald has asked your daughter to marry him, and she has accepted.

Admiral: Rose is a minx, Lady Frederick, and she's much too young to marry.

Lady Frederick: Now don't fly into a passion. We're going to talk it over quite calmly.

Admiral: I tell you I won't hear of it. The boy's penniless.

Lady Frederick: That's why it's so lucky you're rich.

Admiral: Eh?

Lady Frederick: You've been talking of buying a place in Ireland. You couldn't want anything nicer than Gerald's – gravel soil, you know. And you simply dote on Elizabethan architecture.

Admiral: I can't bear it.

Lady Frederick: How fortunate, then, that the house was burnt down in the eighteenth century and rebuilt in the best Georgian style.

Admiral: Ugh.

Lady Frederick: And you'd love to have little grandsons to dandle on your knee.

Admiral: How do I know they wouldn't be girls?

Lady Frederick: Oh, it's most unusual in our family.

Admiral: I tell you I won't hear of it.

Lady Frederick: You know, it's not bad to have the oldest baronetcy in the country but one.

Admiral: I suppose I shall have to pack Rose off to England.

Lady Frederick: And break her heart?

Admiral: Women's hearts are like old china, none the worse for a break or two.

Lady Frederick: Did you ever know my husband, admiral?

Admiral: Yes.

Lady Frederick: I was married to him at seventeen because my mother thought it a good match, and I was desperately in love with another man. Before we'd been married a fortnight he came home blind drunk, and I had never seen a drunken man before. Then I found out he was a confirmed tippler. I was so ashamed. If you only knew what my life was for the ten years I lived with him. I've done a lot of foolish things in my time, but, my God, I have suffered.

Admiral: Yes, I know, I know.

Lady Frederick: And believe me, when two young things love one another it's better to let them marry. Love is so very rare in this world. One really ought to make the most of it when it's there.

Admiral: I'm very sorry, but I've made up my mind.

Lady Frederick: Ah, but won't you alter it – like Nelson. Don't be hard on Rose. She's really in love with Gerald. Do give them a chance. Won't you? Ah, do – there's a dear.

Admiral: I don't want to hurt your feelings, but Sir Gerald is about the most ineligible young man that I've ever come across.

Lady Frederick (*triumphantly*): There, I knew we should agree. That's precisely what I told him this morning.

Admiral: I understand his place is heavily mortgaged.

Lady Frederick: No one will lend a penny more on it. If they would Gerald would borrow it at once.

Admiral: He's got nothing but his pay to live upon.

Lady Frederick: And his tastes are very extravagant.

Admiral: He's a gambler.

Lady Frederick: Yes, but then he's so good looking.

Admiral: Eh?

Lady Frederick: I'm glad that we agree so entirely about him. Now there's nothing left but to call the young things in, join their hands and give them our united blessing.

Admiral: Before I consent to this marriage, madam, I'll see your brother –

Lady Frederick: Damned?

Admiral: Yes, madam, damned.

Lady Frederick: Now listen to me quietly, will you?

Admiral: I should warn you, Lady Frederick, that when I once make up my mind about a thing, I never change it.

Lady Frederick: Now that is what I really admire. I like a man of character. You know, I've always been impressed by your strength and determination.

Admiral: I don't know about that. But when I say a thing, I do it.

Lady Frederick: Yes I know. And in five minutes you're going to say that Gerald may marry your pretty Rose.

Admiral: No, no, no.

Lady Frederick: Now look here, don't be obstinate. I don't like you when you're obstinate.

Admiral: I'm not obstinate. I'm firm.

Lady Frederick: After all, Gerald has lots of good qualities. He's simply devoted to your daughter.

He's been a little wild, but you know you wouldn't give much for a young man who hadn't.

Admiral (*gruffly*): I don't want a milksop for a son-in-law.

Lady Frederick: As soon as he's married, he'll settle into a model country squire.

Admiral: Well, he's a gambler, and I can't get over that.

Lady Frederick: Shall he promise you never to play cards again? Now, don't be horrid. You don't want to make me utterly wretched, do you?

Admiral (*unwillingly*): Well, I'll tell you what I'll do – they shall marry if he doesn't gamble for a year.

Lady Frederick: Oh, you duck. (*She impulsively throws her arms round his neck and kisses him. He is a good deal taken aback.*) I beg your pardon, I couldn't help it.

Admiral: I don't altogether object, you know.

Lady Frederick: Upon my word, in some ways you're rather fascinating.

Admiral: D'you think so, really?

Lady Frederick: I do indeed.

Admiral: I rather wish that proposal of marriage had been on your own behalf.

Lady Frederick: Ah, with me, dear Admiral, experience triumphs over hope. I must tell the children. (*Calling*) Gerald, come here. Rose.

Gerald *and* **Rose** *come in.*

Lady Frederick: I always knew your father was a perfect darling, Rose.

Rose: Oh, papa, you are a brick.

Admiral: I thoroughly disapprove of the marriage, my dear, but – it's not easy to say no to Lady Frederick.

Gerald: It's awfully good of you, Admiral, and I'll do my best to make Rose a ripping husband.

Admiral: Not so fast, young man, not so fast. There's a condition.

Rose: Oh, father!

Lady Frederick: Gerald is to behave himself for a year, and then you may marry.

Rose: But won't Gerald grow very dull if he behaves himself?

Lady Frederick: I have no doubt of it. But dullness is the first requisite of a good husband.

Admiral: Now you must pack off to bed, my dear. I'm going to smoke my pipe before turning in.

Rose (*kissing* **Lady Frederick**): Good-night, dearest, I'll never forget your kindness.

Lady Frederick: You'd better not thank me till you've been married a few years.

Rose (*holding out her hand to* **Gerald**): Good-night.

Gerald (*taking it and looking at her*): Good-night.

Admiral (*gruffly*): You may as well do it in front of my face as behind my back.

Rose (*lifting up her lips*): Good-night.

> *He kisses her, and the* **Admiral** *and* **Rose** *go out.*

Lady Frederick: Oh lord, I wish I were eighteen.

> *She sinks into a chair, and an expression of utter weariness comes over her face.*

Gerald: I say, what's up?

Lady Frederick (*starting*): I thought you'd gone. Nothing.

Gerald: Come, out with it.

Lady Frederick: Oh, my poor boy if you only knew. I'm so worried that I don't know what on earth to do.

Gerald: Money?

Lady Frederick: Last year I made a solemn determination to be economical. And it's ruined me.

Gerald: My dear, how could it?

Lady Frederick: I can't make it out. It seems very unfair. The more I tried not to be extravagant, the more I spent.

Gerald: Can't you borrow.

Lady Frederick (*laughing*): I have borrowed. That's just it.

Gerald: Well, borrow again.

Lady Frederick: I've tried to. But no one's such a fool as to lend me a penny.

Gerald: Did you say I'd sign anything they liked?

Lady Frederick: I was so desperate I said we'd both sign anything. It was Dick Cohen.

Gerald: Oh, lord, what did he say?

Lady Frederick (*imitating a Jewish accent*): What's the good of wathting a nithe clean sheet of paper, my dear lady?

Gerald (*shouting with laughter*): By George, don't I know it.

Lady Frederick: For heaven's sake don't let's talk of my affairs. They're in such a state that if I think of them at all I shall have a violent fit of hysterics.

Gerald: But look here, what d'you really mean?

Lady Frederick: Well, if you want it – I owe my dressmaker seven hundred pounds, and last year I signed two horrid bills, one for fifteen hundred and the other for two thousand. They fall due the day after to-morrow, and if I can't raise the money I shall have to go through the Bankruptcy Court.

Gerald: By George, that's serious.

Lady Frederick: It's so serious that I can't help thinking something will happen. Whenever I've got in a really tight fix something has turned up and put me on my legs again. Last time, Aunt Elizabeth had an apoplectic fit. But of course it wasn't really very profitable because mourning is so desperately expensive.

Gerald: Why don't you marry?

Lady Frederick: Oh, my dear Gerald, you know I'm always unlucky at games of chance.

Gerald: Charlie Mereston's awfully gone on you.

Lady Frederick: That must be obvious to the meanest intelligence.

Gerald: Well, why don't you have him?

Lady Frederick: Good heavens, I'm old enough to be his mother.

Gerald: Nonsense. You're only ten years older than he is, and nowadays no nice young man marries a woman younger than himself.

Lady Frederick: He's such a good fellow. I couldn't do him a nasty turn like that.

Gerald: How about Montgomerie? He simply stinks of money, and he's not a bad sort.

Lady Frederick (*surprised*): My dear boy, I hardly know him.

Gerald: Well, I'm afraid it means marriage or bankruptcy.

Lady Frederick: Here's Charlie. Take him away, there's a dear. I want to talk to Paradine.

Enter **Paradine Fouldes** *with* **Mereston.**

Fouldes: What, still here, Lady Frederick?

Lady Frederick: As large as life.

Fouldes: We've been taking a turn on the terrace.

Lady Frederick (*to* **Mereston**): And has your astute uncle been pumping you, Charlie?

Fouldes: Eh, what?

Mereston: I don't think he got much out of me.

Fouldes (*good-naturedly*): All I wanted, dear boy. There's no one so transparent as the person who thinks he's devilish deep. By the way, what's the time?

Gerald: About eleven, isn't it?

Fouldes: Ah! How old are you, Charlie?

Mereston: Twenty-two.

Fouldes: Then it's high time you went to bed.

Lady Frederick: Charlie's not going to bed till I tell him. Are you?

Mereston: Of course not.

Fouldes: Has it escaped your acute intelligence, my friend, that I want to talk to Lady Frederick?

Mereston: Not at all. But I have no reason to believe that Lady Frederick wants to talk to you.

Gerald: Let's go and have a game of pills, Charlie.

Mereston: D'you want to be left alone with the old villain?

Fouldes: You show no respect for my dyed hairs, young man.

Lady Frederick: I've not seen him for years, you know.

Mereston: Oh, all right. I say, you're coming for a drive to-morrow, aren't you?

Lady Frederick: Certainly. But it must be in the afternoon.

Fouldes: I'm sorry, but Charles has arranged to go to Nice with me in the afternoon.

Mereston (to **Lady Frederick**): That'll suit me A1. I had an engagement, but it was quite unimportant.

Lady Frederick: Then that's settled. Good-night.

Mereston: Good-night.

He goes out with **Gerald.** **Lady Frederick** *turns and good-humouredly scrutinizes* **Paradine Fouldes.**

Lady Frederick: Well?

Fouldes: Well?

Lady Frederick: You wear excellently, Paradine.

Fouldes: Thanks.

Lady Frederick: How do you manage it?

Fouldes: By getting up late and never going to bed early, by eating whatever I like and drinking whenever I'm thirsty, by smoking strong cigars, taking no exercise, and refusing under any circumstances to be bored.

Lady Frederick: I'm sorry you had to leave town in such a hurry. Were you amusing yourself?

Fouldes: I come to the Riviera every year.

Lady Frederick: I daresay, but not so early.

Fouldes: I've never surrendered so far to middle age as to make habits.

Lady Frederick: My dear Paradine, the day before yesterday, Lady Mereston, quite distracted, went to the post office and sent you the following wire: Come at once, your help urgently needed. Charlie in toils designing female, Maud. Am I right?

Fouldes: I never admit even to myself that a well-dressed woman is wrong.

Lady Frederick: So you started post-haste, bent upon protecting your nephew, and were infinitely surprised to learn that the designing female was no other than your humble servant.

Fouldes: You'd be irresistible, Lady Frederick, if you didn't know you were so clever.

Lady Frederick: And now what are you going to do?

Fouldes: My dear lady, I'm not a police office, but a very harmless, inoffensive old bachelor.

Lady Frederick: With more wiles than the mother of many daughters and the subtlety of a company promoter.

Fouldes: Maud seems to think that as I've racketted about a little in my time, I'm just the sort of man to deal with you. Set a thief to catch a thief, don't you know? She's rather fond of proverbs.

Lady Frederick: She should have thought rather of: When Greek meets Greek, then comes the tug of war. I hear Lady Mereston has been saying the most agreeable things about me.

Fouldes: Ah, that's women's fault; they always show their hand. You're the only woman I ever knew who didn't.

Lady Frederick (*with a brogue*): You should have avoided the Blarney Stone when you went to Ireland.

Fouldes: Look here, d'you want to marry Charlie?

Lady Frederick: Why should I?

Fouldes: Because he's got fifty thousand a year, and

you're head over ears in debt. You've got to raise
something like four thousand pounds at once, or
you go under. You've got yourself a good deal
talked about during the last ten years, but people
have stood you because you had plenty of money.
If you go broke they'll drop you like a hot potato.
And I daresay it wouldn't be inconvenient to
change Lady Frederick Berolles into Lady Mereston.
My sister has always led me to believe that it is
rather attractive to be a marchioness.

Lady Frederick: Unlike a duchess, it's cheap without
being gaudy.

Fouldes: You asked me why you might want to marry
a boy from ten to fifteen years younger than yourself,
and I've told you.

Lady Frederick: And now perhaps you'll tell me why
you're going to interfere in my private concerns?

Fouldes: Well, you see his mother happens to be my
sister, and I'm rather fond of her. It's true her
husband was the most sanctimonious prig I've ever
met in my life.

Lady Frederick: I remember him well. He was
president of the Broad Church Union and wore side-
whiskers.

Fouldes: But she stuck to me through thick and thin.
I've been in some pretty tight places in my day,
and she's always given me a leg up when I wanted
it. I've got an idea it would just about break her
heart if Charlie married you.

Lady Frederick: Thanks.

Fouldes: You know, I don't want to be offensive, but
I think it would be a pity myself. And besides,
unless I'm much mistaken, I've got a little score of
my own that I want to pay off.

Lady Frederick: Have you?

Fouldes: You've got a good enough memory not to
have forgotten that you made a blithering fool of me

once. I swore I'd get even with you, and by George, I mean to do it.

Lady Frederick (*laughing*): And how do you propose to stop me if I make up my mind that I'm going to accept Charlie?

Fouldes: Well, he's not proposed yet, has he?

Lady Frederick: Not yet, but I've had to use every trick and device I can think of to prevent him.

Fouldes: Look here, I'm going to play this game with my cards on the table.

Lady Frederick: Then I shall be on my guard. You're never so dangerous as when you pretend to be frank.

Fouldes: I'm sorry you should think so badly of me.

Lady Frederick: I don't. Only it was a stroke of genius when Nature put the soul of a Jesuit priest into the body of a Yorkshire squire.

Fouldes: I wonder what you're paying me compliments for. You must be rather afraid of me.

They look at one another for a moment.

Lady Frederick: Well, let's look at these cards.

Fouldes: First of all, there's this money you've got to raise.

Lady Frederick: Well?

Fouldes: This is my sister's suggestion.

Lady Frederick: That means you don't much like it.

Fouldes: If you'll refuse the boy and clear out – we'll give you forty thousand pounds.

Lady Frederick: I suppose you'd be rather surprised if I boxed your ears.

Fouldes: Now look here, between you and me high falutin's rather absurd, don't you think? You're in desperate want of money, and I don't suppose it would amuse you much to have a young hobbledehoy hanging about your skirts for the rest of your life.

Lady Frederick: Very well, we'll have no high falutin! You may tell Lady Mereston that if I really wanted the money I shouldn't be such an idiot as to take forty thousand down when I can have fifty thousand a year for the asking.

Fouldes: I told her that.

Lady Frederick: You showed great perspicacity. Now for the second card.

Fouldes: My dear, it's no good getting into a paddy over it.

Lady Frederick: I've never been calmer in my life.

Fouldes: You always had the very deuce of a temper. I suppose you've not given Charlie a sample of it yet, have you?

Lady Frederick (*laughing*): Not yet.

Fouldes: Well, the second card's your reputation.

Lady Frederick: But I haven't got any. I thought that such an advantage.

Fouldes: You see, Charlie is a young fool. He thinks you a paragon of all the virtues, and it's never occurred to him that you've rather gone the pace in your time.

Lady Frederick: It's one of my greatest consolations to think that.

Fouldes: Still it'll be rather a shock to Charlie when he hears that this modest flower whom he trembles to adore has. . . .

Lady Frederick: Very nearly eloped with his own uncle. But you won't tell him that story because you hate looking a perfect ass.

Fouldes: Madam, when duty calls, Paradine Fouldes consents even to look ridiculous. But I was thinking of the Bellingham affair.

Lady Frederick: Ah, of course, there's the Bellingham affair. I'd forgotten it.

Fouldes: Nasty little business, that, eh?

Lady Frederick: Horrid.

Fouldes: Don't you think it would choke him off?

Lady Frederick: I think it very probable.

Fouldes: Well, hadn't you better cave in?

Lady Frederick

Lady Frederick (*ringing the bell*): Ah, but you've not seen my cards yet. (*A servant enters.*) Tell my servant to bring down the despatch-box which is on my writing-table.

Servant: Yes, miladi.

Exit.

Fouldes: What's up now?

Lady Frederick: Well, four or five years ago I was staying at this hotel, and Mimi la Bretonne had rooms here.

Fouldes: I never heard of the lady, but her name suggests that she had an affectionate nature.

Lady Frederick: She was a little singer at the Folies Bergères, and she had the loveliest emeralds I ever saw.

Fouldes: But you don't know Maud's.

Lady Frederick: The late Lord Mereston had a passion for emeralds. He always thought they were such pure stones.

Fouldes (*quickly*): I beg your pardon?

Lady Frederick: Well, Mimi fell desperately ill, and there was no one to look after her. Of course the pious English ladies in the hotel wouldn't go within a mile of her, so I went and did the usual thing, don't you know.

> **Lady Frederick's** *man comes in with a small despatch-box which he places on a table. He goes out.* **Lady Frederick** *as she talks, unlocks it.*

Fouldes: Thank God I'm a bachelor, and no ministering angel ever smoothes my pillow when I particularly want to be left alone.

Lady Frederick: I nursed her more or less through the whole illness, and afterwards she fancied she owed me her worthless little life. She wanted to give me the precious emeralds, and when I refused was so heartbroken that I said I'd take one thing if I might.

284

Fouldes: And what was that?

Lady Frederick: A bundle of letters. I'd seen the address on the back of the envelope, and then I recognized the writing. I thought they'd be much safer in my hands than in hers. (*She takes them out of the box and hands them to* **Paradine**.) Here they are.

He looks and starts violently.

Fouldes: 89 Grosvenor Square. It's Mereston's writing. You don't mean? What! Ah, ah, ah. (*He bursts into a shout of laughter.*) The old sinner. And Mereston wouldn't have me in the house, if you please, because I was a dissolute libertine. And he was the president of the Broad Church Union. Good Lord, how often have I heard him say: 'Gentlemen, I take my stand on the morality, the cleanliness and the purity of English Family life.' Oh, oh, oh.

Lady Frederick: I've often noticed that the religious temperament is very susceptible to the charms of my sex.

Fouldes: May I look?

Lady Frederick: Well. I don't know. I suppose so.

Fouldes (*reading*): 'Heart's delight' . . . And he signs himself, 'your darling chickabiddy'. The old ruffian.

Lady Frederick: She was a very pretty little thing.

Fouldes: I daresay, but thank heaven, I have some sense of decency left, and it outrages all my susceptibilities that a man in side-whiskers should call himself anybody's chickabiddy.

Lady Frederick: Protestations of undying affection are never ridiculous when they are accompanied by such splendid emeralds.

Fouldes (*starting and growing suddenly serious*): And what about Maud?

Lady Frederick: Well?

Fouldes: Poor girl, it'd simply break her heart. He preached at her steadily for twenty years, and she worshipped the very ground he trod on. She'd have died of grief at his death except she felt it her duty to go on with his work.

Lady Frederick: I know.

Fouldes: By Jove, it's a good card. You were quite right to refuse the emeralds: these letters are twice as valuable.

Lady Frederick: Would you like to burn them?

Fouldes: Betsy!

Lady Frederick: There's the fire. Put them in.

> *He takes them up in both hands and hurries to the fire. But he stops and brings them back, he throws them on the sofa.*

Fouldes: No, I won't.

Lady Frederick: Why not?

Fouldes: It's too dooced generous. I'll fight you tooth and nail, but it's not fair to take an advantage over me like that. You'll bind my hands with fetters.

Lady Frederick: Very well. You've had your chance.

Fouldes: But, by Jove, you must have a good hand to throw away a card like that. What have you got – a straight flush?

Lady Frederick: I may be only bluffing, you know.

Fouldes: Lord, it does me good to hear your nice old Irish brogue again.

Lady Frederick: Faith, and does it?

Fouldes: I believe you only put it on to get over people.

Lady Frederick (*smiling*): Begorrah, it's not easy to get over you.

Fouldes: Lord, I was in love with you once, wasn't I?

Lady Frederick: Not more than lots of other people have been.

Fouldes: And you did treat me abominably.

Lady Frederick: Ah, that's what they all said. But you got over it very well.

Fouldes: I didn't. My digestion was permanently impaired by your brutal treatment.

Lady Frederick: Is that why you went to Carlsbad afterwards instead of the Rocky Mountains?

Fouldes: You may laugh, but the fact remains that I've only been in love once, and that was with you.

Lady Frederick (*smiling as she holds out her hand*): Good-night.

Fouldes: For all that I'm going to fight you now for all I'm worth.

Lady Frederick: I'm not frightened of you, Paradine.

Fouldes: Good-night.

> *As he goes out,* **Captain Montgomerie** *enters.*

Lady Frederick (*yawning and stretching her arms*): Oh I'm so sleepy.

Captain Montgomerie: I'm sorry for that. I wanted to have a talk with you.

Lady Frederick (*smiling*): I daresay I can keep awake for five minutes, you know – especially if you offer me a cigarette.

Captain Montgomerie: Here you are.

> *He hands her his case and lights her cigarette.*

Lady Frederick (*with a sigh*): Oh, what a comfort.

Captain Montgomerie: I wanted to tell you, I had a letter this morning from my solicitor to say that he's just bought Crowley Castle on my behalf.

Lady Frederick: Really. But it's a lovely place. You must ask me to come and stay.

Captain Montgomerie: I should like you to stay there indefinitely.

Lady Frederick (*with a quick look*): That's charming of you, but I never desert my London long.

Captain Montgomerie (*smiling*): I have a very nice house in Portman Square.

Lady Frederick (*surprised*): Really?

Captain Montgomerie: And I'm thinking of going into Parliament at the next election.

Lady Frederick: It appears to be a very delightful pastime to govern the British nation, dignified without being laborious.

Captain Montgomerie: Lady Frederick, although I've been in the service I have rather a good head for business, and I hate beating about the bush. I wanted to ask you to marry me.

Lady Frederick: It's nice of you not to make a fuss about it. I'm very much obliged but I'm afraid I can't.

Captain Montgomerie: Why not?

Lady Frederick: Well, you see, I don't know you.

Captain Montgomerie: We could spend the beginning of our married life so usefully in making one another's acquaintance.

Lady Frederick: It would be rather late in the day then to come to the conclusion that we couldn't bear the sight of one another.

Captain Montgomerie: Shall I send my banker's book so that you may see that my antecedents are respectable and my circumstances – such as to inspire affection.

Lady Frederick: I have no doubt it would be very interesting – but not to me.

She makes as if to go.

Captain Montgomerie: Ah, don't go yet. Won't you give me some reason?

Lady Frederick: If you insist. I'm not in the least in love with you.

Captain Montgomerie: D'you think that much matters?

Lady Frederick: You're a friend of Gerald's, and he says you're a very good sport. But I really can't marry every one that Gerald rather likes.

Captain Montgomerie: He said he'd put in a good word for me.

288

Lady Frederick: If I ever marry again it shall be to please myself, not to please my brother.

Captain Montgomerie: I hope I shall induce you to change your mind.

Lady Frederick: I'm afraid I can give you no hope of that.

Captain Montgomerie: You know, when I determine to do a thing, I generally do it.

Lady Frederick: That sounds very like a threat.

Captain Montgomerie: You may take it as such if you please.

Lady Frederick: And you've made up your mind that you're going to marry me?

Captain Montgomerie: Quite.

Lady Frederick: Well, I've made up my mind that you shan't. So we're quits.

Captain Montgomerie: Why don't you talk to your brother about it?

Lady Frederick: Because it's no business of his.

Captain Montgomerie: Isn't it? Ask him!

Lady Frederick: What do you mean by that?

Captain Montgomerie: Ask him. Good-night.

Lady Frederick: Good-night. (*He goes out.* **Lady Frederick** *goes to the window that leads on to the terrace and calls.*) Gerald!

Gerald: Hulloa! (*He appears and comes into the room.*)

Lady Frederick: Did you know that Captain Montgomerie was going to propose to me?

Gerald: Yes.

Lady Frederick: Is there any reason why I should marry him?

Gerald: Only that I owe him nine hundred pounds.

Lady Frederick (*aghast*): Oh, why didn't you tell me?

Gerald: You were so worried, I couldn't. Oh, I've been such a fool. I tried to make a *coup* for Rose's sake.

Lady Frederick: Is it a gambling debt?

Gerald: Yes.

Lady Frederick (*ironically*): What they call a debt of
   honour?

Gerald: I must pay it the day after to-morrow without
   fail.

Lady Frederick: But that's the day my two bills fall
   due. And if you don't?

Gerald: I shall have to send in my papers, and I shall
   lose Rosie. And then I shall blow out my silly
   brains.

Lady Frederick: But who is the man?

Gerald: He's the son of Aaron Levitzki, the money-
   lender.

Lady Frederick (*half-comic, half-aghast*): Oh lord!

CURTAIN

Act II

The scene is the same as in **Act I.** *Admiral Carlisle
is sleeping in an armchair with a handkerchief over
his face.* **Rose** *is sitting in a grandfather's chair, and*
Gerald *is leaning over the back.*

Rose: Isn't papa a perfectly adorable chaperon?

   The **Admiral** *snores.*

Gerald: Perfectly.
   A pause.

Rose: I've started fifteen topics of conversation in the
   last quarter of an hour, Gerald.

Gerald (*smiling*): Have you?

Rose: You always agree with me, and there's an end
   of it. So I have to rack my brains again.

Gerald: All you say is so wise and sensible. Of course
   I agree.

Rose: I wonder if you'll think me sensible and wise in ten years.

Gerald: I'm quite sure I shall.

Rose: Why, then, I'm afraid we shan't cultivate any great brilliancy of repartee.

Gerald: Be good, sweet maid, and let who will be clever.

Rose: Oh, don't say that. When a man's in love, he at once makes a pedestal of the Ten Commandments and stands on the top of them with his arms akimbo. When a woman's in love she doesn't care two straws for Thou Shalt and Thou Shalt Not.

Gerald: When a woman's in love she can put her heart on a slide of a microscope and examine how it beats. When a man's in love, what do you think he cares for science and philosophy and all the rest of it!

Rose: When a man's in love he can only write sonnets to the moon. When a woman's in love she can still cook his dinner and darn her own stockings.

Gerald: I wish you wouldn't cap all my observations.

She lifts up her face, and he kisses her lips.

Rose: I'm beginning to think you're rather nice, you know.

Gerald: That's reassuring, at all events.

Rose: But no one could accuse you of being a scintillating talker.

Gerald: Have you ever watched the lovers in the Park sitting on the benches hour after hour without saying a word?

Rose: Why?

Gerald: Because I've always thought that they must be bored to the verge of tears. Now I know they're only happy.

Rose: You're certainly my soldier, so I suppose I'm your nursery-maid.

Gerald: You know, when I was at Trinity College, Dublin.

Rose (*interrupting*): Were you there? I thought you went to Oxford.

Gerald: No, why?

Rose: Only all my people go to Magdalen.

Gerald: Yes.

Rose: And I've decided that if I ever have a son he shall go there too.

> The **Admiral** *starts and pulls the handkerchief off his face. The others do not notice him. He is astounded at the conversation.* **Lady Frederick** *comes in later and stands smiling as she listens.*

Gerald: My darling, you know I hate to thwart you in any way, but I've quite made up my mind that my son shall go to Dublin as I did.

Rose: I'm awfully sorry, Gerald, but the boy must be educated like a gentleman.

Gerald: There I quite agree, Rose, but first of all he's an Irishman, and it's right that he should be educated in Ireland.

Rose: Darling Gerald, a mother's love is naturally the safest guide in these things.

Gerald: Dearest Rose, a father's wisdom is always the most reliable.

Lady Frederick: Pardon my interfering, but – aren't you just a little previous?

Admiral (*bursting out*): Did you ever hear such a conversation in your life between a young unmarried couple?

Rose: My dear, papa, we must be prepared for everything.

Admiral: In my youth young ladies did not refer to things of that sort.

Lady Frederick: Well, I don't suppose they're any the worse for having an elementary knowledge of natural history. Personally I doubt whether ignorance is quite the same thing as virtue, and I'm not quite sure that a girl makes a better wife because she's been brought up like a perfect fool.

Admiral: I am old-fashioned, Lady Frederick; and my idea of a modest girl is that when certain topics are mentioned she should swoon. Swoon, madam, swoon. They always did it when I was a lad.

Rose: Well, father, I've often tried to faint when I wanted something that you wouldn't give me, and I've never been able to manage it. So I'm sure I couldn't swoon.

Admiral: And with regard to this ridiculous discussion as to which University your son is to be sent, you seem to forget that I have the right to be consulted.

Gerald: My dear Admiral, I don't see how it can possibly matter to you.

Admiral: And before we go any further I should like you to know that the very day Rose was born I determined that her son should go to Cambridge.

Rose: My dear papa, I think Gerald and I are far and away the best judges for our son's welfare.

Admiral: The boy must work, Rose. I will have no good-for-nothing as my grandson.

Gerald: Exactly. And that is why I'm resolved he shall go to Dublin.

Rose: The important thing is that he should have really nice manners and that they teach at Oxford if they teach nothing else.

Lady Frederick: Well, don't you think you'd better wait another twenty years or so before you discuss this?

Admiral: There are some matters which must be settled at once, Lady Frederick.

Lady Frederick: You know, young things are fairly independent nowadays. I don't know what they'll be in twenty years' time.

Gerald: The first thing the boy shall learn is obedience.

Rose: Certainly. There's nothing so hateful as a disobedient child.

Admiral: I can't see my grandson venturing to disobey me.

Lady Frederick: Then you're all agreed. So that's settled. I came to tell you your carriage was ready.

Admiral: Go and put on your bonnet, Rose. (*To* **Lady Frederick**) Are you coming with us?

Lady Frederick: I'm afraid I can't. *Au revoir.*

Admiral: *A tout à l'heure.*

    He and **Rose** *go out.*

Gerald: Have you ever seen in your life any one so entirely delightful as Rose?

Lady Frederick (*laughing*): Only when I've looked in the glass.

Gerald: My dear Elizabeth, how vain you are.

Lady Frederick: You're very happy, my Gerald.

Gerald: It's such a relief to have got over all the difficulties. I thought it never would come right. You are a brick, Elizabeth.

Lady Frederick: I really think I am rather.

Gerald: The moment you promised to arrange things I felt as safe as a house.

Lady Frederick: I said I'd do my best, didn't I? And I told you not to worry.

Gerald (*turning round suddenly*): Isn't it all right?

Lady Frederick: No, it's about as wrong as it can possibly be. I knew Cohen was staying here, and I thought I could get him to hold the bills over for a few days.

Gerald: And won't he?

Lady Frederick: He hasn't got them any more.

Gerald (*startled*): What!

Lady Frederick: They've been negotiated, and he swears he doesn't know who has them.

Gerald: But who could have been such a fool?

Lady Frederick: I don't know, that's just the awful part of it. It was bad enough before. I knew the worst Cohen could do, but now . . . It couldn't be Paradine.

Gerald: And then there's Montgomerie.

Lady Frederick: I shall see him to-day.

Gerald: What are you going to say to him?

Lady Frederick: I haven't an idea. I'm rather frightened of him.

Gerald: You know, dear, if the worst comes to the worst . . .

Lady Frederick: Whatever happens you shall marry Rose. I promise you that.

     Paradine Fouldes *appears.*

Fouldes: May I come in?

Lady Frederick (*gaily*): It's a public room. I don't see how we can possibly prevent you.

Gerald: I'm just going to take a stroll.

Lady Frederick: Do.

    He goes out.

Fouldes: Well? How are things going?

Lady Frederick: Quite well, thank you.

Fouldes: I've left Charlie with his mother. I hope you can spare him for a couple of hours.

Lady Frederick: I told him he must spend the afternoon with her. I don't approve of his neglecting his filial duty.

Fouldes: Ah! . . . I saw Dick Cohen this morning.

Lady Frederick (*quickly*): Did you?

Fouldes: It seems to interest you?

Lady Frederick: Not at all. Why should it?

Fouldes (*smiling*): Nice little man, isn't he?

Lady Frederick (*good humouredly*): I wish I had something to throw at you.

Fouldes (*with a laugh*): Well, I haven't got the confounded bills. I was too late.

Lady Frederick

Lady Frederick: Did you try?

Fouldes: Oh – yes. I thought it would interest Charlie to know how extremely needful it was for you to marry him.

Lady Frederick: Then who on earth has them?

Fouldes: I haven't an idea, but they must make you very uncomfortable. Three thousand five hundred, eh?

Lady Frederick: Don't say it all at once. It sounds so much.

Fouldes: You wouldn't like to exchange those letters of Mereston's for seven thousand pounds, would you?

Lady Frederick (*laughing*): No.

Fouldes: Ah . . . By the way, d'you mind if I tell Charlie the full story of your – relations with me?

Lady Frederick: Why should I? It's not I who'll look ridiculous.

Fouldes: Thanks. I may avail myself of your permission.

Lady Frederick: I daresay you've noticed that Charlie has a very keen sense of humour,.

Fouldes: If you're going to be disagreeable to me I shall go. (*He stops.*) I say, are you quite sure there's nothing else that can be brought up against you?

Lady Frederick (*laughing*): Quite sure, thanks.

Fouldes: My sister's very jubilant to-day. What about the Bellingham affair?

Lady Frederick: Merely scandal, my friend.

Fouldes: Well, look out. She's a woman, and she'll stick at nothing.

Lady Frederick: I wonder why you warn me.

Fouldes: For the sake of old times, my dear.

Lady Frederick: You're growing sentimental, Paradine. It's the punishment which the god's inflict on a cynic when he grows old.

Fouldes: It may be, but for the life of me I can't forget that once –

Lady Frederick (*interrupting*): My dear friend, don't rake up my lamentable past.

Fouldes: I don't think I've ever met any one so entirely devoid of sentiment as you are.

Lady Frederick: Let us agree that I have every vice under the sun and have done with it.

A **Servant** *comes in.*

Servant: Madame Claude wishes to see your ladyship.

Lady Frederick: Oh, my dressmaker.

Fouldes: Another bill?

Lady Frederick: That's the worst of Monte. One meets as many creditors as in Bond Street. Say I'm engaged.

Servant: Madame Claude says she will wait till miladi is free.

Fouldes: You make a mistake. One should always be polite to people whose bills one can't pay.

Lady Frederick: Show her in.

Servant: Yes, miladi.

Exit **Servant**.

Fouldes: Is it a big one?

Lady Frederick: Oh, no; only seven hundred pounds.

Fouldes: By Jove.

Lady Frederick: My dear friend, one must dress. I can't go about in fig-leaves.

Fouldes: One can dress simply.

Lady Frederick: I do. That's why it costs so much.

Fouldes: You know, you're devilish extravagant.

Lady Frederick: I'm not. I'm content with the barest necessities of existence.

Fouldes: You've got a maid.

Lady Frederick: Of course I've got a maid. I was never taught to dress myself.

Fouldes: And you've got a footman.

Lady Frederick: I've always had a footman. And my mother always had a footman. I couldn't live a day without him.

Fouldes: What does he do for you?

Lady Frederick: He inspires confidence in tradesmen.

Fouldes: And you have the most expensive suite of rooms in the hotel.

Lady Frederick: I'm in such a dreadful mess. If I hadn't got nice rooms I should brood over it.

Fouldes: Then, as if that weren't enough, you fling your money away at the tables.

Lady Frederick: When you're as poor as I am, a few louis more or less can make absolutely no difference.

Fouldes (*with a laugh*): You're quite incorrigible.

Lady Frederick: It's not really my fault. I do try to be economical, but money slips through my fingers like water. I can't help it.

Fouldes: You want a sensible sort of man to look after you.

Lady Frederick: I want a very rich sort of a man to look after me.

Fouldes: If you were my wife, I should advertise in the papers that I wasn't responsible for your debts.

Lady Frederick: If you were my husband, I'd advertise immediately underneath that I wasn't responsible for your manners.

Fouldes: I wonder why you're so reckless.

Lady Frederick: When my husband was alive I was so utterly wretched. And afterwards, when I looked forward to a little happiness my boy died. Then I didn't care any more. I did everything I could to stupefy myself. I squandered money as other women take morphia – that's all.

Fouldes: It's the same dear scatter-brained, good-hearted Betsy that I used to know.

Lady Frederick: You're the only person who calls me Betsy now. To all the others I'm only Elizabeth.

Fouldes: Look here, what are you going to do with this dressmaker?

Lady Frederick: I don't know. I always trust to the inspiration of the moment.

Fouldes: She'll make a devil of a fuss, won't she?

Lady Frederick: Oh, no; I shall be quite nice to her.

Fouldes: I daresay. But won't she be very disagreeable to you?

Lady Frederick: You don't know what a way I have with my creditors.

Fouldes: I know it's not a paying way.

Lady Frederick: Isn't it? I bet you a hundred louis that I offer her the money and she refuses it.

Fouldes: I'll take that.

Lady Frederick: Here she is.

> **Madame Claude** *enters, ushered in by the* **Servant**. *She is a stout, genteel person, very splendidly gowned, with a Cockney accent. Her face is set to sternness, decision to make a scene, and general sourness.*

Servant: Madame Claude.

> *Exit* **Servant. Lady Frederick** *goes up to her enthusiastically and takes both her hands.*

Lady Frederick: Best of women. This is a joyful surprise.

Madame Claude (*drawing herself up*): I 'eard quite by chance that your ladyship was at Monte.

Lady Frederick: So you came to see me at once. That was nice of you. You're the very person I wanted to see.

Madame Claude (*significantly*): I'm glad of that, my lady, I must confess.

Lady Frederick: You dear creature. That's one advantage of Monte Carlo, one meets all one's friends. Do you know Mr Fouldes? This is Madame Claude, an artist, my dear Paradine, a real artist.

Madame Claude (*grimly*): I'm pleased that your ladyship should think so.

Fouldes: How d'you do.

Lady Frederick: Now, this gown. Look, look, look. In this skirt there's genius, *mon cher*. In the way it hangs my whole character is expressed. Observe the fullness of it, that indicates those admirable virtues which make me an ornament to Society, while the frill at the bottom just suggests these foibles – you can hardly call them faults – which add a certain grace and interest to my personality. And the flounce. Paradine, I beseech you to look at it carefully. I would sooner have designed this flounce than won the Battle of Waterloo.

Madame Claude: Your ladyship is very kind.

Lady Frederick: Not at all, not at all. You remember that rose chiffon. I wore it the other day, and the dear archduchess came up to me and said: 'My dear, my dear.' I thought she was going to have a fit. But when she recovered she kissed me on both cheeks and said: 'Lady Frederick, you have a dressmaker worth her weight in gold.' You heard her, Paradine, didn't you?

Fouldes: You forget that I only arrived last night.

Lady Frederick: Of course. How stupid of me. She'll be perfectly delighted to hear that you're in Monte Carlo. But I shall have to break it to her gently.

Madame Claude (*unmoved*): I'm sorry to intrude upon your ladyship.

Lady Frederick: Now what are you talking about? If you hadn't come to see me I should never have forgiven you.

Madame Claude: I wanted to have a little talk with your ladyship.

Lady Frederick: Oh, but I hope we shall have many little talks. We must go out some drives together. I hope you're going to stay some time.

Madame Claude: That depends on circumstances, Lady Frederick. I 'ave a little business to do here.

Lady Frederick: Then let me give you one warning – don't gamble.

Madame Claude: Oh, no, my lady. I gamble quite
enough in my business as it is. I never know when
my customers will pay their bills – if ever.

Lady Frederick (*slightly taken aback*): Ha, ha, ha.

Fouldes (*with a deep guffaw*): Ho, ho, ho.

Lady Frederick: Isn't she clever? I must tell that to
the archduchess. She'll be so amused. Ha, ha, ha,
ha. The dear archduchess, you know she likes a
little joke? You must really meet her. Will you
come to lunch? I know you'd hit it off together.

Madame Claude (*more genially*): That's very kind of
your ladyship.

Lady Frederick: My dear, you know perfectly well
that I've always looked upon you as one of my
best friends. Now who shall we have? There's you
and me and the archduchess. Then I'll ask Lord
Mereston.

Madame Claude: The Marquess of Mereston, Lady
Frederick?

Lady Frederick: Yes. And Mr Fouldes, his uncle.

Madame Claude: Excuse me, are you the Mr Paradine
Fouldes?

Fouldes (*bowing*): At our service, madam.

Madame Claude: I'm so glad to make your
acquaintance, Mr Fouldes. (*Unctuously*) I've always
heard you're such a bad man.

Fouldes: Madam, you overwhelm me with confusion.

Madame Claude: Believe me, Mr Fouldes, it's not the
ladies that are married to saints who take the trouble
to dress well.

Lady Frederick: Now we want a third man. Shall we
ask my brother – you know Sir Gerald O'Mara, don't
you? Or shall we ask Prince Doniani? Yes, I think
we'll ask the Prince. I'm sure you'd like him. Such
a handsome man! That'll make six.

Madame Claude: It's very kind of you, Lady Frederick,
but – well, I'm only a tradeswoman, you know.

Lady Frederick: A tradeswoman? How can you talk

such nonsense. You are an artist – a real artist, my dear. And an artist is fit to meet a king.

Madame Claude: Well, I don't deny that I'd be ashamed to dress my customers in the gowns I see painted at the Royal Academy.

Lady Frederick: Then it's quite settled, isn't it, Madame Claude – oh, may I call you Ada?

Madame Claude: Oh, Lady Frederick, I should be very much flattered. But how did you know that was my name?

Lady Frederick: Why you wrote me a letter only the other day.

Madame Claude: Did I?

Lady Frederick: And such a cross letter too.

Madame Claude (*apologetically*): Oh, but Lady Frederick, that was only in the way of business. I don't exactly remember what expressions I may have made use of –

Lady Frederick (*interrupting, as if the truth had suddenly flashed across her*): Ada! I do believe you came here to-day about my account.

Madame Claude: Oh, no, my lady, I promise you.

Lady Frederick: You did; I know you did. I see it in your face. Now that really wasn't nice of you. I thought you came as a friend.

Madame Claude: I did, Lady Frederick.

Lady Frederick: No, you wanted to dun me. I'm disappointed in you. I did think, after all the things I've had from you, you wouldn't treat me like that.

Madame Claude: But I assure your ladyship . . .

Lady Frederick: Not another word. You came to ask for a cheque. You shall have it.

Madame Claude: No, Lady Frederick, I wouldn't take it.

Lady Frederick: What is the exact figure, Madame Claude?

Madame Claude: I – I don't remember.

Lady Frederick: Seven hundred and fifty pounds,

seventeen and ninepence. You see, I remember.
You came for your cheque and you shall have it.

She sits down and takes a pen.

Madame Claude: Now, Lady Frederick, I should look
upon that as most unkind. It's treating me like a
very second-rate establishment.

Lady Frederick: I'm sorry, but you should have
thought of that before. Now I haven't got a cheque;
how tiresome.

Madame Claude: Oh, it doesn't matter, Lady
Frederick. I promise you it never entered my 'ead.

Lady Frederick: What shall I do?

Fouldes: You can write it on a sheet of paper, you
know.

Lady Frederick (*with a look, aside to him*): Monster!
(*Aloud*) Of course I can. I hadn't thought of that.
(*She takes a sheet of paper*) But how on earth am I
to get a stamp?

Fouldes (*much amused*): I happen to have one on me.

Lady Frederick: I wonder why on earth you should
have English stamps in Monte Carlo?

Fouldes (*handing her one*): A penny stamp may
sometimes save one a hundred louis.

Lady Frederick (*ironically*): Thanks so much. I write
the name of my bank on the top, don't I? Pay
Madame Claude. . . .

Madame Claude: Now it's no good, Lady Frederick, I
won't take it. After all I 'ave my self-respect to
think of.

Lady Frederick: It's too late now.

Madame Claude (*sniffing a little*): No, no, Lady
Frederick. Don't be too 'ard on me. As one lady to
another I ask you to forgive me. I did come about
my account, but – well, I don't want the money.

Lady Frederick (*looking up good-humouredly*): Well,
well. (*She looks at the cheque.*) It shall be as you
wish. There. (*She tears it up.*)

Madame Claude: Oh, thank you, Lady Frederick. I look upon that as a real favour. And now I really must be getting off.

Lady Frederick: Must you go? Well, good-bye. Paradine, take Madame Claude to her carriage. Ada!

She kisses her on the cheek.

Madame Claude (*going*): I am pleased to have seen you.

> **Paradine** *offers his arm and goes out with* **Madame Claude. Lady Frederick** *goes to the window, stands on a chair and waves her handkerchief. While she is doing this,* **Captain Montgomerie** *enters.*

Captain Montgomerie: How d'you do?

Lady Frederick (*getting down*): How nice of you to come. I wanted to see you.

Captain Montgomerie: May I sit down?

Lady Frederick: Of course. There are one or two things I'd like to talk to you about.

Captain Montgomerie: Yes?

Lady Frederick: First I must thank you for your great kindness to Gerald. I didn't know last night that he owed you a good deal of money.

Captain Montgomerie: It's a mere trifle.

Lady Frederick: You must be very rich to call nine hundred pounds that?

Captain Montgomerie: I am.

Lady Frederick (*with a laugh*): All the same it's extremely good of you to give him plenty of time.

Captain Montgomerie: I told Gerald he could have till to-morrow.

Lady Frederick: Obviously he wants to settle with you as soon as ever he can.

Captain Montgomerie (*quietly*): I often wonder why gambling debts are known as debts of honour.

Lady Frederick (*looking at him steadily*): Of course I

realize that if you choose to press for the money and Gerald can't pay – he'll have to send in his papers.

Captain Montgomerie (*lightly*): You may be quite sure I have no wish to bring about such a calamity. By the way, have you thought over our little talk of last night?

Lady Frederick: No.

Captain Montgomerie: You would have been wise to do so.

Lady Frederick: My dear Captain Montgomerie, you really can't expect me to marry you because my brother has been so foolish as to lose more money at poker than he can afford.

Captain Montgomerie: Did you ever hear that my father was a money-lender?

Lady Frederick: A lucrative profession, I believe.

Captain Montgomerie: He found it so. He was a Polish-Jew called Aaron Levitzki. He came to this country with three shillings in his pocket. He lent half-a-crown of it to a friend on the condition that he should be paid back seven and six in three days.

Lady Frederick: I'm not good at figures, but the interest sounds rather high.

Captain Montgomerie: It is. That was one of my father's specialities. From these humble beginnings his business grew to such proportions that at his death he was able to leave me the name and arms of the great family of Montgomerie and something over a million of money.

Lady Frederick: The result of thrift, industry, and good fortune.

Captain Montgomerie: My father was able to gratify all his ambitions but one. He was eaten up with the desire to move in good society, and this he was never able to achieve. His dying wish was that I should live in those circles which he knew only . . .

Lady Frederick: Across the counter?

Captain Montgomerie: Precisely. But my poor father was a little ignorant in these matters. To him one lord was as good as another. He thought a marquess a finer man than an earl, and a viscount than a baron. He would never have understood that a penniless Irish baronet might go into better society than many a belted earl.

Lady Frederick: And what is the application of this?

Captain Montgomerie: I wanted to explain to you one of the reasons which emboldened me last night to make you a proposal of marriage.

Lady Frederick: But surely you know some very nice people. I saw you lunching the other day with the widow of a city knight.

Captain Montgomerie: Many very excellent persons are glad to have me to dine with them. But I know quite well that they're not the real article. I'm as far off as ever from getting into those houses which you have been used to all your life. I'm not content with third-rate earls and rather seedy dowagers.

Lady Frederick: Forgive my frankness, but – aren't you rather a snob.

Captain Montgomerie: My father, Aaron Levitzki, married an English woman, and I have all the English virtues.

Lady Frederick: But I'm not quite sure that people would swallow you even as my husband.

Captain Montgomerie: They'd make a face, but they'd swallow me right enough. And when I asked them down to the best shoot in England they'd come to the conclusion that I agreed with them very well.

Lady Frederick (*still rather amused*): Your offer is eminently businesslike, but you see I'm not a business woman. It doesn't appeal to me.

Captain Montgomerie: I only ask you to perform such of the duties of a wife as are required by Society. They are few enough in all conscience. I should

wish you to entertain largely and receive my
guests, be polite to me, at least in public, and go
with me to the various places people go to.
Otherwise I leave you entire freedom. You will find
me generous and heedful to all your wishes.

Lady Frederick: Captain Montgomerie, I don't know
how much of all that you have said is meant
seriously. But, surely you're not choosing the right
time to make such a proposal when my brother
owes you so much money that if you care to be
hard you can ruin him.

Captain Montgomerie: Why not?

Lady Frederick: D'you mean to say . . . ?

Captain Montgomerie: I will be quite frank with you.
I should never have allowed Gerald to lose so
much money which there was no likelihood of his
being able to pay, if I had not thought it earned
me some claim upon your gratitude.

Lady Frederick (*shortly*): Gerald will pay every penny
he owes you to-morrow.

Captain Montgomerie (*blandly*): Where d'you
suppose he'll get it?

Lady Frederick: I have no doubt I shall be able to
manage something.

Captain Montgomerie: Have you not tried this
morning, entirely without success?

Lady Frederick (*startled*): What?

Captain Montgomerie: You do not forget that you
have sundry moneys of your own which are payable
tomorrow?

Lady Frederick: How d'you know that?

Captain Montgomerie: I told you that when I took a
thing in hand and I carried it through. You went
to Dick Cohen, and he told you he'd parted with
the bills. Didn't you guess that only one man
could have the least interest in taking them over?

Lady Frederick: You?

Captain Montgomerie: Yes.

Lady Frederick: Oh, God.

Captain Montgomerie: Come, come, don't be worried over it. There's nothing to be alarmed about. I'm a very decent chap – if you'd accepted me right away you would never have known that those bills were in my possession. Think it over once more. I'm sure we should get on well together. I can give you what you most need, money and the liberty to fling it away as recklessly as you choose; you can give me the assured and fixed position on which – my father's heart was set.

Lady Frederick: And if I don't accept, you'll make me a bankrupt and you'll ruin Gerald?

Captain Montgomerie: I refuse to consider that very unpleasant alternative.

Lady Frederick: Oh! I can't, I can't.

Captain Montgomerie (*laughing*): But you must, you must. When shall I come for your answer? To-morrow? I'll come with the bills and Gerald's I.O.U. in my pocket, and you shall burn them yourself. Good-bye.

> *He kisses her hand and goes out.* **Lady Frederick** *remains staring in front of her.* **Mereston** *enters, followed by* **Lady Mereston** *and* **Paradine.**

Mereston (*going to her eagerly*): Hulloa! I wondered what on earth had become of you.

Lady Frederick (*with a laugh*): It's only two hours since I chased you away from me.

Mereston: I'm afraid I bore you to death.

Lady Frederick: Don't be so silly. You know you don't.

Mereston: Where are you going now?

Lady Frederick: I have rather a headache. I'm going to lie down.

Mereston: I'm so sorry.

> **Lady Frederick** *goes out.* **Mereston** *stares after*

her anxiously, and makes a step towards the door.

Lady Mereston (*sharply*): Where are you going, Charlie?

Mereston: I never asked Lady Frederick if I could do anything.

Lady Mereston: Good heavens, there are surely plenty of servants in the hotel to get her anything she wants.

Mereston: Don't you think a drive would do her good?

Lady Mereston (*unable to control herself*): Oh, I have no patience with you. I never saw such a ridiculous infatuation in my life.

Paradine: Steady, old girl, steady.

Mereston: What on earth d'you mean, mother?

Lady Mereston: Presumably you're not going to deny that you're in love with that woman.

Mereston (*growing pale*): Would you mind speaking of her as Lady Frederick?

Lady Mereston: You try me very much, Charlie. Please answer my question.

Mereston: I don't want to seem unkind to you, mother, but I think you have no right to ask about my private affairs.

Fouldes: If you're going to talk this matter over you're more likely to come to an understanding if you both keep your tempers.

Mereston: There's nothing I wish to discuss.

Lady Mereston: Don't be absurd, Charlie. You're with Lady Frederick morning, noon and night. She can never stir a yard from the hotel but you go flying after. You pester her with your ridiculous attentions.

Fouldes (*blandly*): One's relations have always such an engaging frankness. Like a bad looking-glass, they always represent you with a crooked nose and a cast in your eye.

Lady Mereston (*to* Mereston): I have certainly a right to know what you mean by all this and what is going to come of it.

Mereston: I don't know what will come of it.

Fouldes: The question that excites our curiosity is this: are you going to ask Lady Frederick to marry you?

Mereston: I refuse to answer that. It seems to me excessively impertinent.

Fouldes: Come, come, my boy, you're too young to play the heavy father. We're both your friends. Hadn't you better make a clean breast of it? After all, your mother and I are interested in nothing so much as your welfare.

Lady Mereston (*imploring*): Charlie!

Mereston: Of course I'd ask her to marry me if I thought for a moment that she'd accept. But I'm so terrified that she'll refuse, and then perhaps I shall never see her again.

Lady Mereston: The boy's stark, staring mad.

Mereston: I don't know what I should do if she sent me about my business. I'd rather continue in this awful uncertainty than lose all hope for ever.

Fouldes: By George. You're pretty far gone, my son. The lover who's diffident is in a much worse way than the lover who protests.

Lady Mereston (*with a little laugh*): I must say it amuses me that Lady Frederick should have had both my brother and my son dangling at her skirts. Your respective passions are separated by quite a number of years.

Mereston: Lady Frederick has already told me of that incident.

Fouldes: With the usual indiscretion of her sex.

Mereston: It appears that she was very unhappy and you, with questionable taste, made love to her.

Fouldes: Do your best not to preach at me, dear boy. It reminds me of your lamented father.

Mereston: And at last she promised to go away with you. You were to meet at Waterloo Station.

Fouldes: Such a draughty place for an assignation.

Mereston: Your train was to start at nine, and you were going to take the boat over to the Channel Isles.

Fouldes: Lady Frederick has a very remarkable memory. I remember hoping the sea wouldn't be rough.

Mereston: And just as the train was starting her eye fell on the clock. At that moment her child was coming down to breakfast and would ask for her. Before you could stop her she'd jumped out of the carriage. The train was moving, and you couldn't get out, so you were taken on to Weymouth – alone.

Lady Mereston: You must have felt a quite egregious ass, Paradine.

Fouldes: I did, but you need not rub it in.

Lady Mereston: Doesn't it occur to you, Charlie, that a woman who loves so easily can't be very worthy of your affection?

Mereston: But, my dear mother, d'you think she cared for my uncle?

Fouldes: What the dickens d'you mean?

Mereston: D'you suppose if she loved you she would have hesitated to come? D'you know her so little as that? She thought of her child only because she was quite indifferent to you.

Fouldes (crossly): You know nothing about it, and you're an impertinent young jackanapes.

Lady Mereston: My dear Paradine, what can it matter if Lady Frederick was in love with you or not?

Fouldes (calming down): Of course it doesn't matter a bit.

Lady Mereston: I have no doubt you mistook wounded vanity for a broken heart.

Fouldes (acidly): My dear, you sometimes say things

311

which explain to me why my brother-in-law so frequently abandoned his own fireside for the platform of Exeter Hall.

Mereston: It may also interest you to learn that I am perfectly aware of Lady Frederick's financial difficulties. I know she has two bills falling due to-morrow.

Fouldes: She's a very clever woman.

Mereston: I've implored her to let me lend her the money, and she absolutely refuses. You see, she's kept nothing from me at all.

Lady Mereston: My dear Charlie, it's a very old dodge to confess what doesn't matter in order to conceal what does.

Mereston: What do you mean, mother?

Lady Mereston: Lady Frederick has told you nothing of the Bellingham affair?

Mereston: Why should she?

Lady Mereston: It is surely expedient you should know that the woman you have some idea of marrying escaped the divorce court only by the skin of her teeth.

Mereston: I don't believe that, mother.

Fouldes: Remember that you're talking to your respected parent, my boy.

Mereston: I'm sorry that my mother should utter base and contemptible libels on – my greatest friend.

Lady Mereston: You may be quite sure that I say nothing which I can't prove.

Mereston: I won't listen to anything against Lady Frederick.

Lady Mereston: But you must.

Mereston: Are you quite indifferent to the great pain you cause me?

Lady Mereston: I can't allow you to marry a woman who's hopelessly immoral.

Mereston: Mother, how dare you say that?

Fouldes: This isn't the sort of thing I much like, but hadn't you better hear the worst at once?

Mereston: Very well. But if my mother insists on saying things, she must say them in Lady Frederick's presence.

Lady Mereston: That I'm quite willing to do.

Mereston: Good.

He rings a bell. A **Servant** *enters.*

Fouldes: You'd better take care, Maudie. Lady Frederick's a dangerous woman to play the fool with.

Mereston (*to the* **Servant**): Go to Lady Frederick Berolles and say Lord Mereston is extremely sorry to trouble her ladyship, but would be very much obliged if she'd come to the drawing-room for two minutes.

Servant: Very well, my lord.

Exit.

Fouldes: What are you going to do, Maud?

Lady Mereston: I knew there was a letter in existence in Lady Frederick's handwriting which proved all I've said about her. I've moved heaven and earth to get hold of it, and it came this morning.

Fouldes: Don't be such a fool. You're not going to use that?

Lady Mereston: I am indeed.

Fouldes: Your blood be upon your own head. Unless I'm vastly mistaken you'll suffer the greatest humiliation that you can imagine.

Lady Mereston: That's absurd. I have nothing to fear.

Lady Frederick *comes in*

Mereston: I'm so sorry to disturb you. I hope you don't mind?

Lady Frederick: Not at all. I knew you wouldn't have sent for me in that fashion without good cause.

Mereston: I'm afraid you'll think me dreadfully impertinent.

Lady Frederick

Lady Mereston: Really you need not apologize so much, Charlie.

Mereston: My mother has something to say against you, and I think it right that she should say it in your presence.

Lady Frederick: That's very nice of you, Charlie – though I confess I prefer people to say horrid things of me only behind my back. Especially if they're true.

Fouldes: Look here, I think all this is rather nonsense. We've most of us got something in our past history that we don't want raked up, and we'd all better let bygones be bygones.

Lady Frederick: I'm waiting, Lady Mereston.

Lady Mereston: It's merely that I thought my son should know that Lady Frederick had been the mistress of Roger Bellingham. (**Lady Frederick** *turns quickly and looks at her; then bursts into a peal of laughter.* **Lady Mereston** *springs up angrily and hands her a letter.*) Is this in your handwriting?

Lady Frederick (*not at all disconcerted*): Dear me, how did you get hold of this?

Lady Mereston: You see that I have ample proof, Lady Frederick.

Lady Frederick (*handing the letter to* **Mereston**): Would you like to read it? You know my writing well enough to be able to answer Lady Mereston's question.

He reads it through and looks at her in dismay.

Mereston: Good God! . . . What does it mean?

Lady Frederick: Pray read it aloud.

Mereston: I can't.

Lady Frederick: Then give it to me. (*She takes it from him.*) It's addressed to my brother-in-law, Peter Berolles. The Kate to whom it refers was his wife. (*Reads*) *Dear Peter: I'm sorry you should have had a row with Kate about Roger Bellingham. You are*

314

*quite wrong in all you thought. There is
absolutely nothing between them. I don't know
where Kate was on Tuesday night, but certainly
she was not within a hundred miles of Roger. This
I know because* . . .

Mereston (*interrupting*): For God's sake don't go on.

> **Lady Frederick** *looks at him and shrugs her
> shoulders.*

Lady Frederick: It's signed Elizabeth Berolles. And
there's a postscript: *You may make what use of
this letter you like.*

Mereston: What does it mean? What does it mean?

Lady Mereston: Surely it's very clear? You can't want
a more explicit confession of guilt.

Lady Frederick: I tried to make it as explicit as
possible.

Mereston: Won't you say something? I'm sure there
must be some explanation.

Lady Frederick: I don't know how you got hold of this
letter, Lady Mereston. I agree with you, it is
compromising. But Kate and Peter are dead now,
and there's nothing to prevent me from telling the
truth.

> **Paradine Fouldes** *takes a step forward and
> watches her.*

Lady Frederick: My sister-in-law was a meek and mild
little person, as demure as you can imagine, and
no one would have suspected her for a moment of
kicking over the traces. Well, one morning she
came to me in floods of tears and confessed that
she and Roger Bellingham (*with a shrug*) had been
foolish. Her husband suspected that something was
wrong and had kicked up a row.

Fouldes (*drily*): There are men who will make a scene
on the smallest provocation.

Lady Frederick: To shield herself she told the first lie
that came into her head. She said to Peter that

Roger Bellingham was my lover – and she threw herself on my mercy. She was a poor, weak little creature, and if there'd been a scandal she'd have gone to the dogs altogether. It had only been a momentary infatuation for Roger, and the scare had crushed her. At the bottom of her heart she loved her husband still. I was desperately unhappy, and I didn't care much what became of me. She promised to turn over a new leaf and all that sort of thing. I thought I'd better give her another chance of going straight. I did what she wanted. I wrote that letter taking all the blame on myself, and Kate lived happily with her husband till she died.

Mereston: It was just like you.

Lady Mereston: But Lord and Lady Peter are dead?

Lady Frederick: Yes.

Lady Mereston: And Roger Bellingham?

Lady Frederick: He's dead too.

Lady Mereston: Then how can you prove your account of this affair?

Lady Frederick: I can't.

Lady Mereston: And does this convince you, Charlie?

Mereston: Of course.

Lady Mereston (*impatiently*): Good heavens, the boy's out of his senses. Paradine, for Heaven's sake say something.

Fouldes: Well, much as it may displease you, my dear, I'm afraid I agree with Charlie.

Lady Mereston: You don't mean to say you believe this cock-and-bull story?

Fouldes: I do.

Lady Mereston: Why?

Fouldes: Well, you see, Lady Frederick's a very clever woman. She would never have invented such an utterly improbable tale, which can't possibly be proved. If she'd been guilty, she'd have had ready at least a dozen proofs of her innocence.

Lady Mereston: But that's absurd.

Fouldes: Besides, I've known Lady Frederick a long time, and she has at least a thousand faults.

Lady Frederick (*with flashing eyes*): Thanks.

Fouldes: But there's something I will say for her. She's not a liar. If she tells me a thing, I don't hesitate for a moment to believe it.

Lady Frederick: It's not a matter of the smallest importance if any of you believe me or not. Be so good as to ring, Charlie.

Mereston: Certainly.

> *He rings, and a* **Servant** *immediately comes in.*

Lady Frederick: Tell my servant that he's to come here at once and bring the despatch-box which is in my dressing-room.

Servant: Yes, miladi.

> *Exit.*

Fouldes (*quickly*): I say, what are you going to do?

Lady Frederick: This is absolutely no business of yours.

Fouldes: Be a brick, Betsy, and don't give her those letters.

Lady Frederick: I think I've had enough of this business. I'm proposing to finish with it.

Fouldes: Temper, temper.

Lady Frederick (*stamping her foot*): Don't say temper to me, Paradine.

> *She walks up and down angrily.* **Paradine** *sits at the piano and with one finger strums 'Rule Britannia'.*

Mereston: Shut up.

> *He takes a book, flings it at his head and misses.*

Fouldes: Good shot, sir.

Lady Frederick: I often wonder how you got your reputation for wit, Paradine.

Fouldes: By making a point of laughing heartily at other people's jokes.

The **Footman** *enters with the despatch-box, which* **Lady Frederick** *opens. She takes a bundle of letters from it.*

Fouldes: Betsy, Betsy, for heaven's sake don't! Have mercy.

Lady Frederick: Was mercy shown to me? Albert!

Footman: Yes, miladi.

Lady Frederick: You'll go the proprietor of the hotel and tell him that I propose to leave Monte Carlo to-morrow.

Mereston (*aghast*): Are you going?

Footman: Very well, my lady.

Lady Frederick: Have you a good memory for faces?

Footman: Yes, my lady.

Lady Frederick: You're not likely to forget Lord Mereston?

Footman: No, my lady.

Lady Frederick: Then please take note that if his lordship calls upon me in London I'm not at home.

Mereston: Lady Frederick!

Lady Frederick (*to* **Footman**): Go.

Exit **Footman.**

Mereston: What d'you mean? What have I done?

Without answering **Lady Frederick** *takes the letters.* **Paradine** *is watching her anxiously. She goes up to the fire and throws them in one by one.*

Lady Mereston: What on earth is she doing?

Lady Frederick: I have some letters here which would ruin the happiness of a very worthless woman I know. I'm burning them so that I may never have the temptation to use them.

Fouldes: I never saw anything so melodramatic.

Lady Frederick: Hold your tongue, Paradine. (*Turning*

to **Mereston**) My dear Charlie, I came to Monte
Carlo to be amused. Your mother has persecuted
me incessantly. Your uncle – is too well-bred to
talk to his servants as he has talked to me. I've
been pestered in one way and another, and
insulted till my blood boiled, because apparently
they're afraid you may want to marry me. I'm sick
and tired of it. I'm not used to treatment of this
sort; my patience is quite exhausted. And since
you are the cause of the whole thing I have an
obvious remedy. I would much rather not have
anything more to do with you. If we meet one
another in the street you need not trouble to look
my way because I shall cut you dead.

Lady Mereston (in an undertone): Thank God for that.

Mereston: Mother, mother. (To **Lady Frederick**) I'm
awfully sorry. I feel that you have a right to be angry.
For all that you've suffered I beg your pardon most
humbly. My mother has said and done things
which I regret to say are quite unjustifiable.

Lady Mereston: Charlie!

Mereston: On her behalf and on mine I apologize with
all my heart.

Lady Frederick (smiling): Don't take it too seriously.
It really doesn't matter. But I think it's far wiser
that we shouldn't see one another again.

Mereston: But I can't live without you.

Lady Mereston (with a gasp): Ah!

Mereston: Don't you know that my whole happiness
is wrapped up in you? I love you with all my heart
and soul. I can never love anyone but you.

Fouldes (to **Lady Mereston**): Now you've done it.
You've done it very neatly.

Mereston: Don't think me a presumptuous fool. I've
been wanting to say this ever since I knew you,
but I haven't dared. You're brilliant and charming
and fascinating, but I have nothing whatever to
offer you.

Lady Frederick (*gently*): My dear Charlie.

Mereston: But if you can overlook my faults, I daresay you could make something of me. Won't you marry me? I should look upon it as a great honour, and I would love you always to the end of my life. I'd try to be worthy of my great happiness and you.

Lady Frederick: You're very much too modest. Charlie. I'm enormously flattered and grateful. You must give me time to think it over.

Lady Mereston: Time?

Mereston: But I can't wait. Don't you see how I love you? You'll never meet anyone who'll care for you as I do.

Lady Frederick: I think you can wait a little. Come and see me to-morrow at ten, and I'll give you an answer.

Mereston: Very well, if I must.

Lady Frederick (*smiling*): I'm afraid so.

Fouldes (*to* **Lady Frederick**): I wonder what the deuce your little game is now.

> *She smiles triumphantly and gives him a deep, ironical curtsey.*

Lady Frederick: Sir, your much obliged and very obedient, humble servant.

CURTAIN

Act III

Scene: Lady Frederick's *dressing-room. At the back is a large opening, curtained, which leads to the bedroom; on the right a door leading to the passage; on the left a window. In front of the window, of which the blind is drawn, is a dressing-table.* **Lady Frederick's** *maid is in the room, a very neat pretty*

*Frenchwoman. She speaks with a slight accent. She
rings the bell, and the* **Footman** *enters.*

Maid: As soon as Lord Mereston arrives he is to be
shown in.

Footman (*surprised*): Here?

Maid: Where else?

> *The* **Footman** *winks significantly. The* **Maid**
> *draws herself up with dignity, and with a
> dramatic gesture points to the door.*

Maid: Depart.

> *The* **Footman** *goes out.*

Lady Frederick (*from the bedroom*): Have you drawn
the blind, Angélique?

Maid: I will do so, miladi. (*She draws the blind, and
the light falls brightly on the dressing-table.*) But
miladi will never be able to stand it. (*She looks at
herself in the glass.*) Oh, the light of the sun in
the morning! I cannot look at myself.

Lady Frederick (*as before*): There's no reason that you
should – especially in my glass.

Maid: But if 'is lordship is coming, miladi must let
me draw the blind. Oh, it is impossible.

Lady Frederick: Do as you're told and don't interfere.

> *The* **Footman** *enters to announce* **Mereston.**
> *The* **Maid** *goes out.*

Footman: Lord Mereston.

Lady Frederick (*as before*): Is that you, Charlie? You're
very punctual.

Mereston: I've been walking about outside till the
clock struck.

Lady Frederick: I'm not nearly dressed, you know.
I've only just had my bath.

Mereston: Must I go?

Lady Frederick: No, of course not. You can talk to me
while I'm finishing.

Mereston: All right. How are you this morning?

Lady Frederick: I don't know. I haven't looked at myself in the glass yet. How are you?

Mereston: A1, thanks.

Lady Frederick: Are you looking nice?

Mereston (*going to the glass*): I hope so. By Jove, what a strong light. You must be pretty sure of your complexion to be able to stand that.

Lady Frederick (*appearing*): I am.

Mereston (*going forward eagerly*): Ah.

> *She comes through the curtains. She wears a kimono, her hair is all dishevelled, hanging about her head in a tangled mop. She is not made up and looks haggard and yellow and lined. When* **Mereston** *sees her he gives a slight start of surprise. She plays the scene throughout with her broadest brogue.*

Lady Frederick: Good-morning.

Mereston (*staring at her in dismay*): Good-morning.

Lady Frederick: Well, what have you to say to me?

Mereston (*embarrassed*): I hope you slept all right.

Lady Frederick (*laughing*): Did you?

Mereston: I forget.

Lady Frederick: I believe you slept like a top. Charlie. You really might have lain awake and thought of me. What is the matter? You look as if you'd seen a ghost.

Mereston: Oh no, not at all.

Lady Frederick: You're not disappointed already?

Mereston: No, of course not. Only – you look so different with your hair not done.

Lady Frederick (*with a little cry*): Oh, I'd forgotten all about it. Angélique, come and do my hair.

Maid (*appearing*): Yes, miladi.

> **Lady Frederick** *sits down at the dressing-table.*

Lady Frederick: Now, take pains, Angélique. I want

to look my very best. Angélique is a jewel of
incalculable value.

Maid: Miladi is very kind.

Lady Frederick: If I'm light-hearted, she does it one
way. If I'm depressed she does it another.

Maid: Oh, miladi, the perruquier who taught me said
always that a good hairdresser could express every
mood and every passion of the human heart.

Lady Frederick: Good heavens, you don't mean to say
you can do all that?

Maid: Miladi, he said I was his best pupil.

Lady Frederick: Very well. Express – express a great
crisis in my affairs.

Maid: That is the easiest thing in the world, miladi.
I bring the hair rather low on the forehead, and
that expresses a crisis in her ladyship's affairs.

Lady Frederick: But I always wear my hair low on the
forehead.

Maid: Then it is plain her ladyship's affairs are always
in a critical condition.

Lady Frederick: So they are. I never thought of that.

Mereston: You've got awfully stunning hair, Lady
Frederick.

Lady Frederick: D'you like it, really?

Mereston: The colour's perfectly beautiful.

Lady Frederick: It ought to be. It's frightfully
expensive.

Mereston: You don't mean to say it's dyed?

Lady Frederick: Oh, no. Only touched up. That's quite
a different thing.

Mereston: Is it?

Lady Frederick: It's like superstition, you know,
which is what other people believe. My friends dye
their hair, but I only touch mine up. Unfortunately,
it costs just as much.

Mereston: And you have such a lot.

Lady Frederick: Oh, heaps. [*She opens a drawer and*

takes out a long switch.) Give him a bit to look at.

Maid: Yes, miladi.

She gives it to him.

Mereston: Er – yes. *(Not knowing what on earth to say.)* How silky it is.

Lady Frederick: A poor thing, but mine own. At least, I paid for it. By the way, have I paid for it yet, Angélique?

Maid: Not yet, miladi. But the man can wait.

Lady Frederick *(taking it from* **Mereston***):* A poor thing, then, but my hairdresser's. Shall I put it on?

Mereston: I wouldn't, if I were you.

Maid: If her ladyship anticipates a tragic situation, I would venture to recommend it. A really pathetic scene is impossible without a quantity of hair worn quite high on the head.

Lady Frederick: Oh, I know. Whenever I want to soften the hard heart of a creditor I clap on every bit I've got. But I don't think I will to-day. I'll tell you what, a temple curl would just fit the case.

Maid: Then her ladyship inclines to comedy. Very well, I say no more.

> **Lady Frederick** *takes two temple-curls from the drawer.*

Lady Frederick: Aren't they dears?

Mereston: Yes.

Lady Frederick: You've admired them very often, Charlie, haven't you? I suppose you never knew they cost a guinea each?

Mereston: It never occurred to me they were false.

Lady Frederick: The masculine intelligence is so gross. Didn't your mother tell you?

Mereston: My mother told me a great deal.

Lady Frederick: I expect she overdid it. There. Now that's done. D'you think it looks nice.

Mereston: Charming.

Lady Frederick: Angélique, his lordship is satisfied.
You may disappear.
Maid: Yes, miladi.

She goes.

Lady Frederick: Now, tell me you think I'm the most
ravishing creature you ever saw in your life.
Mereston: I've told you that so often.
Lady Frederick (*stretching out her hands*): You are a
nice boy. It was charming of you to say – what
you did yesterday. I could have hugged you there
and then.
Mereston: Could you?
Lady Frederick: Oh, my dear, don't be so cold.
Mereston: I'm very sorry, I didn't mean to be.
Lady Frederick: Haven't you got anything nice to say
to me at all?
Mereston: I don't know what I can say that I've not
said a thousand times already.
Lady Frederick: Tell me what you thought of all night
when you tossed on that sleepless pillow of yours.
Mereston: I was awfully anxious to see you again.
Lady Frederick: Didn't you have a dreadful fear that
I shouldn't be as nice as you imagined? Now, come
– honestly.
Mereston: Well, yes, I suppose it crossed my mind.
Lady Frederick: And am I?
Mereston: Of course.
Lady Frederick: You're sure you're not disappointed?
Mereston: Quite sure.
Lady Frederick: What a relief! You know, I've been
tormenting myself dreadfully. I said to myself:
He'll go on thinking of me till he imagines I'm the
most beautiful woman in the world, and then,
when he comes here and sees the plain reality, it'll
be an awful blow.
Mereston: What nonsense! How could you think
anything of the kind?

Lady Frederick: Are you aware that you haven't shown the least desire to kiss me yet?

Mereston: I thought – I thought you might not like it.

Lady Frederick: It'll be too late in a minute.

Mereston: Why?

Lady Frederick: Because I'm just going to make up, you silly boy.

Mereston: How? I don't understand.

Lady Frederick: You said I must be very sure of my complexion. Of course I am. Here it is.

She runs her fingers over a row of little pots and vases.

Mereston: Oh, I see. I beg your pardon.

Lady Frederick: You don't mean to say you thought it natural?

Mereston: It never occurred to me it might be anything else.

Lady Frederick: It's really too disheartening. I spend an hour every day of my life making the best complexion in Monte Carlo, and you think it's natural. Why, I might as well be a dairymaid of eighteen.

Mereston: I'm very sorry.

Lady Frederick: I forgive you . . . You may kiss my hand. (*He does so.*) You dear boy. (*Looking at herself in the glass*) Oh, Betsy, you're not looking your best today. (*Shaking her finger at the glass*) This won't do, Betsy, my dear. You're very nearly looking your age. (*Turning round quickly*) D'you think I look forty?

Mereston: I never asked myself how old you were.

Lady Frederick: Well, I'm not, you know. And I shan't be as long as there's a pot of rouge and a powder puff in the world. (*She rubs grease paint all over her face.*).

Mereston: What *are* you doing?

Lady Frederick: I wish I were an actress. They have such an advantage. They only have to make up to look well behind the footlights; but I have to expose myself to that beastly sun.

Mereston (*nervously*): Yes, of course.

Lady Frederick: Is your mother dreadfully annoyed with you? And Paradine must be furious. I shall call him Uncle Paradine next time I see him. It'll make him feel so middle-aged. Charlie, you don't know how grateful I am for what you did yesterday. You acted like a real brick.

Mereston: It's awfully good of you to say so.

Lady Frederick (*turning*): Do I look a fright?

Mereston: Oh, no, not at all.

Lady Frederick: I love this powder. It plays no tricks with you. Once I put on a new powder that I bought in Paris, and as soon as I went into artificial light it turned a bright mauve. I was very much annoyed. You wouldn't like to go about with a mauve face, would you?

Mereston: No, not at all.

Lady Frederick: Fortunately I had a green frock on. And mauve and green were very fashionable that year. Still I'd sooner it hadn't been on my face . . . There. I think that'll do as a foundation. I'm beginning to feel younger already. Now for the delicate soft bloom of youth. The great difficulty, you know, is to make both your cheeks the same colour. (*Turning to him*) Charlie, you're not bored, are you?

Mereston: No, no.

Lady Frederick: I always think my observations have a peculiar piquancy when I have only one cheek rouged. I remember once I went out to dinner, and as soon as I sat down I grew conscious of the fact that one of my cheeks was much redder than the other.

Mereston: By George, that was awkward.

Lady Frederick: Charlie, you are a good-looking boy. I had no idea you were so handsome. And you look so young and fresh, it's quite a pleasure to look at you.

Mereston (*laughing awkwardly*): D'you think so? What did you do when you discovered your predicament?

Lady Frederick: Well, by a merciful interposition of Providence, I had a foreign diplomatist on my right side which bloomed like a rose, and a bishop on my left which was white like the lily. The diplomatist told me risky stories all through dinner so it was quite natural that this cheek should blush fiery red. And as the Bishop whispered in my left ear harrowing details of distress in the East End, it was only decent that the other should exhibit a becoming pallor. (*Meanwhile she has been rouging her cheeks.*) Now look carefully, Charlie, and you'll see how I make the Cupid's bow which is my mouth. I like a nice healthy colour on the lips, don't you?'

Mereston: Isn't it awfully uncomfortable to have all that stuff on?

Lady Frederick: Ah, my dear boy, it's woman's lot to suffer in this world. But it's a great comfort to think that one is submitting to the decrees of Providence and at the same time adding to one's personal attractiveness. But I confess I sometimes wish I needn't blow my nose so carefully. Smile, Charlie. I don't think you're a very ardent lover, you know.

Mereston: I'm sorry. What would you like me to do?

Lady Frederick: I should like you to make me impassioned speeches.

Mereston: I'm afraid they'd be so hackneyed.

Lady Frederick: Never mind that. I've long discovered that under the influence of profound emotion a man always expresses himself in the terms of the *Family Herald*.

Mereston: You must remember that I'm awfully inexperienced.

Lady Frederick: Well, I'll let you off this time – because I like your curly hair. (*She sighs amorously.*) Now for the delicate arch of my eyebrows. I don't know what I should do without this. I've got no eyebrows at all really ... Have you ever noticed that dark line under the eyes which gives such intensity to my expression?

Mereston: Yes, often.

Lady Frederick (*holding out the pencil*): Well, here it is. Ah, my dear boy, in this pencil you have at will roguishness and languor, tenderness and indifference, sprightliness, passion, malice, what you will. Now be very quiet for one moment. If I overdo it my whole day will be spoilt. You mustn't breathe even. Whenever I do this I think how true those lines are: The little more and how much it is. The little less and what worlds away. There! Now just one puff of powder, and the whole world's kind. (*Looking at herself in the glass and sighing with satisfaction*) Ah! I feel eighteen. I think it's a success, and I shall have a happy day. Oh, Betsy, Betsy, I think you'll do. You know, you're not unattractive, my dear. Not strictly beautiful perhaps; but then I don't like the chocolate-box sort of woman. I'll just go and take off this dressing-gown. (**Mereston** *gets up*) No, don't move. I'll go into my bedroom. I shall only be one moment. (**Lady Frederick** *goes through the curtains.*) Angélique.

The **Maid** *enters.*

Maid: Yes, miladi.

Lady Frederick: Just clear away those things on the dressing-table.

Maid (*doing so*): Very well, miladi.

Lady Frederick: You may have a cigarette, Charlie.

Mereston: Thanks. My nerves are a bit dicky this morning.

Lady Frederick: Oh, blow the thing! Angélique, come and help me.

Maid: Yes. miladi.

> *She goes out.*

Lady Frederick: At last.

> *She comes in, having changed the kimono for a very beautiful dressing-gown of silk and lace.*

Lady Frederick: Now, are you pleased?

Mereston: Of course I'm pleased.

Lady Frederick: Then you may make love to me.

Mereston: You say such disconcerting things.

Lady Frederick (*laughing*): Well, Charlie, you've found no difficulty in doing it for the last fortnight. You're not going to pretend that you're already at a loss for pretty speeches?

Mereston: When I came here, I had a thousand things to say to you, but you've driven them all out of my head. Won't you give me an answer now?

Lady Frederick: What to?

Mereston: You've not forgotten that I asked you to marry me?

Lady Frederick: No, but you asked me under very peculiar circumstances. I wonder if you can repeat the offer now in cold blood?

Mereston: Of course. What a cad you must think me!

Lady Frederick: Are you sure you want to marry me still – after having slept over it?

Mereston: Yes.

Lady Frederick: You are a good boy, and I'm a beast to treat you so abominably. It's awfully nice of you.

Mereston: Well, what is the answer?

Lady Frederick: My dear, I've been giving it you for the last half-hour.

Mereston: How?

Lady Frederick: You don't for a moment suppose I should have let you into those horrible mysteries of my toilette if I'd had any intention of marrying you? Give me credit for a certain amount of intelligence and good feeling. I should have kept up the illusion, at all events till after the honeymoon.

Mereston: Are you going to refuse me?

Lady Frederick: Aren't you rather glad?

Mereston: No, no, no.

Lady Frederick (*putting her arm through his*): Now let us talk it over sensibly. You're a very nice boy, and I'm awfully fond of you. But you're twenty-two, and heaven only knows my age. You see, the church in which I was baptized was burnt down the year I was born, so I don't know how old I am.

Mereston (*smiling*): Where was it burnt?

Lady Frederick: In Ireland.

Mereston: I thought so.

Lady Frederick: Just at present I can make a decent enough show by taking infinite pains; and my hand is not so heavy that the innocent eyes of your sex can discover how much of me is due to art. But in ten years you'll only be thirty-two, and then, if I married you, my whole life would be a mortal struggle to preserve some semblance of youth. Haven't you seen those old hags who've never surrendered to Anno Domini, with their poor, thin, wrinkled cheeks covered with paint, and the dreadful wigs that hide a hairless pate? Rather cock-eyed, don't you know, and invariably flaxen. You've laughed at their ridiculous graces, and you've been disgusted too. Oh, I'm so sorry for them, poor things. And I should become just like that, for I should never have the courage to let my hair be white so long as yours was brown. But if I

331

don't marry you, I can look forward to the white
hairs fairly happily. The first I shall pluck out, and
the second I shall pluck out. But when the third
comes I'll give in, and I'll throw my rouge and my
poudre de riz and my pencils into the fire.

Mereston: But d'you think I should ever change?

Lady Frederick: My dear boy, I'm sure of it. Can't you
imagine what it would be to be tied to a woman
who was always bound to sit with her back to the
light? And sometimes you might want to kiss me.

Mereston: I think it very probable.

Lady Frederick: Well, you couldn't – in case you
disarranged my complexion. (**Mereston** *sighs
deeply*) Don't sigh, Charlie. I daresay I was horrid
to let you fall in love with me, but I'm only
human, and I was desperately flattered.

Mereston: Was that all?

Lady Frederick: And rather touched. That is why I
want to give a cure with my refusal.

Mereston: But you break my heart.

Lady Frederick: My dear, men have said that to me
ever since I was fifteen, but I've never noticed that
in consequence they ate their dinner less heartily.

Mereston: I suppose you think it was only calf-love?

Lady Frederick: I'm not such a fool as to imagine a
boy can love any less than a man. If I'd thought your
affection ridiculous I shouldn't have been so
flattered.

Mereston: It doesn't hurt any the less because the
wounds you make are clean cut.

Lady Frederick: But they'll soon heal. And you'll fall
in love with a nice girl of your own age, whose
cheeks flush with youth and not with rouge, and
whose eyes sparkle because they love you, and not
because they're carefully made up.

Mereston: But I wanted to help you. You're in such
an awful scrape, and if you'll only marry me it can
all be set right.

Lady Frederick: Oh, my dear, don't go in for self-sacrifice. You must leave that to women. They're so much more used to it.

Mereston: Isn't there anything I can do for you?

Lady Frederick: No, dear. I shall get out of the mess somehow. I always do. You really need not worry about me.

Mereston: You know, you *are* a brick.

Lady Frederick: Then it's all settled, isn't it? And you're not going to be unhappy?

Mereston: I'll try not to be.

Lady Frederick: I'd like to imprint a chaste kiss on your forehead, only I'm afraid it would leave a mark.

> *The* **Footman** *comes in and announces* **Paradine Fouldes.**

Footman Mr Paradine Fouldes.

> *Exit.*

Fouldes: Do I disturb?

Lady Frederick: Not at all. We've just finished our conversation.

Fouldes: Well?

Mereston: If anyone wants to know who the best woman in the world is send 'em to me, and I'll tell them.

Lady Frederick (*taking his hand*): You dear! Good-bye.

Mereston: Good-bye. And thanks for being so kind to me.

> *He goes out.*

Fouldes: Do I see in front of me my prospective niece?

Lady Frederick: Why d'you ask, Uncle Paradine?

Fouldes: Singularly enough because I want to know.

Lady Frederick: Well, it so happens – you don't.

Fouldes: You've refused him?

Lady Frederick: I have.

Fouldes: Then will you tell me why you've been leading us all such a devil of a dance?

Lady Frederick: Because you interfered with me, and I allow no one to do that.

Fouldes: Hoity-toity.

Lady Frederick: You weren't really so foolish as to imagine I should marry a boy who set me up on a pedestal and vowed he was unworthy to kiss the hem of my garments?

Fouldes: Why not?

Lady Frederick: My dear Paradine, I don't want to commit suicide by sheer boredom. There's only one thing in the world more insufferable than being in love.

Fouldes: And what is that, pray?

Lady Frederick: Why, having some one in love with you.

Fouldes: I've suffered from it all my life.

Lady Frederick: Think of living up to the ideal Charlie has of me. My hair would turn a hydrogen yellow in a week. And then to be so desperately adored as all that – oh, it's so dull! I should have to wear a mask all day long. I could never venture to be natural in case I shocked him. And notwithstanding all my efforts I should see the illusions tumbling about his ears one by one till he realized I was no ethereal goddess, but a very ordinary human woman neither better nor worse than anybody else.

Fouldes: Your maxim appears to be, marry anyone you like except the man that's in love with you.

Lady Frederick: Ah, but don't you think I might find a man who loved me though he knew me through and through? I'd far rather that he saw my faults and forgave them than that he thought me perfect.

Fouldes: But how d'you know you've choked the boy off for good?

Lady Frederick: I took good care. I wanted to cure

him. If it had been possible I would have shown him my naked soul. But I couldn't do that, so I let him see. . . .

Fouldes (*interrupting*): What!

Lady Frederick (*laughing*): No, not quite. I had a dressing-gown on and other paraphernalia. But I made him come here when I wasn't made up, and he sat by while I rouged my cheeks.

Fouldes: And the young fool thought there was nothing more in you than a carefully prepared complexion?

Lady Frederick: He was very nice about it. But I think he was rather relieved when I refused him.

There is a knock at the door.

Gerald (*outside*): May we come in?

Lady Frederick: Yes, do.

Enter **Gerald** *and* **Rose** *and the* **Admiral**.

Gerald (*excitedly*): I say, it's all right. The Admiral's come down like a real brick. I've told him everything.

Lady Frederick: What do you mean? Good-morning, dear Admiral.

Admiral: Good-morning.

Gerald: I've made a clean breast of it. I talked it over with Rosie.

Rose: And we went to papa together.

Gerald: And told him that I owed Montgomerie nine hundred pounds.

Rose: And we thought papa would make an awful scene.

Gerald: Raise Cain, don't you know.

Rose: But he never said a word.

Gerald: He was simply ripping over it.

Lady Frederick (*putting her hands to her ears*): Oh, oh, oh. For heaven's sake be calm and coherent.

Gerald: My dear, you don't know what a relief it is.

Rose: I saw Gerald was dreadfully worried, and I wormed it out of him.

Gerald: I'm so glad to be out of the clutches of that brute.

Rose: Now we're going to live happily ever afterwards.

All the while the **Admiral** *has been trying to get a word in, but each time he is about to start one of the others has broken in.*

Admiral: Silence. (*He puffs and blows.*) I never saw such a pair in my life.

Lady Frederick: Now do explain it all, admiral. I can't make head or tail of these foolish creatures.

Admiral: Well, they came and told me that Montgomerie had an I.O.U. of Gerald's for nine hundred pounds and was using it to blackmail you.

Fouldes: Is that a fact?

Lady Frederick: Yes.

Admiral: I never liked the man's face. And when they said his terms were that you were to marry him or Gerald would have to send in his papers, I said . . .

Fouldes: Damn his impudence.

Admiral: How did you know?

Fouldes: Because I'd have said it myself.

Gerald: And the admiral stumped up like a man. He gave me a cheque for the money, and I've just this moment sent it on to Montgomerie.

Lady Frederick (*taking both his hands*): It's awfully good of you, and I'm sure you'll never regret that you gave Gerald a chance.

Admiral: May I have a few words' private conversation with you?

Lady Frederick: Of course. (*To the others*) Make yourselves scarce.

Fouldes: We'll go on the balcony, shall we?

Admiral: I'm sorry to trouble you, but it'll only take three minutes.

> **Gerald** *and* **Rose** *and* **Fouldes** *go on to the balcony.*

Lady Frederick *(when they've gone)*: There.

Admiral: Well, what I wanted to say to you was this: I like Gerald, but I think he wants guiding. D'you follow me?

Lady Frederick: I'm sure he will take your advice always.

Admiral: It's a woman's hand that he wants. Now if you and I were to join forces we could keep him out of mischief, couldn't we?

Lady Frederick: Oh, I'll come and stay with you whenever you ask me. I love giving good advice when I'm quite sure it won't be taken.

Admiral: I was thinking of a more permanent arrangement. Look here, why don't you marry me?

Lady Frederick: My dear admiral!

Admiral: I don't think an attractive woman like you ought to live alone. She's bound to get in a scrape.

Lady Frederick: It's awfully good of you, but . . .

Admiral: You don't think I'm too old, do you?

Lady Frederick: Of course not. You're in the very prime of life.

Admiral: There's life in the old dog yet, I can tell you.

Lady Frederick: I feel sure of that. I never doubted it for a moment.

Admiral: Then what have you got against me?

Lady Frederick: You wouldn't like to commit polygamy, would you?

Admiral: Eh?

Lady Frederick: You see, it's not a question of marrying me only, but all my tradespeople.

Admiral: I hadn't thought of that.

Lady Frederick: Besides, you're Rose's father, and I'm Gerald's sister. If we married I would be my

337

brother's mother-in-law, and my step-daughter
would be my sister. Your daughter would be your
sister-in-law, and your brother would just snap his
fingers at your fatherly advice.

Admiral (*confused*): Eh?

Lady Frederick: I don't know if the prayer-book allows
things like that, but if it does I think it's
hopelessly immoral.

Admiral: Well, shall I tell them I've changed my mind
and they can't marry?

Lady Frederick: Then there'd be no reason for us to –
commit the crime, would there?

Admiral: I hadn't thought of that. I suppose not.

Lady Frederick: You're not cross with me, are you?
I'm very much flattered, and I thank you from the
bottom of my heart.

Admiral: Not at all, not at all. I only thought it might
save trouble.

Lady Frederick (*calling*): Gerald. Come along. (*They
come in.*) We've had our little talk.

Gerald: Everything satisfactory?

Lady Frederick (*with a look at the* **Admiral**): Quite.

Admiral (*gruffly*): Quite.

Lady Frederick's Footman *enters.*

Footman: Captain Montgomerie wishes to know if he
may see your ladyship.

Lady Frederick: I'd forgotten all about him.

Gerald: Let me go to him, shall I?

Lady Frederick: No, I'm not afraid of him any longer.
He can't do anything to you. And as far as I'm
concerned it doesn't matter.

Gerald: Then I'll tell him to go to the devil.

Lady Frederick: No, I'm going to tell him that myself.
(*To the* **Footman**) Ask Captain Montgomerie to
come here.

Footman: Yes, miladi.

Exit.

338

Lady Frederick (*walking up and down furiously*): I'm going to tell him that myself.

Fouldes: Now keep calm, Betsy.

Lady Frederick (*very deliberately*): I shall not keep calm.

Fouldes: Remember that you're a perfect lady.

Lady Frederick: Don't interfere with me. I ate humble pie yesterday, and it didn't agree with me at all.

> **Footman** *enters to announce* **Captain Montgomerie,** *who follows him, and immediately withdraws.*

Footman: Captain Montgomerie.

Captain Montgomerie: How d'you do.

> *He is obviously surprised to see the others.*

Lady Frederick (*pleasantly*): Quite a party, aren't we?

Captain Montgomerie: Yes. (*A pause.*) I hope you don't mind my coming so early?

Lady Frederick: Not at all. You made an appointment for half-past ten.

Captain Montgomerie: I trust you have good news for me.

Lady Frederick: Captain Montgomerie, every one here knows the circumstances that have brought you.

Captain Montgomerie: I should have thought it wiser for both our sakes not to make them too public.

Lady Frederick (*very amiably*): I don't see why you should be ashamed because you made me a proposal of marriage.

Captain Montgomerie: I'm sorry you should think it a laughing matter, Lady Frederick.

Lady Frederick: I don't. I never laugh at an impertinence.

Captain Montgomerie (*taken aback*): I beg your pardon.

Lady Frederick: Surely the receipt of my brother's letter was sufficient answer for you. After that you must have guessed there was no likelihood that I should change my mind.

Captain Montgomerie: What letter? I don't understand.

Gerald: I sent you a note this morning enclosing a cheque for the money I lost to you.

Captain Montgomerie: I've not received it.

Gerald: It must be waiting for you at the hotel.

> **Captain Montgomerie** *pauses and looks meditatively at the assembled company.*

Lady Frederick: I think there's nothing for which I need detain you longer.

Captain Montgomerie (*smiling*): I don't think I've quite finished yet. Has it slipped your memory that the two bills fall due to-day? Allow me to present them.

> *He takes them out of his pocket-book.*

Lady Frederick: I'm very sorry I can't pay them – at present.

Captain Montgomerie: I regret that I can't wait. You must pay them.

Lady Frederick: I tell you it's impossible.

Captain Montgomerie: Then I shall get an order against you.

Lady Frederick: That you may do to your heart's content.

Captain Montgomerie: You realize the consequences. It's not very nice to be an undischarged bankrupt.

Lady Frederick: Much nicer than to marry a rascally money-lender.

Fouldes: May I look at these interesting documents?

Captain Montgomerie: Certainly. (*Blandly*) I haven't the least wish to be offensive.

Fouldes (*taking them*): You fail lamentably in achieving your wish. Three thousand five hundred pounds in all. It seems hardly worth while to make a fuss about so small a sum.

Captain Montgomerie: I'm in urgent need of money.

Fouldes (*ironically*): So rich a man as you?

Captain Montgomerie: Even a rich man may be temporarily embarrassed.

Fouldes: Then be so good as to wait for one moment. (*He sits down at a table and writes a cheque.*) No sight is more affecting than that of a millionaire in financial straits.

Lady Frederick: Paradine!

Fouldes (*handing the cheque*): Now sir, I think that settles it. Will you exchange my cheque for those bills.

Captain Montgomerie: Damn you, I forgot you.

Fouldes: You may not be aware that it's unusual to swear in the presence of ladies.

Captain Montgomerie (*looking at the cheque*): I suppose it's all right.

> **Paradine** *goes to the door and opens it.*

Fouldes: There is the window, and here is the door. Which will you choose?

> **Captain Montgomerie** *looks at him without answering, shrugs his shoulders and goes out.*

Lady Frederick: Oh, Paradine, you are a brick.

Gerald: I say it's awfully good of you.

Fouldes: Nonsense. I've got a strong sense of effect, and I always cultivate the dramatic situation.

Lady Frederick: I shall never be able to pay you back, Paradine.

Fouldes: My dear, I'm not entirely devoid of intelligence.

Admiral: Well, well, I must be off to take my constitutional.

Lady Frederick: And Rose and Gerald must take care of you. We shall all meet at luncheon.

Admiral: Yes, yes.

> *The* **Admiral, Rose** *and* **Gerald** *go out.* **Lady**

Lady Frederick

Frederick goes up to **Paradine** *and takes his hands.*

Lady Frederick: Thanks awfully. You are a good friend.

Fouldes: By George, how your eyes glitter!

Lady Frederick: It's only belladonna, you know.

Fouldes: I'm not such a fool as my nephew, my dear.

Lady Frederick: Why did you do it?

Fouldes: D'you know what gratitude is?

Lady Frederick: Thanks for past favours and a lively sense of benefits to come.

Fouldes: Well, yesterday you had my sister in the hollow of your hand. She gave you great provocation, and you burnt those confounded letters.

Lady Frederick: My dear Paradine, I can't get over my own magnanimity. And what are the benefits to come?

Fouldes: Well, it might be five per cent on the capital.

Lady Frederick: I don't know why you should squeeze my hands all the time.

Fouldes: But it isn't. Look here, don't you get awfully tired of racketting about?

Lady Frederick: Oh, my dear friend, I'm sick to death of it. I've got half a mind to retire from the world and bury myself in a hermitage.

Fouldes: So have I, and I've bought the lease of a little house in Norfolk Street, Park Lane.

Lady Frederick: Just the place for a hermitage – fashionable without being vulgar.

Fouldes: And I propose to live there quite quietly, and I shall just subsist on a few dried herbs, don't you know.

Lady Frederick: But do have them cooked by a really good French chef; it makes such a difference.

Fouldes: And what d'you say to joining me?

Lady Frederick: I?

Fouldes: You.

Lady Frederick: Oh, I *am* a success to-day. That's another proposal of marriage.

Fouldes: It sounds very much like it.

Lady Frederick: I've already had three this morning.

Fouldes: Then I should think you've said no quite often enough.

Lady Frederick: Come at ten o'clock to-morrow, and you shall see me make up.

Fouldes: D'you think that would choke me off? D'you suppose I don't know that behind that very artificial complexion there's a dear little woman called Betsy who's genuine to the bottom of her soul?

Lady Frederick: Oh, don't be so sentimental or I shall cry.

Fouldes: Well, what is it to be?

Lady Frederick (*her voice breaking*): D'you like me still, Paradine, after all these years.

Fouldes: Yes. (*She looks at him, her lips quivering. He stretches out his arms, and she, breaking down, hides her face on his shoulder.*) Now don't be an ass, Betsy . . . I know you'll say in a minute I'm the only man you ever loved.

Lady Frederick (*looking up with a laugh*): I shan't. . . . But what will your sister say?

Fouldes: I'll tell her there was only one way in which I could save Charlie from your clutches.

Lady Frederick: What?

Fouldes: By marrying you myself.

Lady Frederick (*putting up her face*): Monster.

He kisses her lips.

CURTAIN

Methuen World Classics
include

Jean Anouilh (two volumes)
John Arden (two volumes)
Arden & D'Arcy
Brendan Behan
Aphra Behn
Bertolt Brecht (six volumes)
Büchner
Bulgakov
Calderón
Anton Chekhov
Noël Coward (five volumes)
Eduardo De Filippo
Max Frisch
Gorky
Harley Granville Barker
(two volumes)
Henrik Ibsen (six volumes)
Lorca (three volumes)
Marivaux

Mustapha Matura
David Mercer (two volumes)
Arthur Miller (five volumes)
Molière
Musset
Clifford Odets
Joe Orton
A. W. Pinero
Luigi Pirandello
Terence Rattigan
W. Somerset Maugham
(two volumes)
Wole Soyinka
August Strindberg
(three volumes)
J. M. Synge
Ramón del Valle-Inclán
Frank Wedekind
Oscar Wilde

Methuen Contemporary Dramatists
include

Peter Barnes (three volumes)
Sebastian Barry
Edward Bond (six volumes)
Howard Brenton
  (two volumes)
Richard Cameron
Jim Cartwright
Caryl Churchill (two volumes)
Sarah Daniels (two volumes)
David Edgar (three volumes)
Dario Fo (two volumes)
Michael Frayn (two volumes)
Peter Handke
Jonathan Harvey
Declan Hughes
Terry Johnson
Bernard-Marie Koltès
Doug Lucie
David Mamet (three volumes)

Anthony Minghella
  (two volumes)
Tom Murphy (four volumes)
Phyllis Nagy
Peter Nichols (two volumes)
Philip Osment
Louise Page
Stephen Poliakoff
  (three volumes)
Christina Reid
Philip Ridley
Willy Russell
Ntozake Shange
Sam Shepard (two volumes)
David Storey (three volumes)
Sue Townsend
Michel Vinaver (two volumes)
Michael Wilcox

Methuen Classical Greek Dramatists

Aeschylus Plays: One
(Persians, Seven Against Thebes, Suppliants,
Prometheus Bound)

Aeschylus Plays: Two
(Oresteia: Agamemnon, Libation-Bearers, Eumenides)

Aristophanes Plays: One
(Acharnians, Knights, Peace, Lysistrata)

Aristophanes Plays: Two
(Wasps, Clouds, Birds, Festival Time, Frogs)

Aristophanes & Menander: New Comedy
(Women in Power, Wealth, The Malcontent,
The Woman from Samos)

Euripides Plays: One
(Medea, The Phoenician Women, Bacchae)

Euripides Plays: Two
(Hecuba, The Women of Troy, Iphigeneia at Aulis,
Cyclops)

Euripides Plays: Three
(Alkestis, Helen, Ion)

Euripides Plays: Four
(Elektra, Orestes, Iphigeneia in Tauris)

Euripides Plays: Five
(Andromache, Herakles' Children, Herakles)

Euripides Plays: Six
(Hippolytos, Suppliants, Rhesos)

Sophocles Plays: One
(Oedipus the King, Oedipus at Colonus, Antigone)

Sophocles Plays: Two
(Ajax, Women of Trachis, Electra, Philoctetes)

Methuen Student Editions

John Arden	*Serjeant Musgrave's Dance*
Alan Ayckbourn	*Confusions*
Aphra Behn	*The Rover*
Edward Bond	*Lear*
Bertolt Brecht	*The Caucasian Chalk Circle*
	Life of Galileo
	Mother Courage and her Children
Anton Chekhov	*The Cherry Orchard*
Caryl Churchill	*Top Girls*
Shelagh Delaney	*A Taste of Honey*
John Galsworthy	*Strife*
Robert Holman	*Across Oka*
Henrik Ibsen	*A Doll's House*
Charlotte Keatley	*My Mother Said I Never Should*
Bernard Kops	*Dreams of Anne Frank*
Federico García Lorca	*Blood Wedding*
John Marston	*The Malcontent*
Willy Russell	*Blood Brothers*
Wole Soyinka	*Death and the King's Horseman*
August Strindberg	*The Father*
J. M. Synge	*The Playboy of the Western World*
Oscar Wilde	*The Importance of Being Earnest*
Tennessee Williams	*A Streetcar Named Desire*
Timberlake Wertenbaker	*Our Country's Good*

Methuen Modern Plays
include work by

Jean Anouilh
John Arden
Margaretta D'Arcy
Peter Barnes
Sebastian Barry
Brendan Behan
Edward Bond
Bertolt Brecht
Howard Brenton
Simon Burke
Jim Cartwright
Caryl Churchill
Noël Coward
Lucinda Coxon
Sarah Daniels
Nick Dear
Shelagh Delaney
David Edgar
David Eldridge
Dario Fo
Michael Frayn
John Godber
Paul Godfrey
David Greig
John Guare
Peter Handke
David Harrower
Jonathan Harvey
Iain Heggie
Declan Hughes
Terry Johnson
Sarah Kane
Charlotte Keatley
Barrie Keeffe
Howard Korder
Robert Lepage

Stephen Lowe
Doug Lucie
Martin McDonagh
John McGrath
Terrence McNally
David Mamet
Patrick Marber
Arthur Miller
Mtwa, Ngema & Simon
Tom Murphy
Phyllis Nagy
Peter Nichols
Joseph O'Connor
Joe Orton
Louise Page
Joe Penhall
Luigi Pirandello
Stephen Poliakoff
Franca Rame
Mark Ravenhill
Philip Ridley
Reginald Rose
David Rudkin
Willy Russell
Jean-Paul Sartre
Sam Shepard
Wole Soyinka
Shelagh Stephenson
C. P. Taylor
Theatre de Complicite
Theatre Workshop
Sue Townsend
Judy Upton
Timberlake Wertenbaker
Victoria Wood

For a Complete Catalogue of Methuen Drama titles
write to:

Methuen Drama
Random House
20 Vauxhall Bridge Road
London SW1V 2SA